T0137251

Theory and Applications
of Natural Language Processing

Series editors:
Julia Hirschberg
Eduard Hovy
Mark Johnson

Aims and Scope

The field of Natural Language Processing (NLP) has expanded explosively over the past decade: growing bodies of available data, novel fields of applications, emerging areas and new connections to neighboring fields have all led to increasing output and to diversification of research.

"Theory and Applications of Natural Language Processing" is a series of volumes dedicated to selected topics in NLP and Language Technology. It focuses on the most recent advances in all areas of the computational modeling and processing of speech and text across languages and domains. Due to the rapid pace of development, the diversity of approaches and application scenarios are scattered in an ever-growing mass of conference proceedings, making entry into the field difficult for both students and potential users. Volumes in the series facilitate this first step and can be used as a teaching aid, advanced-level information resource or a point of reference.

The series encourages the submission of research monographs, contributed volumes and surveys, lecture notes and textbooks covering research frontiers on all relevant topics, offering a platform for the rapid publication of cutting-edge research as well as for comprehensive monographs that cover the full range of research on specific problem areas.

The topics include applications of NLP techniques to gain insights into the use and functioning of language, as well as the use of language technology in applications that enable communication, knowledge management and discovery such as natural language generation, information retrieval, question-answering, machine translation, localization and related fields.

The books are available in printed and electronic (e-book) form:

* Downloadable on your PC, e-reader or iPad
* Enhanced by Electronic Supplementary Material, such as algorithms, demonstrations, software, images and videos
* Available online within an extensive network of academic and corporate R&D libraries worldwide
* Never out of print thanks to innovative print-on-demand services
* Competitively priced print editions for eBook customers thanks to MyCopy service http://www.springer.com/librarians/e-content/mycopy

More information about this series at http://www.springer.com/series/8899

Marta R. Costa-jussà • Reinhard Rapp •
Patrik Lambert • Kurt Eberle •
Rafael E. Banchs • Bogdan Babych
Editors

Hybrid Approaches to Machine Translation

Springer

Editors

Marta R. Costa-jussà
Universitat Politècnica de Catalunya
Barcelona, Spain

Reinhard Rapp
University of Aix-Marseille and
   University of Mainz
Marseille, France

Patrik Lambert
Pompeu Fabra University
Barcelona
Barcelona, Spain

Kurt Eberle
Lingenio GmbH
Heidelberg
Germany

Rafael E. Banchs
Institute for Infocomm Research
Singapore, Singapore

Bogdan Babych
School of Modern Languages&Cultures
University of Leeds
Leeds, United Kingdom

ISSN 2192-032X   ISSN 2192-0338   (electronic)
Theory and Applications of Natural Language Processing
ISBN 978-3-319-79334-4   ISBN 978-3-319-21311-8   (eBook)
DOI 10.1007/978-3-319-21311-8

This Springer imprint is published by Springer Nature
The registered company is Springer International Publishing AG Switzerland

Foreword

The term Hybrid Machine Translation suggests the existence of pure forms of machine translation, often associated with "statistical" and "rule-based" approaches. However, there is risk that the contrast between the "statistical" and the "rule based" is taken literally and could be interpreted as a mere mismatch between two paradigms: the old and the new. However, I personally think that any clash between the two paradigms has come about merely due to historical reasons. Therefore, this book on hybrid MT should be taken as an effort at combining the obvious merits of both approaches, directly aiming for improved MT performance.

The paradigmatic shift from linguistic theorizing to data-driven methods, which took place two decades ago in computational linguistics, cannot be taken as a license to dismiss the linguistic view on language data. At its core, the data-driven approach (usually called statistical) concentrates on the problem of modeling the expected similarities between training data and future test data. This allows the data-driven approach to target performance phenomena usually shoved aside in traditional linguistic approaches. Examples of such phenomena are ambiguity resolution, the graded scale of idiomatic language use, and the shifting translation distributions depending on the domain of language use (as opposed to so-called broad-coverage systems).

Yet, the mere focus of the data-driven approach on the expected similarities between training and test data carries with it major risks. First and foremost, there is the temptation to forget the nature of language data and consider it as mere streams of bits and bytes. Obviously, caring for the frequent has the risk of forgetting the long tail of low-frequency phenomena. It has often been observed that human language processing exhibits effects pertaining to latent structure, often collectively put in linguistics under recursive and graphical structures. If the data is viewed correctly, it could be that low-frequency phenomena actually belong together with other phenomena and, hence, are not of low frequency after all. Despite major efforts spent on developing hierarchical models, the data-driven approach has yet to prove that it can deal with phenomena, such as the interaction between morphology and syntaco-semantic roles, usually expressed at the surface as word order or morphological markers including agreement.

All along, since the early days of statistical MT, there have been efforts of exploiting statistics over linguistic structures, including syntax, morphology, semantic roles, word senses, and so on. Unfortunately, these efforts have been rewarded with limited measurable success over the linguistically agnostic approach. Admittedly this is not only due to the fact that the measures of success (MT evaluation) themselves are likely too coarse to be meaningful in various scenarios. For example, linguistic syntactic structures could be useful for translating what may be viewed as the "compositional" part of the data. But syntax-driven translation has failed to explain human translators' choices, which is (more often than not) "non-compositional" relative to constituency syntax. Crucially, the aspect of "compositionality" itself depends completely on the choice of structures and the accompanying composition operators. Hence, when syntax is used to enrich (rather than constrain) the statistical approach, it could often give major improvements in translation quality. In other words, within the data-driven approach, linguistic structure is as useful as it can be incorporated to model the similarities between training and test data.

This book on hybrid approaches to MT presents a number of direct efforts at striking a certain balance between existing MT systems of both paradigms. It is undoubtedly driven by an engineering motivation to obtain improved per-formance over systems that do not combine aspects from both paradigms. The hybrid approach, as it is called these days, symbolizes the drive at obtaining improved systems which are useful for the translation industry, which attaches major importance to more effective translation tools. The research avenue leading to linguistically inspired, data-driven MT has rather similar goals but might take a different perspective. In any case, my personal view is that there is truly no contradiction whatsoever between using linguistic structure and the goals of statistical, data-driven modeling. To put it in popularized terminology: Statistics can be pursued as mere counting. Yet, counting must start out from an explicit model which transfers the data from mere bits and bytes to a suitable linguistic space where new regularities are exposed, so that counting becomes more meaningful for language translation.

Chair of Computational Linguistics   Khalil Sima'an
Institute for Logic, Language and Computation (ILLC)
University of Amsterdam (UvA)
Amsterdam
The Netherlands

Preface

Nowadays, most important developments in Machine Translation (MT) are achieved via combining data-driven and rule-based techniques. These combinations typically involve hybridization of different traditional paradigms, such as the introduction of linguistic knowledge into statistical MT paradigms, the incorporation of data-driven components into rule-based paradigms, or statistical and rule-based pre- and post-processing for both types of MT architectures. This volume aims at giving (in an introductory chapter) an overview of the field as well as publishing the latest relevant research conducted by linguists and practitioners from different multidisciplinary areas working on hybrid MT.

The work on hybrid MT is typically scattered over conference proceedings and mixed with other publications about research on MT or text analysis. Therefore, it is difficult for the reader interested in hybrid approaches to get a condensed topic-driven overview on current research in this field. Inspired by the workshop series on Hybrid Approaches to Translation (HyTra), this volume contains some of the most suitable publications from the first three editions, with the aim of providing an overview on some of the most relevant research topics in the area.

In the introductory chapter, the book provides an overview and classification of the different types of hybrid architectures. The other chapters are classified accordingly, so that the reader, e.g., who is interested in the latest research on a specific architectural variant, can quickly find the respective section by following the structure of the book. The book is meant to address the needs of readers who are interested in introductory overviews on a number of topics as well as of readers who would like to be informed about some of the latest research in the respective areas. Thus the book tries to serve two purposes, and it is unique in this respect.

The book will be of interest primarily for specialists in MT, but is also relevant to researchers in computational linguistic, machine learning, and data mining, to translators and managers of translation companies, and to professionals who are interested in recent progress on tools for automating the translation process. The book is organized as follows: the first chapter gives an introduction to hybrid MT, presenting an overview on the history, the state-of-the-art, and the prospects. Then, the remainder of the book is divided into three parts:

- Part I covers approaches that add linguistic knowledge into statistical systems. The chapters in this part include: imbuing statistical MT with linguistic knowledge, hybrid language models, hybrid word alignment, and introducing syntax in statistical MT.
- Part II overviews how adding machine learning can help MT. The chapters are about supplementing rule-based MT using machine learning and about performing language-independent hybrid MT.
- Part III reports on hybrid Natural Language Processing (NLP) tools that have been shown useful for MT. Three chapters explain how to use MT in the following tools: dependency parsers, transductions grammars, and word sense disambiguation.

We would like to thank all contributors to this book, the reviewers, the participants, and the invited speakers of the first three editions of the HyTra workshop. Many thanks also to the publisher, the series editors, and the typesetting and production team. In particular, we would like to highlight the excellent and more than pleasant cooperation with Federica Corradi dell'Acqua and Ed Hovy.

Barcelona, Spain	Marta R. Costa-jussà
Marseille, France	Reinhard Rapp
Barcelona, Spain	Patrik Lambert
Heidelberg, Germany	Kurt Eberle
Singapore, Singapore	Rafael E. Banchs
Leeds, UK	Bogdan Babych
March 2016	

Contents

Hybrid Machine Translation Overview

Cristina España-Bonet and Marta R. Costa-jussà

Abstract This survey chapter provides an overview of the recent research in hybrid Machine Translation (MT). The main MT paradigms are sketched and their integration at different levels of depth is described starting with system combination techniques and followed by integration strategies led by rule-based and statistical systems. System combination does not involve any hybrid architecture since it combines translation outputs. It can be done with different granularities that include sentence, sub-sentential and graph-levels. When considering a deeper integration, architectures guided by the rule-based approach introduce statistics to enrich resources, modules or the backbone of the system. Architectures guided by the statistical approach include rules in pre-/post-processing or at a inner level which means including rules or dictionaries in the core system. This chapter overviewing hybrid MT puts in context, introduces, and motivates the subsequent chapters that constitute this book.

1 Introduction

Machine translation (MT) has been a very active research field specially in the last 15 years. The rise of Statistical MT (SMT) helped in the spreading and diffusion of MT by generating systems that, given availability of parallel corpora, can translate any text with an acceptable quality at least for a basic understanding. But SMT seems to have reached a plateau and, in parallel with its growth, several approaches have been developed to join the best of the different MT paradigms under the label of Hybrid MT (HMT).

C. España-Bonet (✉)
Department of Computer Science, TALP Research Center, Universitat Politècnica de Catalunya – Barcelona Tech, Jordi Girona 1-3, 08034 Barcelona, Spain
e-mail: cristinae@cs.upc.edu

M.R. Costa-jussà
Department of Signal Theory and Communications, TALP Research Center, Universitat Politècnica de Catalunya – BarcelonaTech, Jordi Girona 1-3, Barcelona, Spain
e-mail: marta.ruiz@upc.edu

© Springer International Publishing Switzerland 2016
M.R. Costa-jussà ct al. (eds.), *Hybrid Approaches to Machine Translation*,
Theory and Applications of Natural Language Processing,
DOI 10.1007/978-3-319-21311-8_1

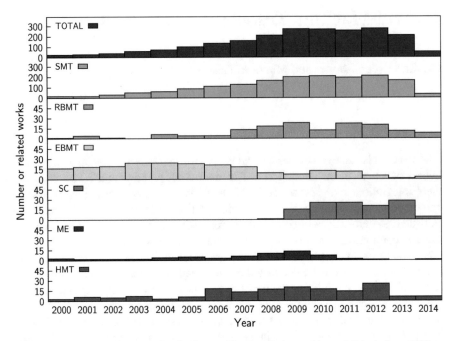

Fig. 1 Number of works appearing in the machine translation archive published since 2000 on different MT paradigms. See text for a wider description

The number of papers published on every topic can be a qualitative measure of the aforementioned. Figure 1 shows the number of works that appear in the Machine Translation Archive[1] related to MT and HMT. The plot begins when the number of HMT articles starts to emerge, back in the 90s there are almost no contributions. The measure is only qualitative for several reasons: (1) although most of conference papers are in the list, not all of the journal articles appear; (2) additional works such as tutorials or invited talks are considered; and (3) there is overlap among lists. The trends seen in the plot are clear. Most of the production in MT is currently due to SMT, the number of works is an order of magnitude higher than for the other MT paradigms. The other leading approach, Rule-based MT (RBMT), is in general more complex, that is, its development is costly and time-consuming. Although these systems are previous to the empirical ones, most of the systems were commercial at the beginning and the production in terms of papers has been smaller. Finally, another empirical approach, Example-based MT (EBMT), was dominant around the turn of the century and up to 2002 the number of works on EBMT was higher than on SMT. Since then, the success of SMT has affected EBMT and its production is currently minor.

---

[1]http://mt-archive.info

During the last decade also hundreds of papers on HMT have been published. The system types in the Archive (those shown in the plot) distinguish among HMT, Multi-Engine systems (ME) and System Combination (SC). The main difference is that for the latter the final output is created by combination of the individual outputs, that is, there is no real integration of the individual engines. If the combination is done in parallel one can talk of ME systems; SC is more general and would also include cases where the combination is done sequentially as a pre/post-edition. In the subsequent state of the art, SC also includes works on ME translation. On the contrary, HMT generally implies an integration of the system architectures. However, limits are fuzzy and some works can be classified within the three groups.

In this survey we discriminate between SC and HMT according the degree of mixture between the individual system architectures. System Combination per se was consolidated with the creation of several editions of devoted tasks into the MT evaluation campaigns. The *NIST Open Machine Translation Evaluation*[2] of 2009 and 2012 had a System Combination Task and so was also the case of the *Workshop on Statistical Machine Translation*[3] between 2009 and 2012. In 2011, in the *Workshop on Applying Machine Learning Techniques to Optimise the Division of Labour in Hybrid Machine Translation*,[4] the organisers defined a shared task where participants were asked to combine the output of several systems of different types.

At the same time, in 2011, the *International Workshop on Using Linguistic Information for Hybrid Machine Translation*[5] took place. This workshop was specific for HMT and covered both HMT systems themselves and their evaluation. Another series of workshops is the trilogy of *Hybrid Approaches to Machine Translation* (HyTra) in 2012,[6] 2013[7] and 2014.[8] Finally, in 2015, an Special Issue on Hybrid Machine Translation: Integration of Linguistics and Statistics, will be published in the Computer Speech and Language Journal. The present volume is an outcome of the HyTra workshops with selected contributions from the authors describing systems and tools.

Before going into these works, the following sections of this chapter present some of the previous approaches to HMT. First, Sect. 2 describes the main characteristics of RBMT and SMT paradigms that will serve to understand how hybrid systems can be build on them. Then, Sect. 3 summarises recent work on SC at three different levels: sentence, subsentencial and search graph levels. Sections 4 and 5 summarise a compilation of hybrid systems lead by an SMT and RBMT engine respectively. Most of the contributions of this volume can be included within this

---

[2]http://www.nist.gov/itl/iad/mig/openmt.cfm

[3]http://www.statmt.org/

[4]http://www.dfki.de/ml4hmt, http://www.eamt.org/news/news_cfp_ml4hmt.php

[5]http://ixa2.si.ehu.es/lihmt2011/

[6]http://www-lium.univ-lemans.fr/esirmt-hytra/hytra.php

[7]http://hytra.barcelonamedia.org/hytra2013/

[8]http://parles.upf.edu/llocs/plambert/hytra/hytra2014/

category. At the end of every of these three sections there is a recap table with the references of the most relevant works. Finally, an overview of the book and future research directions are given in Sect. 6.

2 Machine Translation Paradigms

Fully automated MT systems can be classified according to their main paradigm as seen in Fig. 2 in rule-based and empirical systems. The distinctive characteristic is the resources they use. Rule-based systems mainly use grammars and dictionaries to do the translation. They need a group of human experts to establish the set of rules. This is usually slow, expensive and not portable, but one obtains high quality syntactics for the translated output. Within empirical systems two main approaches can be pointed out, both of them relying on parallel data: example-based MT and statistical MT. For EBMT new translations are formed on the basis of the previously compiled translations, for SMT also a probabilistic model is considered. These systems are specially good with lexical selection and fluency but are worse than the RBMT ones grammatically because long dependencies are not taken into account.

Nowadays, this is a naïve classification since most of the systems use both data and rules at some point. Think for example of how simple rules can be applied to deal with dates in statistical systems or lexicons extracted from parallel corpora can be used in rule-based systems. Those systems that explicitly merge the approaches in a thorougher way can be included within a third family with the denomination of hybrid systems.

In the following subsections we describe the RBMT and SMT paradigms paying special attention to the points that can be complemented with other approaches.

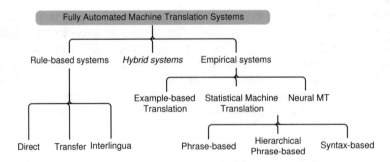

Fig. 2 Taxonomy of fully automated machine translation systems. Hybrid systems combine features from the other architectures. Neural MT is a new MT technology (e.g. Kalchbrenner and Blunsom 2013; Bahdanau et al. 2014). Its discussion goes beyond the scope of this book

2.1   Rule-Based Machine Translation

The amount and the linguistic techniques used in a translation system distinguishes in direct, transfer and interlingua the (RB)MT approaches as was first depicted in the Vauquois triangle (Vauquois 1968) (Fig. 3). The direct method shown at the base of the triangle does a straightforward translation word-by-word. In transfer systems there is a syntactic analysis of the sentences of the source language (SL) which results in an abstract representation of the sentences. This representation is transferred to the abstract representation of the target language (TL), and the output is generated from it. For the interlingua approach, the abstract representation is assumed to be the same for all languages and there is no need for the transfer step.

2.1.1   Transfer Systems

Most of the general-domain RBMT systems are transfer systems; interlingual systems, when built, are more suitable for specific domains or even controlled languages [see for instance Ranta (2011) and Kauers et al. (2002)]. Not all transfer systems analyse the source sentence at the same depth. Shallow transfer systems consider morphology and at most a shallow parsing (syntactic transfer). Deep transfer systems use a complete parse tree and possibly semantics (semantic transfer). In both cases, the sequence analysis-transfer-generation is respected.

During the analysis step, one needs processors in the SL to parse the input, a grammar and a lexicon. Afterwards, a grammar is used for the structural transfer and a bilingual lexicon for the lexical transfer. Finally, a generation grammar and possibly a lexicon in the TL generate the final translation. All these rules and dictionaries that are, in principle, hand-crafted can also be learned from data. In a same way as statistical parsers can be used for the analysis of the source sentence, monolingual or bilingual corpus can be used to obtain bilingual lexicons or learn the transfer rules. It is on this point that techniques used in SMT systems can be

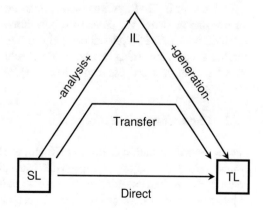

Fig. 3   Schematic Vauquois triangle (Vauquois 1968). (RB)MT systems are divided according to the amount of linguistic analysis applied on the source language (SL). With the deepest analysis, the SL is converted into an abstract interlingual representation (IL) before the generation of the target language (TL)

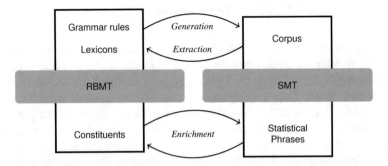

Fig. 4 Shallow loans and exchanges between the resources of RBMT and SMT paradigms (*above*) and their side products (*below*). Some hybrid systems are build by taking advantage of these relations

very useful (Fig. 4). Statistical systems can also be used as a pre-processing or post-processing step in order to help in disambiguation and choose among the different translation options, but, as we will see in the following section, it is more common the other way around and rules are sometimes used as a pre-process in SMT systems to reorder the input sentence or as a post-process to choose grammatically correct sentences.

2.2 Statistical Machine Translation

SMT systems estimate probabilistic models (language and translation models) by frequency counts in corpora. For a language model, monolingual data in the target language is needed; translation probabilities are extracted from relations in both the target and the source language and therefore parallel data are used to build the translation model. At the end, the best translation in a statistical system is that maximising the product of models.

Differences in SMT systems mainly arise from the definition of the minimal unit for translation (word vs. phrase vs. constituent). Dictionaries and/or constituents obtained with RBMT systems can help in the translation as a complement to the parallel corpus, and rules can be used for reordering the input or the output as a pre-process or post-process respectively (Fig. 4).

2.2.1 Phrase-Based Systems

Phrase-based translation (PBSMT) (Koehn et al. 2003) is the natural evolution of word-to-word translation. When considering a phrase instead of a word, the (small) context and the local reordering of every word is taken into account. A phrase here is just a sequence of words but it is not necessarily a linguistic element consistent with a word alignment between the source and the target (Koehn 2010: 131). This is positive because the number of phrases that can be extracted from a corpus is larger than the number of syntactic elements and it allows more freedom in the translation. But on the other hand, the extraction of noisy phrases leads to non-grammatical translations.

2.2.2 Syntax-Based Systems

Syntax-based systems (SSMT) (Wu 1997; Quirk et al. 2005) implement the opposite approach and translate syntactic elements. The basic idea is to use synchronous grammars which are able to generate the source and the target simultaneously. Synchronous grammars are learned from parallel corpus and that makes the approach very slow in comparison to the PBSMT systems.

2.2.3 Hierarchical Phrase-Based Systems

Hierarchical phrase-based systems (HPBSMT) (Chiang 2005) strike a balance between pure lexical PBSMT and SSMT. A hierarchical phrase consists of words and subphrases and this hierarchy is intended to capture reorderings among phrases. The hierarchical phrase pairs are obtained from a synchronous context-free grammar (CFG) learned from parallel corpora without syntactic information. As the authors explain, the system is formally syntax-based as it uses synchronous CFG, but not linguistically syntax-based, because the parallel data does not include syntactic information.

3 System Combination

A popular research direction for bringing together different paradigms in MT is system combination, which consists in selecting the highest quality output among various options from multiple MT engines. Therefore, this type of combination does not aim at integrating system architectures, but only the translation outputs from systems as the ones described in the previous section.

System combination in the field of MT has originally been inspired by previous successful works in the area of speech recognition (Fiscus 1997). Basically, MT outputs may be combined at three different levels: sentence, subsentencial, or search graphs. The combination for the sentence and subsentencial levels takes either the best output sentence of each available system or a list of n-best outputs. In the following, we make an overview of each category and collect references from all categories in Table 1.

Table 1 System combination summary

Granularity	References
Sentence-level	Callison-Burch and Flournoy (2001), Nomoto (2004), Akiba et al. (2002), Costa-jussà et al. (2007), Formiga et al. (2013)
Subsentencial-level	Frederking and Nirenburg (1994), Bangalore et al. (2001), Jayaraman and Lavie (2005), Matusov et al. (2006), Sim et al. (2007), Rosti et al. (2008), He et al. (2008), Mellebeek and van Genabith (2006)
Graph-level	Li et al. (2009), DeNero et al. (2010), Duan et al. (2011), Okita and van Genabith (2012)

3.1   Sentence-Level Combination

This is the level with the lowest granularity. At this level, system combination has been widely influenced by the use of the information provided by n-gram language modelling (Callison-Burch and Flournoy 2001; Nomoto 2004), which assume that the best translation comes from the most fluent translation. Akiba et al. (2002) take a step forward and propose two different methods that use a combination of language and translation models to choose the best translation. The authors in Costa-jussà et al. (2007) combine the outputs of an n-gram-based and a PBSMT system by using the scoring of both systems. These scores include language and translation models as in the previous works, but also the other features of standard SMT systems. Recent approaches such as that in Formiga et al. (2013) use SVMs and random forests together with several confidence measures to re-rank an n-best list of translation outputs.

3.2   Subsentencial-Level Combination

One step further in obtaining the best translation output is done by merging hypothesis at the level of words or phrases. One of the first works in this direction can be found in Frederking and Nirenburg (1994), which combines three MT engines from different nature into a chart data structure. This work is even previous to the first references on sentence-level combination systems, and to obtain the best translations they use several heuristics to estimate the quality of each chunk. Some years later, Bangalore et al. (2001) used a monotonic alignment to construct a confusion network from several translation hypotheses. Alignments are crucial in the combination and, soon after, Jayaraman and Lavie (2005) and Matusov et al. (2006) propose a non-monotonic alignment. In the latter, the context of the whole document is taken into account. Then, Sim et al. (2007) extracts alignments with the Translation Error Rate (TER) measure (Snover et al. 2006). Rosti et al. (2008) uses confidence scores derived from generalised linear models and He et al. (2008) uses indirect HMM alignments.

Within another line of subsentencial combination, Mellebeek and van Genabith (2006) do not rely on word alignments of output hypotheses, but prepare the input sentence for multi-engine processing. They do this by using a recursive decomposition algorithm that produces simple chunks as input to the MT engines. A consensus translation is produced by combining the best chunk translations, selected through majority voting, a trigram language model score and a confidence score assigned to each MT engine.

3.3 Search Graph-Level Combination

At the top level of granularity, there is the proposal of integrating consensus translations at decoding time. This is the most recent approach within system combination and also the one that is closer to HMT. In Li et al. (2009) both partial and full hypotheses are re-ranked during the decoding phase directly using consensus between translations from different systems. According to the authors, this is different from system combination since decoders collaborate by exchanging partial translation results and not final n-best lists, but this is the case for several systems presented in this section. Also the authors in DeNero et al. (2010) define their system as a forest-based technique that unifies consensus decoding and system combination. The approach is able to deal with systems with heterogeneous structures, the only request is that every system to be combined can output a forest or lattice of translations. In both cases, collaborative decoding (Li et al. 2009) and model combination (DeNero et al. 2010), the systems outperform their corresponding baseline in terms of the BLEU score (Papineni 2002).

Work by Duan et al. (2011) presents hypothesis mixture decoding, a new decoding scheme that performs translation reconstruction using hypotheses generated by multiple component systems. This decoding involves two decoding stages: first, each component system decodes the source sentence independently; second, a new search space is constructed by composing existing hypotheses produced by all systems using a set of rules, and a new set of features is used to seek the final best translation within this new constructed search space. Finally, we mention a system combination strategy that uses Minimum Bayes Risk (MBR) decoding. Under certain hypotheses, the authors in Okita and van Genabith (2012) develop a new MBR decoding strategy that exploits a larger hypothesis space compared with previous works. The final system improves from 1 to 10 % on the BLEU score depending on the language pair.

4   Hybridisation Lead by an SMT System

A second way of combining more than one translation engine is by a hybridisation between approaches. This hybridisation is useful to compensate the weak points of an approach with the strong points of another one. Statistical systems can be built whenever there are parallel corpora available and the quality of the translation is affected by the amount of data. Since lexical selection is modelled from these data, a good lexical choice and fluency are the strong points of SMT systems when data on the specific domain is available. On the bad side, syntax and long distance structures are more difficult to catch even with lots of data [see Costa-jussà et al. (2012) for a review].

This section shows how statistical systems try to improve their global syntax and grammaticality. To do so, SMT has integrated features from RBMT systems at different stages including at a superficial level such as using rules at pre/post-processing or at a deep level such as augmenting the phrase table with RBMT entries. See Table 2 for a summary of this classification.

4.1   Pre/Post-processing Integration

There are popular approaches that use pre-processing rules to reorder source sentences to better match target sentences. These approaches include human written rules for different languages (Xia and McCord 2004; Collins et al. 2005; Wang et al. 2007; Patel 2013; Hatakoshi et al. 2014) or automatically extracted rules with non-linguistic knowledge (Costa-jussà and Fonollosa 2006) or with syntactic knowledge (Khalilov and Fonollosa 2011). In the former studies, specific rules are designed for English–French (Xia and McCord 2004), German–English (Collins et al. 2005), Chinese–English (Wang et al. 2007), English–Hindi (Patel 2013) and Japanese–English (Hatakoshi et al. 2014). In the latter cases, when extracting automatic rules, one cannot really say that the system is integrating RBMT knowledge.

A different type of pre-processing rules are those considering normalisation issues in order to deal, for example, with data noise, chat or informal languages

Table 2 Hybrid systems lead by SMT: summary

Integration level	References
Pre/post processing	Xia and McCord (2004), Collins et al. (2005), Wang et al. (2007), Patel (2013), Hatakoshi et al. (2014), Costa-jussà and Fonollosa (2006), Khalilov and Fonollosa (2011), Formiga et al. (2012), Lewis et al. (2013), Rudolf (2014), Farrús et al. (2011)
Core system	Nießen and Ney (2004), Vogel and Monson (2004), Okuma (2008), Eisele et al. (2008), Sánchez-Cartagena et al. (2016), Chen and Eisele (2010), Ahsan et al. (2010), Li et al. (2011)

(Lewis et al. 2013). Normally, this type of pre-processing is done in most of the SMT systems and it may not be considered as a hybrid technique, unless it is quite complete and sophisticated.

There are some approaches that use post-processing rules in standard SMT system to solve morphology generation problems, that is, not being able to generate all morphological variations from the target language. In these cases, the authors have proposed a combination of machine learning and the introduction of dictionaries (Formiga et al. 2012) to generate morphological forms that have not been observed in the training corpus. In the literature, one can find a previous study (Toutanova et al. 2008) in a similar direction, the main differences are the language pairs used, the morphology generalisation and the way of recovering the inflection information. However, the latter study does not use dictionaries and, again, it may not be considered hybrid.

From another perspective, Rudolf (2014) implements an automatic rule-based tool capable of post-editing SMT outputs. This tool, named *Depfix*, integrates several NLP tools to obtain analyses of the input sentences, and it uses a set of rules to correct common or serious errors in MT outputs. *Depfix* is currently implemented only for English-to-Czech translation direction.

Finally, Farrús et al. (2011) have compiled a set of both pre-processing and post-processing rules to solve normalisation problems typical from noisy corpora. This compilation is ad-hoc for Spanish–Catalan. Grammatical categories are used to formulate rules for solving problems with apostrophes, clitics, capital letters at the beginning of sentences, the relative pronoun *cuyo* and polysemy disambiguation.

4.2 Core Integration

SMT systems have also used rules at a deeper level. An early work from 2004 by Nießen and Ney proposes the construction of hierarchical lexicon models on the basis of equivalence classes of words. Both Vogel and Monson (2004) and Okuma (2008) have introduced dictionaries into phrase tables to reduce unknown words. The former augments the dictionary with morphological forms and assigns probabilities in a Chinese-to-English translation system. The latter focuses on the challenge of learning a context for words in dictionaries by using high-frequency words and replacing contexts.

Eisele et al. (2008) increase the standard phrase table with entries obtained from translating the data with several RBMT systems. The resulting phrase table combines statistical phrase pairs with phrase pairs generated by linguistic rules. The work is extended in Chen and Eisele (2010) by integrating a commercial RBMT system with a hierarchical SMT system and extracting rules from RBMT translations. The hybrid system uses the lexicons from both systems as well as local syntactic constructions defined in the RBMT system. Translation quality is improved on out-of-domain tests according to BLEU (~1.5 points). A similar study is conducted by Sánchez-Cartagena et al. (2016) using a shallow-transfer

RBMT system. In this case, both automatic and manual evaluations showed a clear improvement of translation quality when only small corpora are available and when the domain to translate was generic.

In 2010, Ahsan et al. focused on integrating local and long reorderings as well as the generation module from a RBMT system into the core translation model of a standard statistical system. These are key aspects in English–Hindi MT and with the hybridisation they achieved significant improvements in terms of automatic evaluation metrics (BLEU) and subjective metrics [SSER (Nießen 2000)]. A bit later, Li et al. (2011) integrates manual rules into a hierarchical SMT system (Chiang 2007) in the context of patent translation. The key idea is to propose a feedback selecting algorithm for manually acquired rules in patent translation using automatic evaluation, which picks out manually acquired rules that benefit MT quality.

5 Hybridisation Lead by a RBMT System

The last group of hybrid translation systems corresponds to those where the heart of the engine is rule-based. These systems are costly in time and human effort since, traditionally, dictionaries and rules were hand-made. However, with a correct parsing of the source and good generation rules, RBMT systems produce better translations from a syntactic point of view than pure data-based systems, and besides, they are able to deal with long distance dependencies, agreement and constituent reordering. On the other hand, the nature of data-driven systems makes them better at lexical selection and fluency [see Costa-jussà et al. (2012) for a review].

In order to improve the weak points just mentioned, pure RBMT systems use more every day components based on corpora. The essence of the components depends on the characteristics and needs of every system and range from automatising the acquisition of dictionaries or rules to generate translations that keep the syntactic structure but introduce new chunk translations or correct the existing ones. Although there is no standard classification among this kind of systems we have divided the following summary in three classes that take into account the degree of mixture between systems. As in the previous sections, we conclude with the summary (Table 3).

5.1 Enriching Rule-Based Resources

A first approach consists on enriching the basic resources of a RBMT with data gathered from corpora. Traditionally, these systems have been developed in order to improve a specific component of an already operative rule-based system, that is, either the dictionary or the transfer rules. The mixture between systems in this case

Table 3 Hybrids led by RBMT summary

Approach	References
Enrich resources	Eisele et al. (2008), Alegria et al. (2008), Dugast et al. (2009), Enache et al. (2012), Sánchez-Martínez and Forcada (2009)
Data-based modules	Habash et al. (2009), Wolf et al. (2011), Federmann and Hunsicker (2011), Tyers et al. (2012)
RB as backbone	Federmann et al. (2010), Federmann et al. (2011), Sánchez-Martínez et al. (2009), Labaka et al. (2014)

is low. Automatic techniques are used to generate the resources saving in human effort and mostly do not interfere with the engine.

In 2008, Eisele et al. (2008) described an implementation of a hybrid system that enlarged a RBMT lexicon by using bilingual phrases coming from an SMT system. The parallel corpus was annotated with part of speech and lemma and that allowed the authors to filter out non-syntactic phrases. This work was a joint project between the DFKI and the European Patent Office (EPO), and the evaluations within EPO itself showed an increase in lexical coverage when translating patents.

Also the *Matxin* system (Alegria et al. 2007) was adapted to a concrete domain by using Elexbi (Gurrutxaga Hernaiz et al. 2006) for a semiautomatic extraction of terminology from translation memories, and a parallel corpus to tackle lexical selection. The resulting system is analysed in a wider work that uses this domain-adapted version of Matxin for system combination (Alegria et al. 2008).

Similarly, *SYSTRAN*,[9] a pure rule-based system at that time, enlarged its dictionary with noun, verb, adjective and adverb phrases filtered from a phrase table also obtained with a PBSMT (Dugast et al. 2009). In this case, enriching the dictionary with phrases extracted from the Europarl corpus increased the BLEU score in 3 points on an in-domain test set.

In Enache et al. (2012), the authors present a hybrid translation system specifically designed to deal with patents. A grammar-based translator is developed to assure grammatically correct translations and a parallel corpus and SMT alignments are used to build the parallel lexicon of the RBMT translator on the fly for each sentence. In their system, the hybridisation is not only for enriching the dictionary, but an SMT system is on top of the RBMT one to translate those phrases not covered by the grammar. Under this point of view the paper could also fit in Sect. 4. As for the evaluation, both manual and automatic evaluations showed a slight preference for the hybrid system against the individual systems.

These systems have in common the fact that not all SMT phrases are incorporated within a RBMT engine, only linguistic phrases fulfil the requirements of a RBMT

---

[9]http://www.systransoft.com

system. As a result, not all the lexical richness given by a SMT system is transferred to the hybrid system, but the coverage improves. Lexical metrics, however, are usually not able to capture the quality improvements that become apparent with a manual evaluation of the translation quality.

Contrary to the previous works, the authors in Sánchez-Martínez and Forcada (2009) try to use corpora for collecting the transfer rules of the RBMT system instead of building the dictionary. As the authors say "manually building a bilingual dictionary for a language pair is usually much easier than developing shallow structural transfer rules for it". So, they develop a method to automatically infer shallow-transfer rules from parallel corpora that is based on the alignment template approach (Och 2002). These rules are used by the *Apertium MT*[10] engine and include syntactic and lexical changes. Their evaluation shows that the automatically inferred rules perform better than the SMT system.

5.2 Including Data-Based Modules

In some cases there is the need of introducing modules within the standard RBMT process to integrate statistical information. For instance, the RBMT system *Generation-heavy machine translation* (GHMT) (Habash 2003), defined by the authors as a primarily symbolic system, was extended with statistical components. The original GHMT system already uses a language model for the target language, but the work done in Habash et al. (2009) extends the use of probabilities to bilingual components. A PBSMT is used to generate translation tables, and those phrases that correspond to linguistically correct subtrees are used as multi-word dictionaries in GHMT. A deep evaluation of the results showed that the hybrid system was not able to outperform the pure PBSMT one when quantified with standard automatic metrics [BLEU, NIST (Doddington 2002) and METEOR (Banerjee and Lavie 2005)]. However, the grammaticality of the translations was improved if one understands grammaticality as correct verb-argument realizations and long-distance dependency translations, two of the strong points of RBMT systems.

More recently, Wolf et al. (2011) described a hybrid system based on *Comprendium* (Alonso and Thurmair 2003) (*Lucy*'s precursor[11]). The authors move from a hybrid system that uses phrase tables together with lexicons and grammars during transfer, to a final hybrid system that also makes use the RBMT components for linguistic filtering and statistical term extraction. The first system achieved, for instance, a better lexical selection than the pure RBMT one but the number of phrases used was small. With the final hybrid they claim to obtain a better F-score. Although the BLEU and NIST metrics are not able to capture the improvements, a

---

[10]http://www.apertium.org

[11]http://www.lucysoftware.com/

manual evaluation showed around 40–50 % of better translations against a 10–20 % of worse.

A different approach was taken by Federmann and Hunsicker (2011) who modified the analysis phase of the RBMT system by adding a module to compare the output of the phase, a forest of several analysis parse trees, with the tree output of robust probabilistic parser. The Tree Selector Module uses a tree edit distance to estimate the quality of the trees from the analysis forest and the best one is sent to the transfer phase. The statistical tool for terminology extraction described in Wolf et al. (2011) is used later in the generation phase. This system was the best-scoring one according to the manual evaluation at the WMT 2011 shared translation task,[12] but the new modules were counterproductive when evaluating with automatic metrics.

Following the work being done to improve the *Apertium MT* engine, Tyers et al. (2012) describes a new lexical-selection module that consists of rules in the form of constraints. These rules are learnt from a parallel corpus and applied to ambiguous input sentences after the lexical and before the structural transfer steps. The hybrid system achieves a statistically significant improvement in translation quality according to a paired bootstrap resampling test.

5.3 Using Rule-Based Translations as a Backbone

This last group corresponds to the systems where the mixture between individual systems is the largest, but, still, the rule-based one dominates. In these cases, the border between system combination and hybridisation is sometimes fuzzy. Federmann et al. (2010) extended a previous system combination work to build a system that, after a first RBMT translation, substitutes some selected noun phrases by their SMT counterparts. The evaluation is done in terms of BLEU, and the final system although improves the translation quality of the RBMT is in general worse than the pure SMT translator. In later work, Federmann et al. (2011) based the substitution of tokens on several decision factors, such as part-of-speech, local left and right contexts, and language model probabilities to accommodate different translation outputs to a fixed syntactic structure given by the RBMT translation template.

Following the approaches of the previous subsections, Sánchez-Martínez et al. (2009) included bilingual chunks obtained from a parallel corpus within *Apertium* platform. The main difference here is the fact that instead of including them in the dictionary, the system is modified so that the engine can choose, after a translation, among the pure Apertium option or the corpus-extracted one for all of the chunks. The choice is made according to the language model probability. The evaluation of the new system is given also in terms of BLEU and results show a small but not statistically significant improvement.

---

[12]http://www.statmt.org/wmt11/

Finally, the authors in España-Bonet et al. (2011) and Labaka et al. (2014) present a system where, before the transfer step, partial SMT translations are used to enrich the RBMT tree-based representation with more translation alternatives. The final translation is constructed by choosing the most probable combination among the available fragments using monotone statistical decoding. The monotone decoding allows to respect the order given by the RBMT generation parse tree. This hybrid system outperformed the individual translation systems with several lexical metrics, however, a manual evaluation of the translations contradicted this conclusion for out-of-domain test sets.

6   Overview of the Book and Future Research Directions

This introductory chapter has overviewed hybridisation MT strategies by making a classification that could cover most of the studies done in this research direction. This classification should help the reader of the volume understand the context of the subsequent chapters which present studies on hybrid MT from the linguistic and statistical perspectives. To sum up, hybrid MT systems have been approached either from a more rule-based or corpus-based perspective depending on the guiding system used. When hybrid systems have been guided by SMT systems, integration of rules has been made from the pre/post-processing stage up into the core system. When hybrid systems have been guided by RBMT systems, integration of statistics has been used to enrich resources, data-based modules or the backbone of the rule-based system. A much lower level of hybridisation is the system combination, which combines the translation outputs of systems generally from different nature. System combination has been done at the sentence, subsentencial or graph-level. The following subsections report a more detailed overview of the book chapters and outlines possible future research directions in hybrid MT.

6.1   Overview of the Book

As mentioned in Sect. 1, this book is divided in three parts with a total of seven chapters (without counting the present chapter). As follows we are going to give more details on each chapter.

6.1.1   Part I: Adding Linguistic Knowledge in SMT

The three chapters in this part report a core integration of rules into SMT systems. First, Lewis et al. (2014) describe some of the statistical and non-statistical attempts to incorporate linguistic insights into MT systems in the work at Microsoft Research. One of their biggest achievement, as they mention, has been introducing syntax in SMT. Following this line, the paper experiments with both their treelet and phrase-based SMT systems. Second, Pal and Naskar (2014) propose a hybrid word alignment model that combines two unsupervised word alignments, namely GIZA++ and Berkeley aligner, and a rule-based word alignment technique. High improvements are shown when pre-processing Named Entities in the parallel corpus. And, finally, Han et al. (2014) describe two approaches to deal with the translation of language pairs that have different word orders: one is by exploiting regularities in the differences of phrase head locations and formalising rules that reorder branches of constituency trees; the other, by devising rules that reorder word blocks from dependency trees. Experiments show that the latter achieves significant improvements.

6.1.2   Part II: Using Machine Learning in MT

The two chapters in this part show the benefits of using machine learning in MT. Rios and Göhring (2014) improve a RBMT translation system for Spanish-to-Quechua with a module that uses a classifier to predict an ambiguous verb form in case the rules alone cannot disambiguate it. Although the whole translator is not evaluated, the accuracy in the translation of these verbs increases more than a 15 % by the introduction of the hybrid component. Tambouratzis et al. (2014) presents the development of a hybrid MT methodology, which is based on using large quantities of monolingual corpora, very limited use of parallel corpora and a bilingual lemma dictionary.

6.1.3   Part III: Hybrid NLP Tools Useful for MT

Finally, the two chapters in this part present hybrid tools for parsing and Word Sense Disambiguation (WSD). Green (2014) modifies the dependency parser of a syntax-based engine. The authors use a classifier to build the final parsing tree from several inputs and that is used for translation. The engine is based on *TectoMT* (Zabokrtsky et al. 2008), an already hybrid system that combines statistical techniques and linguistic knowledge. Besides the hybridisation in the engine itself, the hybridisation in this case is among dependency parsers. The authors show that the parser accuracy correlates with automatic MT evaluation metrics. Vintar and Fišer (2014) use WordNet-based unsupervised WSD to solve the ambiguity in MT. Since the fine granularity of WordNet is often reported as problematic, the authors compare the performance of UKB (a software for performing graph-based WSD) when using all WordNet senses and when using sense clusters.

6.2   Future Research Directions

All mentioned hybrid strategies in this introductory chapter and book help improving the quality of MT taking advantage of multiple sources of information and paradigms, and most of them agree that research in hybrid MT has still more room from improvement.

Future directions may be led by either rules, statistics or system combination. All of them focus on enhancing the power given by large amount of data with linguistic knowledge. Based on the most recent works in hybridisation, there are several architectures that can be already envisaged as shown in Costa-jussà (2015). For example, for system combination, novel combination strategies may involve deep learning techniques, which are giving impressive results in NLP (Collobert et al. 2011).

When SMT is the core system, as mentioned in the Lewis et al.'s chapter (Lewis et al. 2014), a better integration of morphological features can have a bigger impact and deeper models of semantics can better represent the meaning. Han et al. (2014) suggest that the improvement in parsers could help towards hybridisation of syntax in SMT, which may improve at the same time the hybridisation of dependency parsers done in Green's chapter (Green 2014). Pal and Naskar (2014) foresee integrating knowledge of multi-word expressions into the word alignment step of an SMT system. Novel research, broadly speaking, may lead to non-pipelined approaches by fully integrating hand-written rules, morphology and novel semantic representations in the statistical decoding.

When RBMT is the core system, Rios and Göhring (2014) suggest improving the accuracy of the classifier which decides the verb form by using more advanced techniques. Further generic research lines may involve scoring transfer-rules or adding language models both based on the already mentioned deep learning techniques.

Finally, for none-of-the-previous core systems, future work proposed in Vintar et al.'s chapter (Vintar and Fišer 2014) includes integrating their WSD technique in a standard MT system. According to Tambouratzis et al. (2014), the extension of hybrid MT systems may come from more accurately matching sentence structures, combining sub-sentential parts or augmenting the language models by combination of different techniques.

In any case, given the large potential of hybrid MT, either the approaches envisaged here or new ones will manage to surprise us and will be decisive to give a step forward in MT.

Acknowledgements This work has been partially funded by the Spanish Ministerio de Economía y Competitividad project TACARDI (TIN2012-38523-C02-00) and contract TEC2015-69266-P, and the Seventh Framework Program of the European Commission through the International Outgoing Fellowship Marie Curie Action (IMTraP-2011-29951).

References

Ahsan, A., P. Kolachina, S. Kolachina, D.M. Sharma, and R. Sanga. 2010. Coupling statistical machine translation with rule-based transfer and generation. In *Proceedings of the 9th Conference of the Association for Machine Translation in the Americas*.

Akiba, Y., T. Watanabe, and E. Sumita. 2002. Using language and translation models to select the best among outputs from multiple MT systems. In *Proceedings of the 19th International Conference on Computational Linguistics*, vol. 1, pp. 1–7. Association for Computational Linguistics.

Alegria, I., A. Díaz de Ilarraza, G. Labaka, M. Lersundi, A. Mayor, and K. Sarasola. 2007. Transfer-based MT from Spanish into Basque: Reusability, standardization and open source. *Lecture Notes in Computer Science* 4394:374–384.

Alegria, I., A. Casillas, A.D.D. Ilarraza, J. Igartua, G. Labaka, M. Lersundi, A. Mayor, K. Sarasola, X. Saralegi, E. Fundazioa, B. Laskurain, and S.L. Eleka. 2008. Mixing approaches to MT for basque: Selecting the best output from RBMT, EBMT and SMT. In *MATMT2008 Workshop: Mixing Approaches to Machine Translation*, 27–34.

Alonso, J.A., and Thurmair, G. 2003. The comprendium translator system. In *Proceedings of MT Summit IX*, New Orleans, LA.

Bahdanau, D., K. Cho, and Y. Bengio. 2014. Neural machine translation by jointly learning to align and translate. arXiv preprint arXiv:1409.0473.

Banerjee, S., and A. Lavie. 2005. METEOR: An automatic metric for MT evaluation with improved correlation with human judgments. In *Proceedings of the ACL Workshop on Intrinsic and Extrinsic Evaluation Measures for Machine Translation and/or Summarization*, 65–72. Ann Arbor, MI: Association for Computational Linguistics.

Bangalore, S., G. Bordel, and G. Riccardi. 2001. Computing consensus translation from multiple machine translation systems. In *IEEE Workshop onAutomatic Speech Recognition and Understanding, 2001. ASRU '01*, 351–354. doi:10.1109/ASRU.2001.1034659

Callison-Burch, C., and R.S. Flournoy. 2001. A program for automatically selecting the best output from multiple machine translation engines. In *Proceedings of the Machine Translation Summit VIII*, 63–66.

Chen, Y., and A. Eisele. 2010. Integrating a rule-based with a hierarchical translation system. In *Proceedings of LREC*.

Chiang, D. 2005. A hierarchical phrase-based model for statistical machine translation. In *Proceedings of the 43rd Annual Meeting of the Association for Computational Linguistics (ACL)*, 263–270.

Chiang, D. 2007. Hierarchical phrase-based translation. *Computational Linguists* 33(2):201–228. doi:10.1162/coli.2007.33.2.201. http://dx.doi.org/10.1162/coli.2007.33.2.201.

Collins, M., P. Koehn, and I. Kučerová. 2005. Clause restructuring for statistical machine translation. In *Proceedings of the ACL*, Ann Arbor, 531–540. doi:10.3115/1219840.1219906.

Collobert, R., J. Weston, L. Bottou, M. Karlen, K. Kavukcuoglu, and P. Kuksa. 2011. Natural language processing (almost) from scratch. *Journal of Machine Learning Research* 12:2493–2537. http://dl.acm.org/citation.cfm?id=1953048.2078186.

Costa-jussà, M.R. 2015. How much hybridization does machine translation need? *Journal of the Association for Information Science and Technology* 6(10):2160–2165.

Costa-jussà, M.R., and J.A.R. Fonollosa. 2006. Statistical machine reordering. In *Proceedings of the 2006 Conference on Empirical Methods in Natural Language Processing, EMNLP '06*, 70–76. Stroudsburg, PA: Association for Computational Linguistics. http://dl.acm.org/citation. cfm?id=1610075.1610086.

Costa-jussà, M.R., J.M. Crego, D. Vilar, J.A.R. Fonollosa, J.B. Mariño, and H. Ney. 2007. Analysis and system combination of phrase- and n-gram-based statistical machine translation systems. In *Human Language Technologies 2007: The Conference of the North American Chapter of the Association for Computational Linguistics*, Companion volume, Short Papers, 137–140.

Costa-jussà, M.R., M. Farrús, J.B. Mariño, and J.A.R. Fonollosa. 2012. Study and comparison of rule-based and statistical Catalan-Spanish machine translation systems. *Computing and Informatics* 31(2):245–270.

DeNero, J., S. Kumar, C. Chelba, and F. Och. 2010. Model combination for machine translation. In *Human Language Technologies: The 2010 Annual Conference of the North American Chapter of the Association for Computational Linguistics*, 975–983. Association for Computational Linguistics.

Doddington, G. 2002. Automatic evaluation of machine translation quality using n-gram co-occurrence statistics. In *Proceedings of the 2nd International Conference on Human Language Technology (HLT)*, San Diego, CA, 138–145.

Duan, N., M. Li, and M. Zhou. 2011. Hypothesis mixture decoding for statistical machine translation. In *Proceedings of the 49th Annual Meeting of the Association for Computational Linguistics: Human Language Technologies*, vol. 1, pp. 1258–1267. Association for Computational Linguistics.

Dugast, L., J. Senellart, and P. Koehn. 2009. Selective addition of corpus-extracted phrasal lexical rules to a rule-based machine translation system. In *Proceedings of MT Summit XII*, Ottawa.

Eisele, A., C. Federmann, H. Saint-Amand, M. Jellinghaus, T. Herrmann, and Y. Chen. 2008. Using moses to integrate multiple rule-based machine translation engi nes into a hybrid system. In *Proceedings of the Third Workshop on Statistical Machine Translation, StatMT '08*, 179–182. Stroudsburg, PA: Association for Computational Linguistics.

Eisele, A., C. Federmann, H. Uszkoreit, H. Saint-Amand, M. Kay, M. Jellinghaus, S. Hunsicker, T. Herrmann, and Y. Chen. 2008. Hybrid machine translation architectures within and beyond the euromatrix project. In *Hybrid MT methods in practice: Their use in multilingual extraction, cross-language information retrieval, multilingual summarization, and applications in hand-held devices*, ed. J. Hutchins, W. Hahn. *Proceedings of the European Machine Translation Conference*, 27–34. European Association for Machine Translation, HITEC e.V.

Enache, R., C. España-Bonet, A. Ranta, and L. Màrquez. 2012. A hybrid system for patent translation. In *Proceedings of the 16th Annual Conference of the European Association for Machine Translation (EAMT12)*, Trento, 269–276.

España-Bonet, C., G. Labaka, A. Díaz de Ilarraza, L. Màrquez, and K. Sarasola. 2011. Hybrid machine translation guided by a rule-based system. In *Proceedings of the 13th Machine Translation Summit (MT-Summit)*, Xiamen, 554–561.

Farrús, M., M.R. Costa-jussà, J. Mariño, M. Poch, A. Hernández, C. Henríquez, and J. Fonollosa. 2011. Overcoming statistical machine translation limitations: Error analysis and proposed solutions for the Catalan-Spanish language pair. *Language Resources and Evaluation* 45(2):181–208. doi:10.1007/s10579-011-9137-0.

Federmann, C., and S. Hunsicker. 2011. Stochastic parse tree selection for an existing RBMT system. In *Proceedings of the Sixth Workshop on Statistical Machine Translation*, 351–357. Edinburgh: Association for Computational Linguistics.

Federmann, C., A. Eisele, Y. Chen, S. Hunsicker, J. Xu, and H. Uszkoreit. 2010. Further experiments with shallow hybrid MT systems. In *Proceedings of the Joint Fifth Workshop on Statistical Machine Translation and MetricsMATR*, 77–81. Uppsala: Association for Computational Linguistics.

Federmann, C., Y. Chen, S. Hunsicker, and R. Wang. 2011. DFKI system combination using syntactic information at ML4HMT-2011. In *Proceedings of the International Workshop on Using Linguistic Information for Hybrid Machine Translation (LIHMT 2011) and of the Shared Task on Applying Machine Learning Techniques to Optimise the Division of Labour in Hybrid Machine Translation (ML4HMT-11)*, Barcelona, 104–109.

Fiscus, J.G. 1997. A post-processing system to yield reduced word error rates: Recognizeroutput voting error reduction (ROVER). In *Proceedings of the Conference on Automatic Speech Recognition and Understanding (ASRU)*, 347–354.

Formiga, L., A. Hernández, J.B. Mariño, and E. Monte. 2012. Improving English to Spanish out-of-domain translations by morphology generalization and generation. In *AMTA Workshop on Monolingual Machine Translation*.

Formiga, L., M. Gonzàlez, A. Barrón-Cedeño, J.A.R. Fonollosa, and L. Marquez. 2013. The TALP-UPC approach to system selection: Asiya features and pairwise classification using random forests. In *Proceedings of the Eighth Workshop on Statistical Machine Translation*, 359–364. Sofia: Association for Computational Linguistics. http://www.aclweb.org/anthology/W13-2244.

Frederking, R., and S. Nirenburg. 1994. Three heads are better than one. In *Proceedings of the Fourth Conference on Applied Natural Language Processing, ANLC '94*, 95–100. Stroudsburg, PA: Association for Computational Linguistics. doi:10.3115/974358.974380. http://dx.doi.org/10.3115/974358.974380.

Green, N.D. 2014. Creating hybrid dependency parsers for syntax-based MT. In *Hybrid approaches to translation*. Berlin: Springer.

Gurrutxaga Hernaiz, A., X. Saralegi Urizar, S. Ugartetxea, and I. Alegría Loinaz. 2006. Elexbi, a basic tool for bilingual term extraction from Spanish-basque parallel corpora. In *Atti del XII Congresso Internazionale di Lessicografia*, ed. E. Corino, C. Marello, C. Onesti. Torino, 159–165.

Habash, N.Y. 2003. Generation-heavy hybrid machine translation. Ph.D. thesis, College Park, MD. AAI3094491.

Habash, N., B. Dorr, and C. Monz. 2009 Symbolic-to-statistical hybridization: Extending generation-heavy machine translation. *Machine Translation* 23:23–63.

Han, D., P. Martínez-Gómez, and Y. Miyao. 2014. Syntax-based pre-reordering for Chinese-to-Japanese statistical machine translation. In *Hybrid approaches to translation*. Berlin: Springer.

Hatakoshi, Y., G. Neubig, S. Sakti, T. Toda, and S. Nakamura. 2014. Rule-based syntactic preprocessing for syntax-based machine translation. In *Syntax, semantics and structure in statistical translation*, 34.

He, X., M. Yang, J. Gao, P. Nguyen, and R. Moore. 2008. Indirect-hmm-based hypothesis alignment for combining outputs from machine translation systems. In *Proceedings of the Conference on Empirical Methods in Natural Language Processing, EMNLP '08*, 98–107. Stroudsburg, PA: Association for Computational Linguistics. http://dl.acm.org/citation.cfm?id=1613715.1613730.

Jayaraman, S., and A. Lavie. 2005. Multi-engine machine translation guided by explicit word matching. In *Proceedings of the ACL 2005 on Interactive Poster and Demonstration Sessions, ACLdemo '05*, 101–104. Stroudsburg, PA: Association for Computational Linguistics. doi:10.3115/1225753.1225779. http://dx.doi.org/10.3115/1225753.1225779.

Kalchbrenner, N., and P. Blunsom. 2013. Recurrent continuous translation models. *EMNLP* 3(39):413.

Kauers, M., S. Vogel, C. Fügen, and A. Waibel. 2002. Interlingua based statistical machine translation. In *7th International Conference on Spoken Language Processing, ICSLP2002 - INTERSPEECH 2002*, Denver, CO, September 16–20, 2002. http://www.isca-speech.org/archive/icslp_2002/i02_1909.html.

Khalilov, M., and J.A.R. Fonollosa. 2011. Syntax-based reordering for statistical machine translation. *Computer Speech and Language* 25(4):761–788. doi:10.1016/j.csl.2011.01.001. http://dx.doi.org/10.1016/j.csl.2011.01.001.

Koehn, P., F.J. Och, and D. Marcu. 2003. Statistical phrase-based translation. In *Proceedings of the 2003 Conference of the North American Chapter of the Association for Computational Linguistics on Human Language Technology- Volume 1, NAACL '03*, 48–54. Stroudsburg, PA: Association for Computational Linguistics. doi:10.3115/1073445.1073462. http://dx.doi.org/10.3115/1073445.1073462.

Koehn, P. 2010. *Statistical machine translation*. Cambridge: Cambridge University Press.

Labaka, G., C. España-Bonet, L. Màrquez, and K. Sarasola. 2014. A hybrid machine translation architecture guided by syntax. *Machine Translation* 28:1–35. doi:10.1007/s10590-014-9153-0. http://dx.doi.org/10.1007/s10590-014-9153-0.

Lewis, W., and C. Quirk. 2013. Controlled ascent: Imbuing statistical MT with linguistic knowledge. In *Proceedings of the Second Workshop on Hybrid Approaches to Translation*, 51–66. Sofia: Association for Computational Linguistics. http://www.aclweb.org/anthology/W13-2809.

Lewis, W.D., C. Quirk, and Q. Gao. 2014. Controlled ascent: Imbuing statistical MT with linguistic knowledge. In *Hybrid approaches to translation*. Berlin: Springer.

Li, M., N. Duan, D. Zhang, C. Li, and M. Zhou. 2009. Collaborative decoding: Partial hypothesis re-ranking using translation consensus between decoders. In *ACL 2009, Proceedings of the 47th Annual Meeting of the Association for Computational Linguistics and the 4th International Joint Conference on Natural Language Processing of the AFNLP*, Singapore, 2–7 August 2009, 585–592. http://www.aclweb.org/anthology/P09-1066.

Li, X., Y. Lü, Y. Meng, Q. Liu, and H. Yu. 2011. Feedback selecting of manually acquired rules using automatic evaluation. In *Proceedings of the 4th Workshop on Patent Translation*, MT Summit XIII, Xiamen, September 2011, 52–59.

Matusov, E., N. Ueffing, and H. Ney. 2006. Computing consensus translation for multiple machine translation systems using enhanced hypothesis alignment. In *Proceedings of the EACL*.

Mellebeek, B., and J. van Genabith. 2006. Multi-engine machine translation by recursive sentence decomposition. In *Proceedings of the 7th Biennial Conference of the Association for Machine Translation in the Americas*, 110–118.

Nießen, S., and H. Ney. 2004. Statistical machine translation with scarce resources using morpho-syntactic information. *Computational Linguists* 30(2):181–204. doi:10.1162/089120104323093285. http://dx.doi.org/10.1162/089120104323093285.

Nießen, S., F.J. Och, G. Leusch, and H. Ney. 2000. An evaluation tool for machine translation: Fast evaluation for MT research. In *Proceedings of the 2nd International Conference on Language Resources and Evaluation*, Athens, 39–45.

Nomoto, T. 2004. Multi-engine machine translation with voted language model. In *Proceedings of the 42Nd Annual Meeting on Association for Computational Linguistics, ACL '04*. Stroudsburg, PA: Association for Computational Linguistics. doi:10.3115/1218955.1219018. http://dx.doi.org/10.3115/1218955.1219018.

Och, F.J. 2002. Statistical machine translation: From single-word models to alignment templates. Ph.D. thesis, RWTH Aachen University, Computer Science Department, RWTH Aachen University, Aachen.

Okita, T., and J. van Genabith. 2012. Minimum bayes risk decoding with enlarged hypothesis space in system combination. In *Computational linguistics and intelligent text processing*, 40–51. Berlin: Springer.

Okuma, H., H. Yamamoto, and E. Sumita. 2008. Introducing a translation dictionary into phrase-based SMT. *IEICE - Transactions on Information and Systems* E91-D(7):2051–2057. doi:10.1093/ietisy/e91-d.7.2051.

Pal, S., and S.K. Naskar, 2014. Hybrid word alignment. In *Hybrid approaches to translation*. Berlin: Springer.

Papineni, K., S. Roukos, T. Ward, and W. Zhu. 2002. BLEU: A method for automatic evaluation of machine translation. In *Proceedings of the 40th Annual Meeting of the Association for Computational Linguistics*, Philadelphia, 311–318.

Patel, R.N., R. Gupta, P.B. Pimpale, and M. Sasikumar. 2013. Reordering rules for English-Hindi SMT. In *Proceedings of the Second Workshop on Hybrid Approaches to Translation*, 34–41. Sofia: Association for Computational Linguistics. http://www.aclweb.org/anthology/W13-2807.

Quirk, C., A. Menezes, and C. Cherry. 2005. Dependency treelet translation: Syntactically informed phrasal SMT. In *Proceedings of the 43rd Annual Meeting of the Association for Computational Linguistics (ACL'05)*, Association for Computational Linguistics, 271–279. http://www.aclweb.org/anthology/P05-1034.

Ranta, A. 2011 *Grammatical framework: Programming with multilingual grammars*. Stanford: CSLI Publications. ISBN-10: 1-57586-626-9 (Paper), 1-57586-627-7 (Cloth).

Rios, A., and A. Göhring. 2014. Machine learning applied to rule-based machine translation. In *Hybrid approaches to translation*. Berlin: Springer.

Rosti, A.V.I., B. Zhang, S. Matsoukas, and R. Schwartz. 2008. Incremental hypothesis alignment for building confusion networks with application to machine translation system combination. In *Proceedings of the Third Workshop on Statistical Machine Translation, StatMT '08*, 183–186. Stroudsburg, PA: Association for Computational Linguistics. http://dl.acm.org/citation.cfm?id=1626394.1626423.

Rudolf, R. 2014. Depfix, a tool for automatic rule-based post-editing of SMT. *The Prague Bulletin of Mathematical Linguistics* 102(1):47–56.

Sánchez-Martínez, F., and M.L. Forcada. 2009. Inferring shallow-transfer machine translation rules from small parallel corpora. *Journal of Artificial Intelligence Research* 34:605–635.

Sánchez-Martínez, F., M.L. Forcada, and A. Way. 2009. Hybrid rule-based example-based MT: Feeding apertium with sub-sentential translation units. In *Proceedings of the 3rd Workshop on Example-Based Machine Translation*, Dublin, ed. M.L. Forcada, A. Way, 11–18.

Sánchez-Cartagena, V.M., J.A. Pérez-Ortiz, and F. Sánchez-Martínez. 2016. Integrating rules and dictionaries from shallow-transfer machine translation into phrase-based statistical machine translation. *Journal of Artificial Intelligence Research* 55:17–61.

Sim, K.C., W.J. Byrne, M.J. Gales, H. Sahbi, and P.C. Woodland. 2007. Consensus network decoding for statistical machine translation system combination. In *IEEE International Conference on Acoustics, Speech and Signal Processing, 2007. ICASSP 2007*, vol. 4, pp. IV–105. New York: IEEE.

Snover, M., B. Dorr, R. Schwartz, L. Micciulla, and J. Makhoul. 2006. A study of translation edit rate with targeted human annotation. In *Proceedings of the Seventh Conference of the Association for Machine Translation in the Americas (AMTA 2006)*, Cambridge, 223–231.

Tambouratzis, G., M. Vassiliou, and S. Sofianopoulos. 2014. Language-independent hybrid MT: Comparative evaluation of translation quality. In *Hybrid approaches to translation*. Berlin: Springer.

Toutanova, K., H. Suzuki, and A. Ruopp. 2008. Applying morphology generation models to machine translation. In *Proceedings of ACL-08: HLT*, 514–522. Columbus, OH: Association for Computational Linguistics. http://www.aclweb.org/anthology/P/P08/P08-1059.

Tyers, F.M., F. Sánchez-Martínez, and M.L. Forcada. 2012. Flexible finite-state lexical selection for rule-based machine translation. In *Proceedings of the 16th Annual Conference of the European Association for Machine Translation*, Trento, 213–220.

Vauquois, B. 1968. A survey of formal grammars and algorithms for recognition and transformation in mechanical translation. In *IFIP Congress* (2), 1114–1122.

Vintar, V., and D. Fišer. 2014. Using wordnet-based word sense disambiguation to improve MT performance. In *Hybrid approaches to translation*. Berlin: Springer.

Vogel, S., and C. Monson. 2004. Augmenting manual dictionaries for statistical machine translation systems. In *2003 Proceedings of LREC*, 1593–1596.

Wang, C., M. Collins, and P. Koehn. 2007. Chinese syntactic reordering for statistical machine translation. In *EMNLP-CoNLL*, ACL, 737–745.

Wolf, P., U. Bernardi, C. Federmann, and S. Hunsicker. 2011. From statistical term extraction to hybrid machine translation. In *Proceedings of the 15th Annual Conference of the European Association for Machine Translation. Annual Conference of the European Association for Machine Translation (EAMT-11)*, Leuven, May 30–31, 225–231. Leuven: European Association for Machine Translation. http://www.mt-archive.info/EAMT-2011-Wolf.pdf.

Wu, D. 1997. Stochastic inversion transduction grammars and bilingual parsing of parallel corpora. *Computational Linguistics* 23(3):377–403.

Xia, F., and M. McCord. 2004. Improving a statistical MT system with automatically learned rewrite patterns. In *Proceedings of the 20th International Conference on Computational Linguistics, COLING '04*. Stroudsburg, PA: Association for Computational Linguistics. doi:10.3115/1220355.1220428. http://dx.doi.org/10.3115/1220355.1220428.

Zabokrtsky, Z., J. Ptacek, and P. Pajas. 2008. Tectomt: Highly modular MT system with tectogrammatics used as transfer layer. In *Proceedings of the Third Workshop on Statistical Machine Translation*, 167–170. Columbus, OH: Association for Computational Linguistics. http://www.aclweb.org/anthology/W08-0325.

Part I
Adding Linguistics into SMT

Controlled Ascent: Imbuing Statistical MT with Linguistic Knowledge

William D. Lewis, Chris Quirk, and Qin Gao

Abstract We explore the intersection of rule-based and statistical approaches in machine translation, with a particular focus on past and current work at Microsoft Research. Until about 10 years ago, the only machine translation systems worth using were rule-based and linguistically-informed. Along came statistical approaches, which use large corpora to directly guide translations toward expressions people would actually say. Rather than making local decisions when writing and conditioning rules, goodness of translation was modeled numerically and free parameters were selected to optimize that goodness. This led to huge improvements in translation quality as more and more data was consumed. By necessity, the pendulum is swinging back towards the inclusion of linguistic features in MT systems. We describe some of our statistical and non-statistical attempts to incorporate linguistic insights into machine translation systems, showing what is currently working well, and what isn't. We also look at trade-offs in using linguistic knowledge ("rules") in pre- or post-processing by language pair, with a particular eye on the return on investment as training data increases in size.

1 Introduction

Machine translation has undergone several paradigm shifts since its original conception. Early work considered the problem as cryptography, imagining that a word replacement cipher could find the word correspondences between two languages. Clearly Weaver was decades ahead of his time in terms of both computational power and availability of data: only now is this approach gaining some traction (Knight 2013).[1] In his time, however, this direction did not appear promising, and work turned toward rule-based approaches.

---

[1] For the original 1949 *Translation* memorandum by Weaver see Weaver (1955).

W.D. Lewis (✉) • C. Quirk • Q. Gao
Microsoft Research, One Microsoft Way, Redmond, WA 98052, USA
e-mail: wilewis@microsoft.com; chrisq@microsoft.com; qigao@microsoft.com

© Springer International Publishing Switzerland 2016
M.R. Costa-jussà et al. (eds.), *Hybrid Approaches to Machine Translation*,
Theory and Applications of Natural Language Processing,
DOI 10.1007/978-3-319-21311-8_2

Effective translation needs to handle a broad range of phenomena. Word substitution ciphers may address lexical selection, but there are many additional complexities: morphological normalization in the source language, morphological inflection in the target language, word order differences, and sentence structure differences, to name a few. Many of these could be captured, at least to a first degree of approximation, by rule-based approaches. A single rule might capture the fact that English word order is predominantly SVO and Japanese word order is predominantly SOV. While many exceptions exist, such rules handle many of the largest differences between languages rather effectively. Therefore, rule-based systems that did a reasonable job of addressing morphological and syntactic differences between source and target dominated the marketplace for decades.

With the broader usage of computers, greater amounts of electronic data became available. Example-based machine translation systems, which learn corpus-specific translations based on data, began to show substantial improvements in the core problem of lexical selection. This task was always quite difficult for rule-based approaches: finding the correct translation in context requires a large amount of knowledge. In practice, nearby words are effective disambiguators once a large amount of data has been captured.

Phrase-based statistical machine translation systems formalized many of the intuitions in example-based machine translation approaches, replacing heuristic selection functions with robust statistical estimators. Effective search techniques developed originally for speech recognition were strong starting influences in the complicated realm of MT decoding. Finally, large quantities of parallel data and even larger quantities of monolingual data allowed such phrasal methods to shine even in broad domain translation.

Translations were still far from perfect, though. Phrasal systems capture local context and local reordering well, but struggle with global reordering. Over the past decade, statistical machine translation has begun to be influenced by linguistic information once again. Syntactic models have shown some of the most compelling gains. Many systems leverage the syntactic structure of either the source or the target sentences to make better decisions about reordering and lexical selection.

Our machine translation group has been an active participant in many of these latest developments. The first MSR MT system used deep linguistic features, often with great positive effect. Inspired by the successes and failures of this system, we invested heavily in syntax-based SMT. However, our current statistical systems are still linguistically impoverished in comparison.

This paper attempts to document important lessons learned, highlight current best practices, and identify promising future directions for improving machine translation. A brief review of our earlier generation of machine translation technology sets the stage; this older system remains relevant given renewed interest in semantics (e.g., http://amr.isi.edu/). Next we describe some of our statistical and non-statistical attempts to incorporate linguistic insights into machine translation systems, showing what is currently working well, and what is not. We also look at trade-offs in using linguistic knowledge ("rules") in pre- or post-processing by language pair, with a particular eye on the return on investment as training data increases in size. Systems built on different architectures, particularly those incorporating some linguistic information, may have different learning curves on data. The advent of social media and big data presents new challenges; we review some effective research in this area. We conclude by exploring promising directions for improving translation quality, especially focusing on areas that stand to benefit from linguistic information.

2 Logical Form Translation

Machine translation research at Microsoft Research began in 1999. Analysis components had been developed to parse surface sentences into deep *logical forms*: predicate-argument structures that normalized away many morphological and syntactic differences. This deep representation was originally intended for information mining and question answering, allowing facts to reinforce one another, and simplifying question and answer matching. These same normalizations helped make information more consistent across languages: machine translation was a clear potential application. Consider the deep representations of the sentence pairs in Fig. 1: many of the surface differences, such as word order and morphological inflection, are normalized away, potentially easing the translation process.

The linguistic theory behind the system was related to other approaches at the time, and is built in the tradition of generative grammar. This separation of syntactic structure and semantic structure bears a strong resemblance to Lexical Functional Grammar (Dalrymple 2001), where the syntactic tree plays a role similar to c-structure, and the logical form is similar to f-structure, for instance. Jensen et al. (1992) documents the early theory and practice of this system.

Substantial differences remained, however. Many words and phrases have non-compositional contextually-influenced translations. Commercial systems of the time relied on complex, hand-curated dictionaries to make this mapping. Yet example-based and statistical systems had already begun to show promise, especially in the case of domain-specific translations. Microsoft in particular had large internal demand for "technical" translations. With increasing language coverage and continuing updates to product documentation and support articles came increasing translation costs. Producing translations tailored to this domain would have been an expensive task for a rule-based system; a corpus-based approach was pursed.

This was truly a hybrid system. Source and target language surface sentences were parsed into deep logical forms using rule-based analyzers.[2] Likewise a rule-based target language generation component could find a surface realization of

---

[2] These parsers were developed with a strong focus on corpora, though. George Heidorn, Karen Jensen, and the NLP research group developed a tool chain for quickly parsing a large bank of test sentences and comparing against the last best result. The improvements and regressions resulting from a change to the grammar could be manually evaluated, and the changes refined until the end result. The end result was a data driven but not statistical approach to parser development.

```
To please reviewers is difficult.
be1 (+Pres +Proposition)
  \Tobj——difficult1 (+Proposition +F0)
            \Tsub——please1 (+Inf +Psych)
                      \Tsub——_X1
                      \Tind——reviewer1 (+Plur)
Reviewers are difficult to please.
be1 (+Pres +Proposition)
  \Tobj——difficult1 (+Proposition +B3)
            \Tsub——please1 (+Inf +Psych)
                      \Tsub——_X1
                      \Tind——reviewer1 (+Plur)
Pleasing reviewers is difficult.
be1 (+Pres +Proposition)
  \Tobj——difficult1 (+Proposition +F0)
            \Tsub——please1 (+Verbnoun +Psych)
                      \Tsub——_X1
                      \Tind——reviewer1 (+Plur)
```

Fig. 1 This figure demonstrates how sentences with very different surface forms may have (nearly) identical logical form representations. After each of the three sentences in *black*, the automatically produced logical form is displayed. This graph with labeled, directed edges represents the sentence content; the nodes shown in *red* (e.g. 'be', 'difficult', 'please', 'reviewer', and the zero pronoun 'X'), and the edge labels shown in *blue* (here 'Tobj' represents the typical object relation, Tsub is the typical subject, and Tind is the indirect object). Despite substantial differences in surface order and syntactic structure, the resulting graphs are isomorphic; for instance, in every case, 'reviewer' is the indirect object of 'please'. In addition, each node has a set of binary attributes (or 'bits', here shown in *gray*) that capture syntactic and surface information: '+Pres' indicates that the verb is present tense, '+Plur' indicates that a noun is plural, etc. These binary attributes were very useful in the translation process

a deep logical form. However, the mapping from source language logical form fragments to target language logical form fragments was learned from parallel data.

2.1 Details of the LF-Based System

Training started with a parallel corpus. First, the source and target language sentences were parsed. Then the logical forms of the source and target were aligned (Menezes and Richardson 2001). These aligned logical forms were partitioned into minimal non-compositional units, each consisting of some non-empty subset of the source and target language nodes and relations. Much like in example-based or phrasal systems, both minimal and composed versions of these units were then stored as possible translations. A schematic of the this data flow is presented in Fig. 2.

At runtime, an input sentence was first parsed into a logical form. Units whose source sides matched the logical form were gathered. A heuristic search found a set

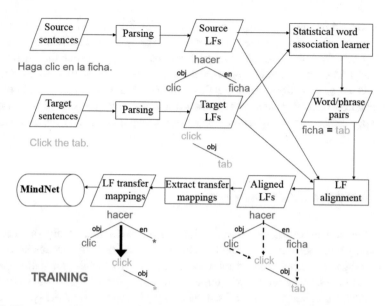

Fig. 2 The process of learning translation information from parallel data in the LF system

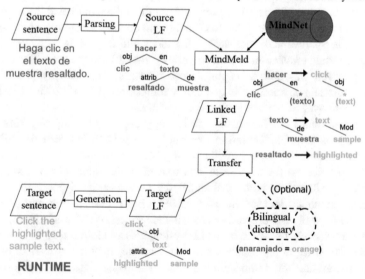

Fig. 3 The process of translating a new sentence in the LF system

of fragments that: (a) covered every input node at least once, and (b) were consistent in their translation selections. If some node or relation was not uncovered, it was copied from source to target. The resulting target language logical form was then fed into a generation component, which produced the final string. A schematic diagram is presented in Fig. 3.

This overview sweeps many fine details under the rug. Many morphological and syntactic distinctions were represented as binary features ("bits") in the LF; mapping bits was difficult. The logical form was a graph rather than a tree—in "John ate and drank", *John* is the DSUB (deep subject) of both *eat* and *drink*—which led to complications in transferring structure. Many such complications were often handled through rules; these rules grew more complex over time. Corpus-based approaches efficiently learned many non-compositional and domain specific issues.

2.2 Results and Lessons Learned

The system was quite successful at the time. MSR used human evaluation heavily, performing both absolute and relative quality evaluations. In the absolute case, human judges gave each translation a score between 1 (terrible translation) and 4 (perfect). For relative evaluations, judges were presented with two translations in randomized order, and were asked whether they preferred system A, system B, or neither. In its training domain, the LF-based system was able to show substantial improvements over rule-based systems that dominated the market at the time.

Much of these gains were due to domain- and context-sensitivity of the system. Consider the Spanish verb "activar". A fair gloss into English is "activate", but the most appropriate translation in context varies ("signal", "flag", etc.). The example-based approach was able to capture those contexts very effectively, leading to automatic domain customization given only translation memories. This was a huge improvement over rule-based systems of the time.

During this same era, however, statistical approaches (Och and Ney 2004) were showing great promise. Therefore, we ran a comparison between the LF-based system and a statistical system without linguistic information. Both systems were trained and tuned on the same data, and translated the same unseen test set. The linguistic system had the additional knowledge sources at its disposal: morphological, lexical, syntactic, and semantic information. Regardless, the systems performed nearly equally well on average. Each had distinct strengths and weaknesses, though.

Often the success or failure of the LF-system was tied to the accuracy of its deep analysis. When these representations were accurate, they could lead to effective generalizations and better translations of rare phenomena. Since surface words were lemmatized and syntactic differences normalized, unseen surface forms could still be translated as long as their lemma was known (see Fig. 4a). Yet mistakes in identifying the correct logical form could lead to major translation errors, as in Fig. 4b. Evaluation of LF accuracy was somewhat difficult as the formalism was substantially different than other resources (e.g. the Penn Treebank). One attempt to compare syntactic structure (Ringger et al. 2004) found that parsing accuracy

(a) Effecitve LF translation. Note how the LF system is able to translate "se lleveban a cabo" even though that particular surface form was not present in the training data.

    SRC: La tabla muestra además dónde se llevaban a cabo esas tareas en Windows NT versión 4.0.

    REF: The table also shows where these tasks were performed in Windows NT version 4.0.

     LF: The table shows where, in addition, those tasks were conducted on Windows NT version 4.0.

    STAT: The table also shows where llevaban to Windows NT version 4.0.

(b) Parsing errors may degrade translation quality; the parser interprted '/' as coordination.

    SRC: La sintaxis del operador / tiene las siguientes partes:

    REF: The / operator syntax has these parts:

     LF: The operator syntax it has the parts:

    STAT: The / operator syntax has these parts:

(c) Graph-like structures for situations such as coordination are difficult to transfer (see the parenthesized group in particular); selecting the correct form at generation time is difficult in the absence of a target language model.

    SRC: Debe ser una consulta de selección (no una consulta de tabla de referencias cruzadas ni una consulta de acción).

    REF: Must be a select query (not a crosstab query or action query).

     LF: You must not be a select query neither not a query in table in cross-references nor not an action query.

    STAT: Must be a select query (not a crosstab query or an action query).

Fig. 4 Example source Spanish sentences, English reference translations of those sentences, translations from the LF system, and translations from a statistical translation system without linguistic features

was close to start of the art statistical parsers of the time. However, no databases of semantic representations existed for comparison at the time, so only syntactic parsing was compared.

Likewise the lack of statistics in the components could cause problems. Statistical approaches found great benefits from the target language model. Using a rule-based generation component made it difficult to leverage a target language model. Often, even if a particular translation was presented tens, hundreds, or thousands of times in the data, the LF-based system could not produce it because the rule-based generation component would not propose the common surface form, as in Fig. 4c.

We drew several lessons from this system when developing our next generation of machine translation systems. It was clear to us that syntactic representations can help translation, especially in reordering and lexical selection: appropriate representations allows better generalization. However, over-generalization can lead to translation error, as can parsing errors.

3 The Next Generation MSR MT Systems

Research in machine translation at Microsoft has been strongly influenced by this prior experience with the LF system. First we must notice that there is a huge space of possible translations. Consider human reference translations: unless tied to a specific domain or area, they seldom agree completely on lexical selection and word order. If our system is to produce reasonable output, it should consider a broad range of translation options, preferring outputs most similar to language used by humans. Why do we say "order of magnitude" rather than "magnitude order", or "master of ceremonies" rather than "ceremonies master"? Many choices in language are fundamentally arbitrary, but we need to conform to those arbitrary decisions if we are to produce fluent and understandable output. Second, while there is leverage to be gained from deep features, seldom do we have a component that identifies these features with perfect accuracy. In practice it seems that the error rate increases as the depth of component analysis increases. Finally, we need a representation of "good translations" that is understandable by a computer. When forced to choose between two translations, the system needs to make a choice: an ordering.

Therefore, our data-driven systems crucially rely on several components. First, we must efficiently search a broad range of translations. Second, we must rank according to both our linguistic intuitions and the patterns that emerge from data.

We use a number of different systems based on the availability of linguistic resources. So-called *phrasal* statistic machine translation systems, which model translations using no more than sequences of contiguous words, perform surprisingly well and require nothing but tokenization in both languages. In language pairs for which we have a source language parser, a parse of the input sentence is used to guide reordering and help select relevant non-contiguous units; this is the *Treelet* system (Quirk and Menezes 2006). Regardless of which system we use, however, target language models score the fluency of the output, and have a huge positive impact on translation quality.

We are interested in means of incorporating linguistic intuition deeper into such a system. As in the case of the Treelet system, this may define the broad structure of the system. However, there are also more accessible ways of influencing existing systems. For instance, linguists may author features that identify promising or problematic translations. We describe one such attempt in the following system.

3.1   Like and DontLike

Even in our linguistically-informed Treelet system (Quirk and Menezes 2006), which uses syntax in its translation system, many of the individual mappings are clearly bad, at least to a human. When working with linguistic experts, one gut response is to write rules that inspect the translation mappings and discard those translation mappings that appear dangerous. Perhaps they seem to delete a verb, perhaps they use a speculative reordering rule—something makes them look bad to a linguist. However, even if we are successful in removing a poor translation choice, the remaining possibilities may be even worse—or perhaps no translation whatsoever remains.

Instead, we can soften this notion. Imagine that a linguist is able to say that this mapping is not preferred because of some property. Likewise, a skilled linguist might be able to identify mappings that look particularly promising, and prefer those mappings to others; see Fig. 5 for an example.

This begs the question: how much should we weight such influence? Our answer is a corpus driven one. Each of these linguistic preferences should be noted, and

```
/* DISPREFER LOST VERBS */
// if this mapping contains verbs not marked as auxiliaries...
if (forany(NodeList(rMapping),[Cat=="Verb" & ^Aux(SynNode(InputNode))])) {
      // find the list of mappings where that verb is mapped into punctuation or a coordination
      // (something that does not contain content).
      list {segrec} bad_target=sublist(keeplist,
            [forall(NodeList, [pure_punk(Lemma) | coord_conjunction(foreign_language,Lemma)])]);
      // if there are mappings like this...
      if (bad_target) {
            segrec rec;
// then for each such mapping, mark the mapping that effectively deletes the verb as DontLike
            foreach (rec; bad_target) {
                  +DontLike(rec);
            }
      }
}
```

Fig. 5 An example rule for marking mappings as "DontLike". In this case, the rule searches for source verbs that are not auxiliaries and that are translated into lemmas or punctuation. Such translations are marked as DontLike

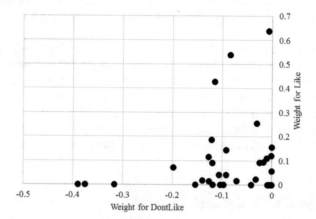

Fig. 6 A plot of the weights for +Like mapping count and +DontLike mapping count. Each point represents a single language pair. Although the weights differ substantially across language pairs, Like is generally assigned a positive weight (sometimes quite positive), and DontLike is assigned a negative weight. In our system, weights are L1 normalized (the sum of the absolute values of the weights is equal to one), so feature weights greater than 0.1 are very influential. This demonstrates that preferences encoded by a linguist can be weighted using automatic methods such as MERT, allowing the system to balance linguistic preferences with statistical models

the weight of these preferences should be tuned with all others to optimize the goodness of translation. Already our statistical system has a number of signals that attempt to gauge translation quality: the translation models attempt to capture fidelity of translation; language models focus on fluency; etc. We use techniques such as MERT (Och 2003) and PRO (Hopkins and May 2011) to tune the relative weight of these signals. Why not tune indicators from linguists in the same manner?

When our linguists mark a mapping as +Like or +DontLike, we track that throughout the search. Each final translation incorporates a count of Like mappings and a count of DontLike mappings, just as it accumulates a language model score, translation model scores, word penalties, and so on. These weights are tuned to optimize some approximate evaluation metric. In Fig. 6, the weight of Like and

DontLike is shown for a number of systems, demonstrating how optimization may be used to tune the effect of hand-written rules. Removing these features degrades the performance of an MT system by at least 0.5 BLEU points, though the degradations are often even more visible to humans.

This mechanism has been used to capture a number of effects in translation commonly missed by statistical methods. It is crucial yet challenging to maintain negation during translation, especially in language pairs where negation is expressed differently: some languages use a free morpheme (Chinese tends to have a separate word), others use a bound morpheme (English may use prefixes), others require two separated morphemes (French has negation agreement); getting any of these wrong can lead to poor translations. Rules that look at potentially distant words can help screen away negation errors. Likewise rules can help ensure that meaning is preserved, by preventing main verbs mapping to punctuation, or screening out mappings that seem unlikely, especially when those mappings involve unusual tokens.

These two features are a rather coarse means of introducing linguistic feedback. As our parameter estimation techniques scale to larger features more effectively, we are considering using finer-grained feedback from linguists to say not only that they like or don't like a particular mapping, but why. The relative impact of each type of feedback can be weighted: perhaps it is critical to preserve verbs, but not so important to handle definiteness. Given recent successes in scaling parameter estimation to larger and larger values, this area shows great promise.

3.2 Linguistic Component Accuracy

Another crucial issue is the quality of the linguistic components. We would certainly hope that better quality of linguistic analysis should lead to better quality translations. Indeed, in certain circumstances it appears that this correlation holds.

In the case of the Treelet system, we hope to derive benefit from linguistic features via a dependency tree. To investigate the impact of the parse quality, we can degrade a Treebank-trained parser by limiting the amount of training data made available. As this decreases, the parser quality should degrade. If we hold all other information in the MT system fixed (parallel and monolingual training data, training regimen, etc.), then all differences should be due to the changes in parse quality. Table 1 presents the results of an experiment of this form (Quirk and Corston-Oliver 2006). As the amount of training data increase, we see a substantial increase in parse quality.

Another way to mitigate parser error is to maintain syntactic ambiguity through the translation process. For syntax directed translation systems, this can be achieved by translating forests rather than single trees, ideally including the score of parse as part of the translation derivation. In unpublished results, we found that this made a substantial improvement in translation quality; the effect was corroborated in other syntax directed translation systems (Mi et al. 2008). Alternatively, allowing

Table 1 Comparison of
BLEU scores as linguistic
information is varied

System	English-German	English-Japanese
Phrasal	31.7	32.9
Right branching	31.4	28.0
250 instances	32.8	34.1
2500 instances	33.0	34.6
25,000 instances	33.7	35.7
39,082 instances	33.8	36.0

A phrasal system provides a baseline free of linguistic information. Next we consider a Treelet system with a very weak baseline: a right branching tree is always proposed. This baseline is much worse than a simple phrasal system. The final four rows evaluate the impact of a parser trained on increasing amounts of sentences from the English Penn Treebank. Even with a tiny amount of training data, the system gets some benefit from syntactic information, and the returns appear to increase with more training data

a neighborhood of trees similar to some predicted tree can handle ambiguity even when the original parser does not maintain a forest. This also allows translation to handle phenomena that are systematically mis-parsed, as well as cases where the parser specification is not ideal for the translation task. Recent work in this area has show substantial improvements (Zhang et al. 2011).

4 Evaluation

4.1 Fact or Fiction: BLEU is Biased Against Rule-Based or Linguistically-Informed Systems?

It has generally been accepted as common wisdom that BLEU favors statistical MT systems and disfavors those that are linguistically informed or rule-based. Surprisingly, the literature on the topic is rather sparse, with some notable exceptions (Riezler and Maxwell 2005; Farrús et al. 2012; Carpuat and Simard 2012). We too have made this assumption, and had a few years ago coined the term *Treelet penalty* to indicate the degree by which BLEU favored our phrasal systems over our Treelet systems. We had noted on a few occasions that Treelet systems had lower BLEU scores than our phrasal systems over the same data (the "penalty"), but when compared against one another in human evaluation, there was little difference, or often, Treelet was favored. A notable case was on German-English, where we noted a three-point difference in BLEU between equivalent Treelet and phrasal systems (favoring phrasal), and a ship/no-ship decision was dependent on the resulting human eval. The general consensus of the team was that the phrasal system was markedly better, based on the BLEU result, and the Treelet system should be pulled. However, after a human eval was conducted, we discovered that the Treelet system was significantly better than the phrasal. From that point forward, we talked about the *Treelet penalty* for German being three points, a "fact" that has lived in the lore of our team ever since.

What was really missing, however, was systematic experimental evidence showing the differences between Treelet and phrasal systems. We talked about the Treelet penalty as a given, but there was slow rumble of counter evidence suggesting that maybe the assumptions behind the "penalty" were actually unfounded, or minimally, misinformed.

One piece of evidence was from experiments done by Xiaodong He and an intern that showed an interaction in quality differences between Treelet and phrasal gated by the length of the sentence. Xiaodong He was able to show that phrasal systems tended to do better on longer sentences and Treelet on shorter: for Spanish-English, he showed a difference in BLEU of 1.29 on "short" content on a general domain test set, and 1.77 for short content on newswire content (the NIST08 test set). The BLEU difference diminished as the length of the content increased, until there was very little difference (less than 1/2 point) for longer content.[3] An interaction between decoder type and sentence length means that there might also be an interaction between decoder type and test set, especially if particular test sets contain a lot of long-ish sentences, e.g., WMT and Europarl). To the contrary, most IT text, which is quite common in Microsoft-specific localization content, tends to be shorter.

The other was based on general impressions between Treelet and phrasal systems. Because Treelet systems are informed by dependency parses built over the source sentences—a parse can help constrain a search space of possible translations, and prune undesirable mappings e.g., constrain to nominal types when the source is a noun—and, as noted earlier, because the parses allow linguists to pre- or post-process content based on observations in the parse, we have tended to see more "fluent" output in Treelet than phrasal. However, as the sizes of data have grown steadily over the years, the quality of translations in our phrasal systems have grown proportionally with the increase in data. The question arose: is there also an interaction between the size of our training data and decoder type? In effect, does the quality of phrasal systems catch-up to the quality of Treelet systems when trained over very large sets of data?

---

[3] These results were not published, but were provided to the authors in a personal conversation with Xiaodong He. In a related paper (He et al. 2008), He and colleagues showed significant improvements in BLEU on a system combination system, but no diffs in human eval. Upon analysis, the researchers were able to show that the biggest benefit to BLEU was in short content, but the same preference was not exhibited on the same content by the human evaluators. In other words, the improvements observed in the short content that BLEU favored had little impact on the overall impressions of the human evaluators.

4.2 Treelet Penalty Experiments

We ran a set of experiments to measure the differences between Treelet and phrasal systems over varying sizes of data, in order to measure the size of the Treelet penalty and its interaction with training data size. Our assumption was that such a penalty existed, and that the penalty decreased as training data size increased, perhaps converging on zero for very large systems.

We chose two languages to run these experiments on, Spanish and German, which we ran in both directions, that is, English-to-target (EX) and target-to-English (XE). We chose Spanish and German for several reasons, first among them being that we have high-quality parsers for both languages, as we do for English. Further, we have done significant development work on pre- and post-processing for both languages over the past several years. Both of these facts combined meant that the Treelet systems stood a real chance of being strong contenders in the experiments against the equivalent phrasal systems. Further, although the languages are typologically close neighbors of English, the word order differences and high distortion rates of English to or from German might favor a parser-based approach.

We had four baseline systems that were built over very large sets of data. For Spanish $\rightleftarrows$ English, the baseline systems were trained on over 22M sentence pairs; for German $\rightleftarrows$ English, the baseline systems were trained on over 36M sentence pairs.[4] We then created five samples of the baseline data for each language pair, consisting of 100K, 500K, 1M, 2M, and 5M sentence pairs (the same samples were used for both EX and XE for the respective languages). We then trained both Treelet and phrasal systems in both directions (EX and XE) over each sample of data. Language models were trained on all systems over the target-side data.

For dev data, we used development data from the 2010 WMT competition (Callison-Burch et al. 2010), and we used MERT (Och 2003) to tune each system. We tested each system against three different test sets: two were from the WMT competitions of 2009 and 2010, and the other was one locally constructed from 5000 sentences of content translated by users of our production service (http://bing.com/translator), which we subsequently had manually translated into the target languages. The former two test sets are somewhat news focused; the latter is a random sample of miscellaneous translations, and is more generally focused.

The results of the experiments are shown in Tables 2 and 3, with the relevant graphs in Figs. 7, 8, 9, and 10. The reader will note that in *all* cases—Spanish and German, EX and XE—the Treelet systems scored higher than the related phrasal systems. This result surprised us, since we thought that Treelet systems would score *less* than phrasal systems, especially at lower data sizes. That said, in the Spanish systems, there is a clear convergence as data sizes increased: on the WMT09 test set for English-Spanish, for instance, the difference starts at 1.46 BLEU (Treelet minus

---

[4] A sizable portion of the data for each were scraped from the Web, but there were other sources used as well, such as Europarl, data from TAUS, MS internal localization data, UN content, WMT news content, etc.

Table 2 BLEU Score results for the Spanish Treelet Penalty experiments

	Treelet			Phrasal			Diff—T-P		
	Req log	WMT 2009	WMT 2010	Req log	WMT 2009	WMT 2010	Req log	WMT 2009	WMT 2010
EX									
100K	26.49	21.52	23.69	23.10	20.06	21.19	3.39	1.46	2.50
500K	28.61	22.85	25.20	25.64	21.47	22.86	2.97	1.38	2.34
1M	30.52	24.82	27.74	28.36	24.17	26.28	2.16	0.65	1.46
2M	31.61	25.59	28.54	29.48	24.76	26.91	2.13	0.83	1.63
5M	32.86	26.37	30.14	30.89	25.84	28.56	1.97	0.53	1.58
22M	33.80	27.01	30.61	32.55	26.89	30.12	1.25	0.12	0.49
XE									
100K	27.72	21.76	23.21	26.18	20.80	21.78	1.54	0.96	1.43
500K	29.89	22.86	24.89	28.16	22.15	23.44	1.73	0.71	1.45
1M	32.18	24.76	27.14	31.32	24.32	26.02	0.86	0.44	1.12
2M	33.31	25.44	28.09	32.77	25.26	27.38	0.54	0.18	0.71
5M	34.47	26.17	29.10	34.18	26.10	28.74	0.29	0.07	0.36
22M	35.88	27.16	30.20	36.21	27.26	30.48	-0.33	-0.10	-0.28

Table 3 BLEU Score results for the German Treelet Penalty experiments

	Treelet			Phrasal			Diff (T-P)		
	Req log	WMT 2009	WMT 2010	Req log	WMT 2009	WMT 2010	Req log	WMT 2009	WMT 2010
EX									
100K	18.98	11.13	12.19	18.22	10.81	11.53	0.76	0.32	0.66
500K	22.13	13.18	14.33	21.09	12.74	13.68	1.04	0.44	0.65
1M	23.23	13.98	15.12	21.89	13.51	14.27	1.34	0.47	0.85
2M	23.72	14.77	15.87	23.11	14.04	15.03	0.61	0.73	0.84
5M	24.82	15.31	16.58	24.35	15.00	16.01	0.47	0.31	0.57
36M	26.72	16.72	18.20	25.83	16.33	17.18	0.89	0.39	1.02
XE									
100K	27.42	15.91	16.37	26.75	15.83	16.28	0.67	0.08	0.09
500K	30.98	18.25	19.16	29.80	18.11	19.09	1.18	0.14	0.07
1M	32.30	19.16	20.40	31.26	19.06	20.18	1.04	0.10	0.22
2M	33.40	19.95	21.48	32.25	19.65	21.06	1.15	0.30	0.42
5M	34.86	21.14	22.55	33.91	20.67	22.13	0.95	0.47	0.42
36M	37.31	22.72	24.97	36.08	21.99	23.85	1.23	0.73	1.12

Fig. 7 English-Spanish
BLEU graph across different
data sizes, Treelet vs. Phrasal

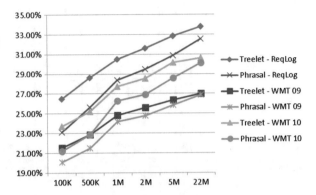

Fig. 8 Spanish-English
BLEU graph across different
data sizes, Treelet vs. Phrasal

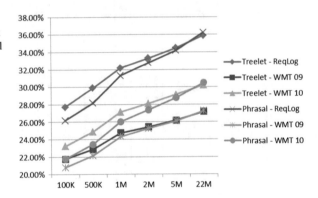

Fig. 9 English-German
BLEU graph across different
data sizes, Treelet vs. Phrasal

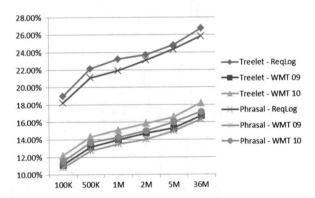

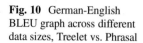
Fig. 10 German-English
BLEU graph across different
data sizes, Treelet vs. Phrasal

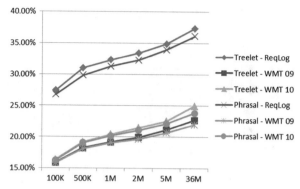

phrasal) for the 100K sentence system, with a steady convergence to near zero (0.12) for the full-data baseline. The other test sets show the same steady convergence, although they do not approach zero quite as closely. (One might ask whether they would converge to zero with more training data.) The other direction is even more dramatic: on all test sets the diffs converge on negative values, indicating that phrasal systems surpass the quality of the associated Treelet systems at the largest data points. This is a nice result since it shows, at least in the case of Spanish, that there is an interaction between decoder type and the amount of data: Treelet clearly does better at lower data amounts, but phrasal catches up with, and can even pass, the quality of equivalent Treelet given sufficient data. With larger data, phrasal may, in fact, be favored over Treelet.

The German systems do not tell quite as nice a story. While it is still true that Treelet has higher BLEU scores than phrasal throughout, and that systems trained using both decoders improve in quality as more data is added (and the trajectory is similar), there is no observable convergence as data size increases. For German, then, we can only say that more data helps either decoder, but we cannot say that phrasal benefits from larger data more than Treelet. Why the difference between Spanish and German? We suspect there may be an interaction with the parsers, in that two separate teams developed them. Thus, it could be the fact that the strength of the respective parsers affected how "linguistically informed" particular systems are. There could also be an interaction with the number of word types vs. tokens in the German data—given German's rampant compounding—which increases data sparsity, dampening effects until much larger amounts of data are used.

Since human evaluation is the gold standard we seek to achieve with our quality measures, and since BLEU is only weakly correlated with human eval (Coughlin 2003), we ran human evals against both the English-Spanish and English-German output. Performing human evaluation gives us two additional perspectives on the data: (1) do humans perceive a qualitative difference between Treelet and phrasal, as we see with BLEU, and (2), if the difference is perceptible, what is its magnitude relative to BLEU. If the magnitude of the difference is much larger than that of BLEU, and especially does not show convergence in the Spanish cases, then we still have a strong case for the Treelet penalty. In fact, if human evaluators perceive a

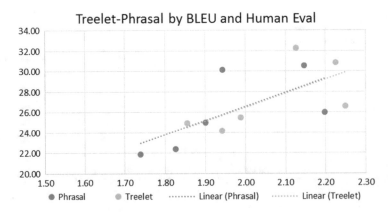

Fig. 11 Scatterplot showing Treelet vs Phrasal systems across different data sizes, plotting BLEU (Y) against Human Eval scores (X)

difference in the Spanish cases on the full data systems, the case where we show convergence, then the resulting differences could be described as the penalty value.

Unfortunately, our human evaluation data on the Treelet penalty effect was inconclusive. Our evaluations show a strong correlation between BLEU and human evaluation, something that is attested to in the literature [e.g., the first paper on BLEU (Papineni et al. 2002), and a deeper exploration in Coughlin (2003)]. However, the effect we were looking for—that is, a difference between human evaluations across decoders—was not evident. In fact, the human evaluations followed the differences we saw in BLEU between the two decoders very closely. Figure 11 shows data points for each data size for each decoder, plotting BLEU against human evaluation. When we fit a regression line against the data points for each decoder, we see complete overlap.[5]

In summary, we show a strong effect of Treelet systems performing better than phrasal systems trained on small data sizes. That difference, however, generally diminishes as data sizes increase, and in the case of Spanish (both directions), there is a convergence in very large data sizes. These results are not completely surprising, but still are a nice systematic confirmation that linguistically informed systems really do better in lower-data environments. Without enough data, statistical systems cannot learn the generalizations that might otherwise be provided by a parse, or codified in rules. What we failed to show, at least with Spanish and German, is a confirmation of the existence of the Treelet penalty. Given the small number of samples, a larger study which includes many more language pairs and data sizes, may once and for all confirm the Penalty. Thus far, human evaluations do not show qualitative differences between the two decoders—at least, not divergent from BLEU. However, we did additional analyses over noisy data and data of varying

---

[5] Clearly, the sample is *very* small, so the regression line should be taken with a grain of salt. We would need a lot more data to be able to draw any strong conclusions.

lengths, in order to explore other interactions between the two decoder types. These are discussed in the next two sections (Sects. 4.3 and 4.4).

4.3   Interaction Between Decoder Type and Sentence Length

When comparing the differences between decoders, another area to pay special attention to is systematic differences in behavior as input content is varied. For example, we may expect a phrasal decoder to do better on noisier, less grammatical data than a parser-informed decoder, since in the latter case the parser may fail to parse; the failure could ripple through subsequent processes, and thus lessen the quality of the output. Likewise, a parser-informed decoder may do better on content that is short and easy to parse. If we were to do a coarse-grained separation of data into length buckets, making the very gross assumption that short equals easy-to-parse and long not, then we may see some qualitative differences between the decoders across these buckets.

To see length-based effects across decoder types, we designed a set of experiments on German and Spanish in both directions, where we separated the WMT 2010 test data into length-based word-count buckets: 0–10, 10–20, 20–30, 30–40, and 40+ words. We then calculated the BLEU scores on each of these buckets, the results for which are shown in Fig. 12.

Treelet does better than phrasal in almost all conditions (except one). That is not surprising, given the results we observed in Sect. 4.2. What is interesting is to see how much stronger Treelet performs on short content than phrasal: Treelet does the best on the shortest content, with quality dropping off anywhere between 10 and 30 words.

One conclusion that can be drawn from these data is that Treelet performs best on short content precisely because the parser can easily parse the content, as we hypothesized earlier, and the parse is effective in informing subsequent processes. The most sustained benefit is observable in English-German, with a bump up at 10–20, and a slow tapering off thereafter. Processing the structural divergence between the two languages, especially when it comes to word order, may benefit more from

Fig. 12 Treelet-Phrasal BLEU differences by bucket across language pair

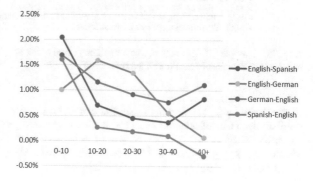

a parse. In other words, the parser can help inform alignment where there are long-distance distortion effects; a phrasal system's view is too local to catch them. However, at longer sentence sizes, the absence of good parses lessen the Treelet advantage. In fact, in English-German (and in Spanish-English) at 40+, there is no observable benefit of Treelet over phrasal.[6]

4.4   Treelet Penalty and Noisy Data

The "domain" of data used in training and/or testing also may interact with decoder type, and may give us further insight into the existence of the Treelet penalty. As noted in Sect. 4.2, a crucial component of the Treelet decoder is the parser, since each parse it produces provides generalizations about the language that otherwise would have to be learned from large amounts of data. But if the parser is less successful at parsing the data, Treelet's primary advantage over the phrasal decoder is lost.

In this section, we extend our experiments to output from the speech translation domain, where the input to the decoder is the output from a automatic speech recognition (ASR) engine. In this domain, linguistic knowledge (i.e., from the parser) is less helpful because spontaneous speech contains significant numbers of speech artifacts and speech recognition errors. The source language we chose for our test set is English, where we recorded 291 utterances, consisting of 454 sentences and 3000 words. Some examples are shown in Fig. 13. We human translated the English test data into Chinese, Spanish, German, French and Italian to generate reference sentences.

We then evaluated Treelet and phrasal systems trained on the same data against the test sets. The results are shown in Table 4.[7] As we can observe, the phrasal systems perform consistently better as measured by BLEU than the Treelet systems. However, when we look at the human evaluation we see a different picture: we see no significant difference in the human evaluation when the BLEU difference

- what would you think of a food would you go back?
- so, what kind of desserts they have.
- i heard that the happening place where most people go out.
- it is in clinton bell, which is, i am just north of the ohio state university campus.
- what did you get there like a can of soda?

Fig. 13 Examples of ASR output. These are then passed to the MT decoders directly. Translations are evaluated against human translated references

---

[6] The bump up at 40+ on English-Spanish and German-English is inexplicable, but may be attributable to the difficulty that either decoder has in processing such long content. There is also likely an interaction with statistical noise cause by such small sample sizes.

[7] *Note*: The English-Spanish and English-German systems shown in Table 4 are trained on the same data for the "full" systems discussed in Sect. 4.2.

Table 4 BLEU score and Human score of speech translation task in four languages

Langauge	Treelet		Phrasal		Diffs	Diffs	Significant
	BLEU	Human score	BLEU	Human score	BLEU	Human score	preference
Chinese	29.56	2.19	24.96	2.01	4.60	0.18	Phrasal
German	9.96	2.13	9.48	2.22	0.48	−0.09	Treelet
Spanish	24.94	2.41	21.18	2.36	3.76	0.04	Phrasal
French	22.86	1.95	21.04	1.93	1.82	0.01	Equal
Italian	14.35	1.79	12.88	1.80	1.47	0.00	Equal

Source language is English in all cases. The **Diffs** columns shows the difference between Treelet and phrasal systems for Human or BLEU scores, and the "Significant Preference" column shows the system that are significantly better than the other based on human evaluation

is just below 2 points (e.g., French and Italian), significance in favor of phrasal when the BLEU gap is much greater than 3 points (e.g., Spanish and Chinese), and significance in favor of Treelet when the BLEU score difference is around 1/2 point (e.g., German).[8]

Results from these experiments against these test sets not only show evidence for a Treelet penalty, but also show the penalty to be somewhere in the neighborhood of two to three points. More experiments would be needed to truly isolate the penalty value(s) (at least for this domain).

Summarizing the results in Sect. 4, we do see some evidence for a Treelet penalty. In Sect. 4.2, although we could not explicitly identify a penalty, it is clear that data size interacts with the relative quality of the two decoder types. With large sets of data, phrasal systems are more effectively able to learn knowledge through rote memorization and catch up with the advantage that linguistic knowledge gives Treelet. Likewise, in Sect. 4.3 we showed an interaction between decoder type and sentence length. Here we show evidence that longer sentences are translated better by the phrasal decoder, since the Treelet parser likely has difficulty parsing such long input, thus favoring phrasal. When we move to noisy ASR output in Sect. 4.4, we see the strongest evidence for a Treelet penalty, more pronounced in a domain where much of the data may be difficult to parse. In total, the Treelet penalty appears to be fact rather than fiction, but the interaction of multiple factors influence its impact.

5 The Data Gap

All Statistical Machine Translation work relies on data, and the manipulation of the data as a pre-process can often have significant effects downstream. "Data munging", as we like to call it, is every team's "secret sauce", something that can often lead to multi-point differences in BLEU. For most teams, the heuristics that are

---

[8] The word error rate of the test set is 17.09.

applied are fairly ad hoc, and highly dependent on the kind of data being consumed. Since data sources are often quite noisy, e.g., the Web, noise reduction is a key component of many of the heuristics. Here is a list of common heuristics applied to data. Some of these are drawn from our own pre-processing, some are mentioned explicitly in other literature, in particular, Denkowski et al. (2012).

- Remove lines containing escape characters, invalid Unicode, and other non-linguistic noise.
- Remove content where the ratio of certain content passes some threshold, e.g., alphabetic/numeric ratio, script ratio (percentage of characters in wrong form passes some threshold, triggering removal).
- Normalize space, hyphens, quotes, etc. to standard forms.
- Normalize Unicode characters to canonical forms, e.g., Form C, Form KC.
- In parallel data, measure the degree of ratio of length imbalance (e.g., character or word count) between source and target, as a test for misalignments. Remove sentence pairs that pass some threshold.
- Remove content where character count for any token, or token count across a sentence, exceeds some threshold (the assumption being that really long content is of little benefit due to complications it causes in downstream processing).

The point of *data cleaning* heuristics is to increase the value of training data. Each data point that is noisy increases the chance of learning something that could be distracting or harmful. Likewise, each data point that is cleaned reduces the level of data sparsity (e.g., through normalizations or substitutions) and improves the chances that the models will be more robust. Although it has been shown that increasing the amount of training data for SMT improves results (Brants et al. 2007), not all data is beneficial, and clean data is best of all.

Crucially, most data munging is done through heuristics, or rules, although thresholds or constraints can be tuned by data. A more sophisticated example of data cleaning is described in Denkowski et al. (2012) where the authors used machine learning methods for measuring quality estimation to select the "best" portions of a corpus. So, rather than training their SMT on an entire corpus, they trained an estimator that selected the best portions, and used only those. In their entry in the 2012 WMT competition, they used only 60 % of the English-French Gigaword corpus[9] and came in first in the shared translation task for the pair.

Another important aspect of data as it relates to SMT is task-dependence: what domain or genre of data will an SMT engine be applied to? For instance, will an SMT engine be used to translate IT content, news content, subtitles, or Europarl proceedings? If the engine itself is trained on data that is dissimilar to the desired goal, then results may be less than satisfying. This is a common problem in the field, and a cottage industry has been built around customization and domain-adaptation, e.g., Moore and Lewis (2010), Axelrod et al. (2011), Wang et al. (2012). In general,

---

[9] The English-French Gigaword corpus is described in Callison-Burch et al. (2009).

the solution is to adapt an SMT engine to the desired domain using a set of seed data in that domain.

A more difficult problem is when there is very little parallel data in the desired domain, which is a problem we will look at in the next section.

5.1 No Parallel Data, No Problem!!

A couple of years ago, Facebook activated a translation feature in their service, which directly calls Bing Translator. This feature has allowed users to translate pages or posts not in their native language with a *See Translation* option. An example is shown in Fig. 14.

The real problem with translating "FB-speak" ("Facebook speak"), or content from virtually any kind of social media, is the paucity of parallel data in the domain. This flies in the face of the usual way problems are tackled in SMT, that is, locate (lots of) relevant parallel data, and then train up an engine. Outside of a few slang dictionaries, there is almost no FB-like parallel content available.

Given the relatively formal nature of the text that most of our engines are trained on, the mismatch between FB content and translation models often led to very poor translations. Yet, given the absence of in-domain parallel data, it was not possible for us to train-up FB-specific SMT engines. Table 5 shows sample translations passed through our engines from native FB content, and the same after being "repaired" to more standard English. In the first column, the reader will note that the translations are quite poor, and nearly unintelligible. The repaired translations, on the other hand, are quite interpretable.

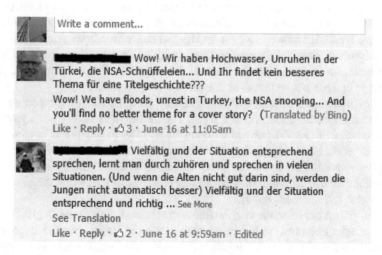

Fig. 14 Two Facebook posts: the first translated, the second showing the *See Translation* option

Table 5 One English FB sentence with and without normalizations, translated to various languages

Language	Unrepaired	Repaired
Original English	i'l do cuz ma parnts r ma lyf	I'll do because my parents are my life
To Italian	i'l fare cuz ma parnts r ma lyf	lo far perch i miei genitori sono la mia vita
To German	i'l tun Cuz Ma Parnts R Ma lyf	Ich werde tun, weil meine Eltern mein Leben sind
To Spanish	traer hacer cuz ma parnts r ma lyf	voy a hacer porque mis padres son mi vida

One approach for dealing with domain- or style-shifted content is to adapt tools to the new domain or style. Examples of this can be seen in Ritter et al. (2012), who describe an event-extraction and categorization system for Twitter, relying on tools specifically tailored to "Twitter-speak". Also relevant is recent work by Gimpel et al. (2011), who describe a custom-built POS tagger for Twitter content. For MT, however, we are still left with the paucity of relevant parallel training data. One could conceivably train language models over monolingual social media content, which could then score output from an SMT engine. However, the absence of relevant candidates in the n-best output generated by the engine's translation models would significantly degrade the resulting output.

Another option is to make the new style or domain look like conventional data, in other words, perform repairs like those shown in Table 5. If we transform social media input into conventional language, and then translate this content, we may provide much better results. Effectively, then, we'd be treating "FB-speak" as a dialect of the source language, and alter vocabulary as necessary to produce good source language candidates. This approach has significant merit. Although it is true that social media introduces new vocabulary and new expressions, many show up as altered forms of standard expressions, and much of the introduced vocabulary has direct correlates in the standard dialect of the language. This fact can work to our advantage in a transformational, or "repair"-driven, approach.

Table 6 gives some examples of FB content on the left, and the more conventional representation of the same on the right. The reader will note some systematic characteristics of the FB content as compared to the conventional content, e.g., vowel or consonant lengthening for emphasis, shortened expressions for easy of typing, sound-alike and other phonetic substitutions, abbreviated multi-word expressions treated as stand-alone words, or combinations of all of the above (see also Hassan and Menezes 2013).

Given that most of these altered forms correspond directly to English words, a very simple approach would be to apply string or regex (regular expression) substitutions directly to the FB input, and then use the resulting text as a "repaired source" for translation. A very simple set of regex repairs are shown in Table 7.

Table 6 FB speak with English references

FB speak	English translation	Comment
goooood morniiing	good morning	Extended characters for emphasis or dramatic effect
wuz up bro	What's up brother	"Phonetic" spelling to reflect local dialect or usage
cm to c my luv	Come to see my love	Remove vowels in common words, sound-alike sequences
4get, 2morrow	Forget, tomorrow	Sound-alike number substitution
r u 4 real?	Are you for real?	Sound-alike letter and number substitutions
LMS	Like my status	Single 'word' abbreviations for multi-word expressions
IDK	I don't know	
ROFL	Rolling on the floor laughing	

Table 7 Some example regexes to "fix" FaceBook content

Regex	Output
frnd[sz]	Friends
plz+	Please
yess*	Yes
be?c[uo][sz]	Because
nuff	Enough
wo?u?lda	Would have
srr+y	Sorry

Our first pass at the problem was to try such a rule-based approach. To determine the extent to which such "rules" could repair FB content, we tokenized the FB logs (logs of actual Facebook translation requests), then sorted the resulting word table by frequency. For the 1000 most frequent expressions, we concocted string and regex substitutions, and then applied these to a held-out test set of FB content. A target set of the same content had been transformed manually to standard English as a reference. Precision for this rule-based approach was very high, at 97.07 %. Recall, however, was dismally low, at 15.02 %. Clearly, this content had a very long tail, more than we could capture even with a large ranked frequency list. Further, we also noted regressions in the output that were undesirable, the most notable being the substitution of *u* to *you*. U is a very common expression in English social media content, and thus a repair is highly desirable. However, *u* is also ambiguous, and blanket replacement has ill-effects, e.g., transforming *U.S.A.* to *You.S.A.*. Although one could counter this problem with bigram substitutions, e.g., *u r going to you are*, or *u* followed by any punctuation not being transformed, etc., the set of bigrams with *u* is quite large. Finally, a rule-based solution such as this does not scale to additional languages and scenarios.

To address these deficiencies, we sought a more data-driven approach. But we had to be creative since, as noted, our standard "hammer" of parallel data did not

Table 8 Comparison
between Rule-based and ML
approaches to repairing FB
content

Method	Prec.	Recall	F-scr
Regex rules	97.07	15.02	52.03
TextCorrector	96.51	57.90	72.38

exist. Our intuition was that there were distributional regularities in the FB content that could help automatically discover a mapping for a given target word, e.g., the distribution of *plzzz* in the FB content might be similar to *please* in our non-FB content. To that end, Hany Hassan developed a TextCorrector tool that is, as he put it, "based on constructing a lattice from possible normalization candidates and finding the best normalization sequence according to an n-gram language model using a Viterbi decoder", where he developed an "unsupervised approach to learn the normalization candidates from unlabeled text data" (Hassan and Menezes 2013). He then used a Random Walk strategy to walk a contextual similarity graph. There are two principal benefits of this approach. First, it did not require parallel training data. Two large monolingual corpora *are* required, one for the "noisy" data (i.e., FB content) and one for the clean data (i.e., our large supply of language model training data), but they do not need to be parallel. Secondly it did not require labeled data (i.e., , the algorithm is unsupervised). After several iterations over very large corpora (tens of millions of sentences in both styles) he arrived at a solution that had comparable precision to the regex method but had much higher recall: at the time of this writing, the best iteration achieved 96.51 % precision and 72.38 % recall. A comparison between the best TextCorrector approach and the regex approach are shown in Table 8. Crucially, as the size of the data increases, the TextCorrector continues to show improvement.[10]

The end result was a much better User Experience for FB users. Rather than badly mangled translations, or worse, no translations at all, users get translations generated by our standard, very large statistical engines (for English source, notably, our *Treelet* engines).

6   Conclusions and Future Directions

A crucial lesson from the work on the FB corrections described in Sect. 5.1 is its analog to Machine Learning as a whole: rule-based approaches often achieve very high precision, but often at the sacrifice of recall. The same is true in Machine Translation: rule-based MT is often more accurate when it was accurate, resulting in more precise and grammatical translations. However, it tends to be somewhat brittle and does not do as well on cases not explicitly coded for. SMT, on the other

---

[10] For a complete description of TextCorrector, please see Hassan and Menezes (2013). Also, TextCorrector is directly available through our API. See the following for more details: http:// www.microsoft.com/en-us/translator/developers.aspx.

hand, tends to be more malleable and adaptable, but often less precise. Tapping rule-based approaches in a statistical framework can really give us the best of both worlds, giving us higher precision *and* higher recall.

Finding an appropriate mix is difficult, though. As in the case of parsing, we can see how errors can substantially degrade translation quality, especially if we only consider the single best analysis. By making our analysis components as robust as possible, quantifying our degree of certainty with scoring mechanisms, and preserving ambiguity of the analysis, we can achieve a better return on investment. Making this linguistic information be included *softly* as features is a powerful way of surfacing linguistic generalizations to the system while not forcing its hand.

Some of the greatest successes in mixing linguistic and statistical methods have been in syntax. There is much ground to cover still. Morphology is integrated weakly into current SMT systems, mostly as broad features (Jeong et al. 2010) though sometimes with more sophistication (Chahuneau et al. 2013). Better integration of morphological features could have great effect, especially in agglutinative languages such as Finnish and Turkish.

Deeper models of semantics present a rich challenge to the field. As we proceed into deeper models, picking the correct representation is a significant issue. Humans can generally agree on words, mostly on morphology, and somewhat on syntax. But semantics touches on issues of meaning representation: how should we best represent semantic information? Should we attempt to faithfully represent all the information in the source language, or gather only a simple model that suffices to disambiguate information? Others are focusing on lexical semantics using continuous space representations (Mikolov et al. 2013), a softer means of representing meaning.

Regardless of the details, one point is very clear: future work in MT will require dealing with data. Systems, whether statistical or rule-based, will need to work with and learn from the increasing volumes of information available to computers. Effective hybrid systems will be no exception—tempering the keen insights of experts with the noisy wisdom of big data from the crowd holds great promise.

References

Axelrod, Amittai, Xiaodong He, and Jianfeng Gao. 2011. Domain adaptation via pseudo in-domain data selection. In *Proceedings of EMNLP*, 355–362.

Brants, Thorsten, Ashok C. Popat, Peng Xu, Franz J. Och, and Jeffrey Dean. 2007. Large language models in machine translation. In *Proceedings of the 2007 Joint Conference on Empirical Methods in Natural Language Processing and Computational Natural Language Learning (EMNLP-CoNLL)*, Prague, June, 858–867. Association for Computational Linguistics.

Callison-Burch, Chris, Philipp Koehn, Christof Monz, and Josh Schroeder. 2009. Findings of the 2009 workshop on statistical machine translation. In *Proceedings of the Fourth Workshop on Statistical Machine Translation*, Athens, March, 1–28. Association for Computational Linguistics.

Callison-Burch, Chris, Philipp Koehn, Christof Monz, Kay Peterson, Mark Przybocki, and Omar Zaidan. 2010. Findings of the 2010 joint workshop on statistical machine translation and metrics for machine translation. In *Proceedings of the Joint Fifth Workshop on Statistical Machine Translation and Metricsmatr*, Uppsala, July, 17–53. Association for Computational Linguistics.

Carpuat, Marine, and Michel Simard. 2012. The trouble with SMT consistency. In *Proceedings of the Seventh Workshop on Statistical Machine Translation*, Montréal, June, 442–449. Association for Computational Linguistics.

Chahuneau, Victor, Noah A. Smith, and Chris Dyer. 2013. Knowledge-rich morphological priors for Bayesian language models. In *Proceedings of the 2013 Conference of the North American Chapter of the Association for Computational Linguistics: Human Language Technologies*, Atlanta, GA, June, 1206–1215. Association for Computational Linguistics.

Coughlin, Deborah A. 2003. Correlating automated and human assessments of machine translation quality. In *Proceedings of MT Summit IX*, New Orleans, September, LA. The Association for Machine Translation in the Americas (AMTA).

Dalrymple, Mary. 2001. *Lexical functional grammar. Syntax and semantics series*, vol. 42. New York: Academic.

Denkowski, Michael, Greg Hanneman, and Alon Lavie. 2012. The CMU-Avenue French-English translation system. In *Proceedings of the NAACL 2012 Workshop on Statistical Machine Translation*.

Farrús, Mireia, Marta R. Costa-Jussá, and Maja Popovic. 2012. Study and correlation analysis of linguistic, perceptual and automatic machine translation evaluations. *Journal of the American Society for Information Science and Technology* 63(1):174–84.

Gimpel, Kevin, Nathan Schneider, Brendan O'Connor, Dipanjan Das, Daniel Mills, Jacob Eisenstein, Michael Heilman, Dani Yogatama, Jeffrey Flanigan, and Noah A. Smith. 2011. Part-of-speech tagging for twitter. In *Proceedings of ACL*, Portland, OR.

Hassan, Hany, and Arul Menezes. 2013. Social text normalization using contextual graph random walks. In *Proceedings of the 51st Annual Meeting of the Association for Computational Linguistics*, Sofia, August. Association for Computational Linguistics.

He, Xiaodong, Mei Yang, Jianfeng Gao, Patrick Nguyen, and Robert Moore. 2008. Indirect-HMM-based hypothesis alignment for combining outputs from machine translation systems. In *Proceedings of EMNLP*.

Hopkins, Mark, and Jonathan May. 2011. Tuning as ranking. In *Proceedings of the 2011 Conference on Empirical Methods in Natural Language Processing*, Edinburgh, July, 1352–1362. Association for Computational Linguistics.

Jensen, Karen, George E. Heidorn, and Stephen D. Richardson. 1992. *Natural language processing: The PLNLP approach*. Boston: Kluwer Academic Publishers.

Jeong, Minwoo, Kristina Toutanova, Hisami Suzuki, and Chris Quirk. 2010. A discriminative lexicon model for complex morphology. In *The Ninth Conference of the Association for Machine Translation in the Americas (AMTA-2010)*.

Knight, Kevin. 2013. Tutorial on decipherment. In *ACL 2013*, Sofia, August.

Menezes, Arul, and Stephen D. Richardson. 2001. A best-first alignment algorithm for automatic extraction of transfer mappings from bilingual corpora. Stroudsburg: Association for Computational Linguistics. doi:dx.doi.org/10.3115/1118037.1118043.

Mi, Haitao, Liang Huang, and Qun Liu. 2008. Forest-based translation. In *Proceedings of ACL-08: HLT*, Columbus, OH, June, 192–199. Association for Computational Linguistics.

Mikolov, Tomas, Wen-tau Yih, and Geoffrey Zweig. 2013. Linguistic regularities in continuous space word representations. In *Proceedings of the 2013 Conference of the North American Chapter of the Association for Computational Linguistics: Human Language Technologies*, Atlanta, GA, June, 746–751. Association for Computational Linguistics.

Moore, Robert C, and William D. Lewis. 2010. Intelligent selection of language model training data. In *Proceedings of the ACL 2010 Conference Short Papers*, Uppsala, July.

Och, Franz Josef, and Hermann Ney. 2004. The alignment template approach to statistical machine translation. *Computational Linguisitics* 30(4):417–449.

Och, Franz Josef. 2003. Minimum error rate training in statistical machine translation. In *Proceedings of the 41st ACL*, Sapporo.

Papineni, Kishore, Salim Roukos, Todd Ward, and Wei-Jing Zhu. 2002. BLEU: A method for automatic evaluation of machine translation. In *Proceedings of the 40th ACL*, Philadelphia, PA.

Quirk, Chris, and Simon Corston-Oliver. 2006. The impact of parse quality on syntactically-informed statistical machine translation. In *Proceedings of the 2006 Conference on Empirical Methods in Natural Language Processing*, Sydney, July, 62–69. Association for Computational Linguistics.

Quirk, Chris, and Arul Menezes. 2006. Dependency Treelet translation: The convergence of statistical and example-based machine translation? *Machine Translation* 20:43–65.

Riezler, Stefan, and John T. Maxwell. 2005. On some pitfalls in automatic evaluation and significance testing for MT. In *Proceedings of the ACL Workshop on Intrinsic and Extrinsic Evaluation Measures for Machine Translation and/or Summarization*, Ann Arbor, MI, June, 57–64. Association for Computational Linguistics.

Ringger, Eric, Robert C. Moore, Eugene Charniak, Lucy Vanderwende, and Hisami Suzuki. 2004. Using the Penn Treebank to evaluate non-treebank parsers. In *Proceedings of LREC*, May. European Language Resources Association.

Ritter, Alan, Mausam, Oren Etzioni, and Sam Clark. 2012. Open domain event extraction from twitter. In *Proceedings of the 18th International Conference on Knowledge Discovery and Data Mining (KDD)*, Beijing.

Wang, Wei, Klaus Macherey, Wolfgang Macherey, Franz Och, and Peng Xu. 2012. Improved domain adaptation for statistical machine translation. In *Proceedings of AMTA*.

Weaver, Warren. 1955. Translation. In *Machine translation of languages*, eds. William N. Locke, and A. Donald Booth, 15–23. Cambridge, MA: MIT Press.

Zhang, Hao, Licheng Fang, Peng Xu, and Xiaoyun Wu. 2011. Binarized forest to string translation. In *Proceedings of the 49th Annual Meeting of the Association for Computational Linguistics: Human Language Technologies*, Portland, OR, June, 835–845. Association for Computational Linguistics.

Hybrid Word Alignment

Santanu Pal and Sudip Kumar Naskar

Abstract This paper proposes a hybrid word alignment model for Phrase-Based Statistical Machine Translation (PB-SMT). The proposed hybrid word alignment model provides most informative alignment links, which are offered by both unsupervised and semi-supervised word alignment models. Two unsupervised word alignment models, namely GIZA++ and Berkeley aligner, and a rule based word alignment technique are combined together. The unsupervised alignment models are trained on the surface form as well as the root form of the training data and provide alignment tables for the corresponding training data. The rule-based aligner is aimed towards aligning named entities (NEs) and syntactically motivated chunks. NEs are aligned through transliteration using a joint source-channel model. Chunks are aligned employing a bootstrapping approach by translating the source chunks into the target language using a baseline PB-SMT model and subsequently validating the chunk hypotheses using a fuzzy matching technique against the target corpus. Experiments are carried out after single-tokenizing the multiword NEs. The effectiveness of the proposed hybrid alignment model was extrinsically evaluated on the MT quality by using well-known automatic MT evaluation metrics, such as BLUE and NIST. Our best system provided significant improvements over the baseline as measured by BLEU.

1 Introduction

Word alignment is the backbone of PB-SMT systems or any data driven approaches to Machine Translation (MT) and it has received a lot of attention in the area of statistical machine translation (SMT) (Brown et al. 1993; Och et al. 2003; Koehn et al. 2003) as the success of SMT or any other data driven approaches to MT is

S. Pal (✉)
Universität Des Saarlandes, Saarbrücken, Germany
e-mail: santanu.pal@uni-saarland.de

S.K. Naskar
Jadavpur University, Kolkata, India
e-mail: sudip.naskar@cse.jdvu.ac.in

© Springer International Publishing Switzerland 2016   57
M.R. Costa-jussà et al. (eds.), *Hybrid Approaches to Machine Translation*,
Theory and Applications of Natural Language Processing,
DOI 10.1007/978-3-319-21311-8_3

essentially reliant on the quality of word alignment. Word alignment is not an end task in itself and is usually used as an intermediate step in SMT. Word alignment is the task of detecting correspondences between words that are translations of each other from parallel sentences. Existing statistical word alignment algorithms do not cope well with many-to-many word links and SMT Models suffer from this shortcoming of alignment algorithms to process such links.

Existing unsupervised word alignment models are based on IBM models 1–5 (Brown et al. 1993) and the HMM model (Vogel et al. 1996; Och et al. 2003). IBM Models 3, 4 and 5 are based on fertility-based models, which are asymmetric. To improve word alignment quality, the Berkeley Aligner uses the symmetric property by intersecting alignments induced in each translation direction.

In addition, in any language, Multiword Expressions (MWEs) cause major problems and they pose big challenge in statistical machine translation. MWE can be roughly defined as idiosyncratic interpretations that cross word boundaries (Sag et al. 2002). The meaning of MWEs cannot be always derived from their component words; each of which have their own separate meanings when they occur independently.

Named Entity is considered as MWEs, because it contains more than one words and used as a single semantic unit in a sentence. Named entities (NE), particularly multiword NEs, on the source and the target sides of the parallel corpus should be aligned and translated as a whole. This is also true for multiword expressions (MWE) and complex predicates in general (Pal et al. 2011). However, in the state-of-the-art PB-SMT systems, the constituents of such multiword expressions are often marked and aligned as part of consecutive phrases since PB-SMT (or any other approaches to SMT) does not generally treat multiword expressions as special tokens. This motivated us to consider NEs for special treatment in this work by converting them into single tokens that makes sure that PB-SMT also treats them as a whole.

Word alignment is one of the most difficult as well as critical tasks in SMT. Sometimes some source words, appearing in both the input as well as the training set, do not correctly get translated into the SMT output because of their mapping to NULL token or erroneous mapping during word alignment. Verb phrase translation has proven itself to be a larger challenge in SMT. The words inside verb phrases are generally not aligned one-to-one; the alignments of the words inside source and target verb phrases are mostly many-to-many, particularly so for the English—Bengali language pair.

In the present work, we propose improvement of word alignment quality by combining several word alignment models and tables: (1) surface-to-surface GIZA++ alignment, (2) surface-to-surface Berkeley alignment, (3) root-to-root GIZA++ alignment, (4) root-to-root Berkeley alignment and (5) rule based alignment.

The first objective of the present work is to see how single tokenization and prior alignment of NEs affect the overall MT quality. The second objective is to see whether a hybrid word alignment model combining both unsupervised and semi-supervised techniques can enhance the quality of translation in SMT.

We carried out the experiments on an English—Bengali translation task. Bengali shows high morphological richness at lexical level. Language resources in Bengali are also very scarce.

The hybrid word alignment method combines three different kinds of word alignments—Giza++ word Alignment with grow-diag-final-and (GDFA) heuristic (Koehn et al. 2003), Berkeley aligner and rule-based aligner. We have followed two different strategies to combine the three different word alignment tables: union and add additional alignment algorithm. We implemented a rule based alignment model by considering several types of chunks, which are automatically identified on the source side. Each individual source chunk is translated using a baseline PB-SMT system and validated with the target chunks on the target side. The validated source-target chunks are added in the rule based alignment table. Work has been carried out into three directions: (1) several alignment tables are combined together by taking their union; (2) extra alignment pairs are added into the alignment table which is a well-known practice in domain adaptation in SMT (Eck et al. 2004; Wu et al. 2008) and (3) the alignment table is updated through semi-supervised alignment technique. The rule based alignment table is also improved using the updated hybrid word alignment model and then we further improve the entire model during the second pass of the experiment.

The correctness of the alignments is verified by manually checking the performance of the various alignment systems. We start with the combined alignment table which is produced by the add additional alignment algorithm which is described in Sect. 3.4. Initially, we take a subset of the alignments by manually inspecting from the combined alignment table. Then we train the Berkeley supervised aligner with this labeled data. A subset of the unlabeled data from the combined alignment table is aligned with the supervised model. The output is then added as additional labeled training data for the supervised training method for the next iteration. Using this bootstrapping approach, the amount of labeled training data for the supervised aligner is gradually increased. The process is continued until there are no more unlabeled training data. In this way we establish word alignments for the entire parallel corpus. The process is carried out in a semi-supervised manner.

We carried out evaluation of the proposed model using automatic evaluation metrics and observed significant improvements over the baseline models.

The remainder of the paper is organized as follows. Section 2 discusses related work. The proposed hybrid word alignment model is described in Sect. 3. Section 4 presents the tools and resources used for the various experiments. Section 5 includes the results obtained, together with some analysis. Section 6 concludes and provides avenues for further work.

2 Related Works

A multilingual filtering algorithm that generates bilingual chunk alignments from Chinese-English parallel corpus was proposed in (Zhu 2005). The algorithm has three steps. First, the most frequent bilingual chunks are extracted from the parallel corpus. Secondly, the participating chunks for alignments are combined into a cluster and finally one English chunk is generated corresponding to a Chinese chunk by analyzing the highest co-occurrences of English chunks. Bilingual knowledge can be extracted using chunk alignment (Zhu 2005). Another method of chunk alignment with bootstrapping approach described in (Pal and Bandyopadhyay 2012); they used an SMT based model for chunk translation and then aligned the source-target chunk pairs after validating the translated chunk.

To automatically extract bilingual MWEs, a log likelihood ratio based hierarchical reducing algorithm was proposed in (Ren et al. 2009). The usefulness of these bilingual MWEs in SMT is examined by integrating bilingual MWEs into the Moses decoder (Koehn et al. 2007). They also observed the highest improvement with an additional feature that identifies whether or not a bilingual phrase contains bilingual MWEs. While in (Ma et al. 2007), the authors simplified the task of automatic word alignment as several consecutive words together correspond to a single word in the opposite language by using the word aligner itself, i.e., by bootstrapping on its output. Extracting bilingual multiword expressions and using them in statistical machine translation was first proposed by (Lambert et al. 2005). They applied their MWE extraction technique on the Verbmobil corpus and found that the integration of these bilingual MWEs into the statistical alignment improves word alignment quality as well as translation accuracy. The term: pseudo-word, a kind of multiword expression, was introduced in (Duan et al. 2010). Pseudo-word is defined as a minimal sequence of consecutive words in terms of translation. They considered these pseudo-words as a translational unit and then fed into the Chinese-to-English PB-SMT Model. The model significantly outperformed the baseline PB-SMT model in both travel domain and news domain. Bilingual lexicon construction of MWES from a French—English parallel corpus using a hybrid approach was presented in (Bouamor et al. 2012). They integrated this bilingual MWE lexicon into PB-SMT and reported improvement in translation quality. However, their algorithm works only for many to many alignments and deals with highly and weakly correlated MWES in a given sentence pair. A Maximum Entropy model based approach for English—Chinese NE alignment that significantly outperforms IBM Model4 and HMM was proposed by (Feng et al. 2004). They considered 4 features: translation score, transliteration score, source NE and target NE's co-occurrence score and the distortion score for distinguishing identical NEs in the same sentence. Capitalization cues have also been used for identifying NEs on the English side. Statistical techniques are applied to decide which portion of the target language corresponds to the specified English NE, for simultaneous NE identification and translation (Moore and Robert 2003).

To improve the learning process of unlabeled data using labeled data (Chapelle et al. 2006), semi-supervised learning method is a very useful learning technique. Researchers have begun to explore semi-supervised word alignment models that use both labeled and unlabeled data. A semi-supervised training algorithm was described in (Fraser et al. 2006), where the weighting parameters are learned from discriminative error training on labeled data, and the parameters are estimated by maximum-likelihood EM training on unlabeled data. They also used a log-linear model, which is trained on the available labeled data to improve performance. Interpolating human alignments with automatic alignments has been proposed by (Callison-Burch et al. 2004), where the alignments of higher quality gained much higher weight than the lower quality alignments. Two separate models of standard EM algorithm, which learn separately from both labeled and unlabeled data, were developed by (Wu et al. 2006). These two models are then interpolated as a learner in the semi-supervised Ada-Boost algorithm to improve word alignment. To identify highly uncertain or most informative alignment links, active learning query strategies were applied under an unsupervised word alignment model in (Ambati et al. 2010).

Intuitively, multiword NEs on the source and the target sides should be both aligned in the parallel corpus and translated as a whole. However, in the state-of-the-art PB-SMT systems, the constituents of multiword NE are marked and aligned as parts of consecutive phrases, since PB-SMT (or any other approaches to SMT) does not generally treat multiword NEs as special tokens. This is the motivation behind considering NEs for special treatment in this work by converting them into single tokens that makes sure that PB-SMT also treats them as a whole.

Another problem with SMT systems is the erroneous word alignment. Sometimes some words are not translated in the SMT output sentence because of the mapping to NULL token or erroneous mapping during word alignment. It can often be observed that verb phrase translation poses a major challenge in SMT, particularly so for English to Indic languages. The alignments between the words inside source and target verb phrases for such language pairs are mostly found to be many-to-many.

3 Hybrid Word Alignment Model

The hybrid word alignment model is described as the combination of three word alignment models as follows:

3.1 *Word Alignment Using GIZA++*

GIZA++ (Och et al. 2003) is a statistical word alignment tool, which incorporates all the IBM 1-5 models. GIZA++ facilitates fast development of statistical machine translation (SMT) systems. In case of low-resource language pairs the quality of word alignments is typically quite low and it also deviates from the independence assumptions made by the generative models. Although huge amount of parallel data enables the model parameters to acquire better estimation, a large number of language pairs still lack from the unavailability of sizeable amount of parallel data. GIZA++ has some drawbacks. It allows at most one source word to be aligned with each foreign word. To resolve this issue, some techniques have already been applied, such as the following one. The parallel corpus is aligned bidirectionally; then the two alignment tables are reconciled using different heuristics, e.g., intersection, union, and most recently grow-diagonal-final and grow-diagonal-final-and heuristics have been applied. In spite of these heuristics, the word alignment quality for low-resource language pairs still remain low and calls for further improvement. We describe our approach of improving word alignment quality in the following three subsections.

3.2 Word Alignment Using Berkley Aligner

A recent advancement in word alignment is implemented in Berkeley Aligner (Liang et al. 2006) which allows both unsupervised and supervised approach to align word from parallel corpus. We initially train the model using unsupervised technique. We make a few manual corrections to the alignment table produced by the unsupervised aligner. Then we apply this corrected alignment table as gold standard training data for the supervised aligner. The Berkeley aligner is an extension of the Cross Expectation Maximization word aligner. Berkeley aligner is a very useful word aligner because it allows for supervised training, enabling us to derive knowledge from an already aligned parallel corpus or we can use the same corpus by updating the alignments using some rule based methods. Our approach deals with the latter case. The supervised technique of Berkeley aligner helps us to align those words, which could not be aligned by our rule-based word aligner.

3.3 Rule Based Word Alignment

The proposed rule based aligner aligns named entities and chunks. Figure 1 shows the architecture of the rule-based system. For NE alignment, we first identify NEs from the source side (i.e. English) using Stanford NER. The NEs on the target side

Fig. 1 System architecture of rule based aligner

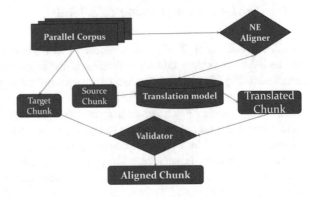

(i.e. Bengali) are identified using a method described in (Ekbal and Bandyopadhyay 2009). The accuracy of the Bengali named entity recognizers (NER) is much poorer than that of English NER due to several reasons: (1) there is no capitalization cue for NEs in Bengali; (2) most of the common nouns in Bengali are frequently used as proper nouns; (3) suffixes (case markers, plural markers, emphasizers, specifiers) get attached to proper names in Bengali. Bengali shallow parser has been used to improve the performance of NE identification by considering proper names as NE. Therefore, NER and shallow parser are jointly employed to detect NEs from the Bengali sentences. The source NEs are then transliterated using a modified joint source-channel model (Ekbal et al. 2006) and aligned to their target side equivalents following the approach of (Pal et al. 2010). Since Bengali NEs differ in their choice of 'matras' (vowel modifiers), both the NEs found in the Bengali sentence as well the transliterated (i.e., Bengali) NEs are transformed into a canonical form after omitting their *matras*. The transliterated NEs are then matched with the corresponding parallel target NEs and finally we align the NEs if a match is found.

After identification of multiword NEs on both sides, we pre-processed the corpus by replacing space with the underscore character ('_'), this ensures that the multiword NEs are single tokenized and considered as a single unit. We have used underscore ('_') instead of hyphen ('-') since there already exists some hyphenated words in the corpus. The use of the underscore ('_') character also facilitates to detokenize the single-tokenized NEs after decoding.

3.3.1 Automatic Alignments of NEs Through Transliteration

We extract the source and target (single token) NEs from the NE-tagged parallel translations in which both sides contain at least one NE. Then we first create an NE parallel corpus. In the example mentioned below, we extract the NE translation pairs given in (2) from the sentence pair shown in (1), where the NEs are shown in italics.

(1a) *Kirti_Mandir*, where *Mahatma_Gandhi* was born, today houses a photo exhibition on the life and times of the *Mahatma*, a library, a prayer hall and other memorabilia.

(1b) *কীর্তি_মন্দির* , যেখানে *মহাত্মা_গান্ধী* জন্মেছিলেন , বর্তমানে সেখানে *মহাত্মার* জীবন ও সেই সময়ের ঘটনাসমূহের একটি চিত্রপ্রদর্শনশালা , একটি লাইব্রেরী ও একটি প্রার্থনা ঘর এবং অন্যান্য স্মৃতিবিজড়িত জিনিসপত্র আছে ।

(2a) Kirti_Mandir Mahatma_Gandhi Mahatma

(2b) কীর্তি_মন্দির মহাত্মা_গান্ধী মহাত্মার

Next, we try to align the extracted source and target NEs, as illustrated in (2). If both sides contain only one NE then the alignment is trivial, and we add such NE pairs to seed another parallel NE corpus that contains examples having only one token in both side. Otherwise, we establish alignments between the source and target NEs using transliteration. We use the joint source-channel model of transliteration (Ekbal et al. 2006) for this purpose.

If both the source and target side contains n number of NEs, and the alignments of n-1 NEs can be established through transliteration or by means of already existing alignments, then the nth alignment is trivial. Similarly, for multiword NEs, intra-NE word alignments are established through transliteration or by means of already existing alignments. For a multiword source NE, if we can align all the words inside the NE with words inside a target NE, then we assume they are translations of each other.

Since the source side NER is much more reliable than the target side NER, we transliterate the English NEs, and try to align them with the Bengali NEs. We take the 5 best transliterations produced by the transliteration system for an English word, and compare them against the Bengali words. Here, we first normalize both Bengali words: target NEs and the transliterated ones, because Bengali NEs often differ in their choice of *matras* (vowel modifiers). Thus we transform Bengali NE word into a canonical form by dropping the *matras*, and then compare the results; if they match, then we align the English NE word with the Bengali NE word.

(3) নিরজ (ন্ + ি + র্ + জ্ঞ) -- নীরাজ (ন্ + ী + র্ + া + জ্ঞ)

The example in (3) illustrates the procedure. Assume we are trying to align "Niraj" with "নীরাজ". The transliteration system produces "নিরজ" from the English word "Niraj" and we compare "নিরজ" with "নীরাজ". Since the consonant sequences match in both words, "নিরজ" is considered a spelling variation of "নীরাজ", and the English word "Niraj" is aligned to the Bengali word "নীরাজ".

In this way, we achieve word-level alignments, as well as NE-level alignments. (4) shows the alignments established from (1). The word-level alignments help to establish new word/NE alignments. Word and NE alignments obtained in this way are added to the parallel corpus as additional training data.

(4a) Kirti-Mandir—কিতী-মন্দির
(4b) Kirti—কিতী
(4c) Mandir—মন্দির
(4d) Mahatma-Gandhi—মহাত্মা-গান্ধী
(4e) Mahatma—মহাত্মা
(4f) Gandhi—গান্ধী
(4g) Mahatma—মহাত্মার

3.3.2 Automatic Chunk Alignment

For chunk alignment, the source sentences of the parallel corpus are parsed using Stanford POS tagger. The chunks of the sentences are extracted using CRF chunker. The chunker detects the boundaries of noun, verb, adjective, adverb and prepositional chunks from the sentences. In case of prepositional phrase chunks, we have taken a special attention: we have expanded the prepositional phrase chunk by examining a single noun chunk followed by a preposition or a series of noun chunks separated by conjunctions such as 'comma', 'and' etc. For each individual chunk, the head word is identified. Similarly, target side sentences are parsed using a shallow parser. The individual target side Bengali chunks are extracted from the parsed sentences. The head words for all individual chunks on the target side are also marked. If the translated head word of a source chunk matches with the headword of a target chunk then we hypothesize that these two chunks are translations of each other.

The extracted source chunks are translated using a baseline SMT model trained on the same corpus. The translated chunks are validated against the target chunks found in the corresponding target sentence. During the validation process, if any match is found between the translated chunk and a target chunk then the source chunk is directly aligned with the original target chunk. Otherwise, the source chunk is ignored in the current iteration for any possible alignment and is considered in the next iterations.

The extracted chunks on the source side may not have a one to one correspondence with the target side chunks. The alignment validation process is focused on the proper identification of the head words and not between the translated source chunk and target chunk. The matching process has been carried out using a fuzzy matching technique. If both sides contain only one chunk after aligning the remaining chunks then the alignment is trivial. After aligning the individual chunks, we also establish word alignments between the matching words in those aligned chunks. Thus we get a sentence level source-target word alignment table.

Figure 2 shows how word alignments are established between a source-target sentence pair using the rule based method. Figure 2a shows the alignments obtained through rule-based method. The solid links are established through transliteration (for NEs) and translation. The dotted arrows are also probable candidates for intra-

Fig. 2 Establishing alignments through rule based methods. (**a**) Rule based alignments. (**b**) Gold standard alignments

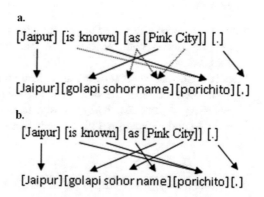

chunk word alignments; however they are not considered in the present work. Figure 2b shows the gold standard alignments for this sentence pair.

3.4 Hybrid Word Alignments Model

The hybrid word alignment method combines word alignments produced by three different kinds of word aligners—Giza++ with grow-diag-final-and (GDFA) heuristic, Berkeley aligner and rule based aligner. We have followed two different strategies to combine the three different word alignment tables.

3.4.1 Union

In the union method all the alignment tables are united together and duplicate entries are removed. Taking union of the alignments should improve the recall of the word alignment.

3.4.2 ADD Additional Alignments

In this method, we consider either of the alignments generated by GIZA++ (A_1) or Berkeley aligner (A_2) as the standard alignment as the rule-based aligner (A_3) fails to align many words in the parallel sentences. For any set of alignments $\{A_1, A_2, \ldots A_n\}$, we propose an alignment combination method as described in Algorithm 1.

Algorithm 1

Step 1:   Choose a Standard alignment table (A_s) from the set of alignment tables $\{A_1, A_2 \ldots A_n\}$ with the exception that any rule based alignment cannot be assigned to A_s.

Step 2:   Correct the alignments in A_s using the remaining (n-1) alignment tables. Take intersection of the other n-1 alignment tables. E.g., for three alignment tables A_1, A_2 and A_3, if A_2 is assigned to A_s then find additional alignments from A_1 and A_3 using $A_1 \cap A_3$ and add these additional entries to A_s.

3.5 Berkeley Semi-Supervised Alignment

The correctness of the alignments is verified by manually checking the performance of the various alignment systems. We start with the combined alignment table, which is produced by Algorithm 1. Initially, we take a subset of the alignments, a set of

500 alignments from the combined alignment table, which was manually inspected and corrected. Then we train the Berkeley supervised aligner with this labeled data. A subset of the unlabeled data, i.e., alignments collected from the combined alignment table, is aligned with this supervised model. The output is then added as additional labeled training data for the supervised training method for the next iteration. Using this bootstrapping approach, the amount of labeled training data for the supervised aligner is gradually increased. The process is continued until there are no more unlabeled training data left. In this way we refine the whole alignment table for the entire parallel corpus. The process is carried out in a semi-supervised manner.

The manual correction process involves correction of one-to-one, one-to-many, many-to-one and many-to-many alignments. To optimize the manual effort involved we focus only on one-to-one alignment correction, other types of correction are automatically taken care of by the system during the iterative process. We manually inspected 500 alignments and observed that the quality of the one-to-one alignments is better than the other kinds of alignments. Table 1 shows statistics over the 500 manually inspected alignments.

Since the one-to-one alignment list has better accuracy, the one-to-one alignments are considered initially for correction in the 1st Iteration. In the 1st iteration of the statistical model, the manually checked 500 alignments are used with the large set of alignment. At the end of Iteration 1, it was found that the accuracy of both the one-to-one and one-to-many mapped word alignments increases as more and more words are now correctly aligned. After an in depth study of the one-to-one aligned pairs for a few word, it was found that the number of incorrectly aligned entries before the 1st iteration were more than the correctly aligned entries. A detailed analysis of the word alignment quality after 1st iteration exposed that not only this process improves the accuracy of one-to-one world alignments, the accuracy of other kinds of word alignments also improves. The example given below depicts the improvement the in word alignment.

English sentence: This variety is replicated in the food, architecture, music and culture of Brazil.

Bengali Sentence (English gloss): Brajilera khadya, parikaṭhamo, sangita, sanskṛtite ei baicitra pratiphalita haya.

The example in Table 2 shows that, before the first iteration the word "replicated" is aligned to 3 Bengali words in the target side while the word "culture" remains unaligned. After the first iteration, the word "culture" is correctly

Alignment	Accuracy (%)
1:1	83.2
1:2	67.4
1:3	49.1

Table 1 Word alignment accuracy

Table 2 Word alignment improvement with iterations

Word	Alignment	
	Iteration 1	Iteration 2
NULL	7	7
This	9	9
variety	10	10
is	NA	12
replicated	8 11 12	11
in	NA	NA
the	NA	NA
food	2	2
,	NA	NA
architecture	4	4
,	5	5
music	NA	NA
and	NA	NA
culture	NA	8
of	NA	NA
Brazil	1	1
.	13	13

mapped to the target word "sangaskritite", as these one-to-one mapped words are manually corrected in the training alignment set, the system identifies the correct alignment pairs during the successive iterations. In iteration 2, the system correctly aligns "culture" with "sangaskritite", "is" with "hay" and "replicated" with "pratiPalita".

For the successive iterations the correction of one-to-one mapped word alignments are preferred again. During successive iterations, the correction effort is gradually less and the accuracy of the one-to-many as well as other types of word alignment increases.

The hybrid word alignment model has been incorporated into the SMT workflow as shown in Fig. 3.

4   Tools and Resources Used

A sentence-aligned English-Bengali parallel corpus containing 23,492 parallel sentences from the travel and tourism domain has been used in the present work. The corpus has been collected from the consortium-mode project "Development of

Fig. 3 Translation model
using hybrid word alignment

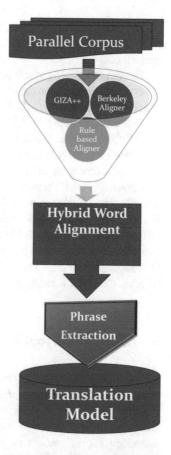

Table 3 Corpus statistics

Corpus		# Sentence	# Words
Training	English	22,492	561,881
	Bengali	22,492	478,568
Development	English	500	10,945
	Bengali	500	9881
Monolingual	Bengali	33,597	506,859
Test	English	500	11,328
	Bengali	500	9894

English to Indian Languages Machine Translation (EILMT) System—Phase II" .[1]
Table 3 presents the statistics about the dataset.

---

[1]The EILMT project is funded by the Department of Electronics and Information Technology (DEITY), Ministry of Communications and Information Technology (MCIT), Government of India.

The Stanford Parser[2] and CRF chunker[3] have been used for identifying chunks and Stanford NER has been used to identify named entities in the source side of the parallel corpus.

The target side (Bengali) sentences are parsed by using the tools obtained from the consortium mode project "Development of Indian Language to Indian Language Machine Translation (IL-ILMT) System - Phase II[4]".

NEs in Bengali are identified using the NER system of (Ekbal and Bandyopadhyay 2009). We use the Stanford Parser, Stanford NER and the NER for Bengali along with the default model files provided, i.e., with no additional training.

The effectiveness of the present work has been tested by using the standard log-linear PB-SMT model as our baseline system: phrase-extraction heuristics described in (Koehn et al. 2003), MERT (minimum-error-rate training) (Och and Franz 2003) on a held-out development set, target language model trained using SRILM toolkit (Stolcke 2002) with Kneser-Ney smoothing (Kneser and Ney 1995) and the Moses decoder (Koehn et al. 2007) have been used in the present study. Statistical significance tests were carried out using bootstrap resampling method (Koehn 2004) considering $p = 0.05$.

5   Experiments and Results

We randomly selected 500 sentences each for the development set and the test set from the initial parallel corpus. The rest are considered as the training corpus. The training corpus was filtered with the maximum allowable sentence length of 100 words and sentence length ratio of 1:2 (either way). Finally the training corpus contained 22,492 sentences. In addition to the target side of the parallel corpus, a monolingual Bengali corpus containing 506,895 words from the tourism domain was used for building the target language model. We experimented with different n-gram settings for the language model and the maximum phrase length and found that a 4-gram language model and a maximum phrase length of 7 produced the optimum baseline result. We carried out the rest of the experiments using these settings.

We experimented with the system over various combinations of word alignment models. Our hypothesis focuses mainly on the theme that improvement in word alignment will result in improvement of the system performance in terms of translation quality, particularly so for language pairs having only small amount of training data.

---

[2]http://nlp.stanford.edu/software/lex-parser.shtml

[3]http://crfchunker.sourceforge.net/

[4]The IL-ILMT project is funded by the Department of Electronics and Information Technology (DEITY), Ministry of Communications and Information Technology (MCIT), Government of India.

Table 4 Evaluation results for different experimental setups

Experiment	Exp. no.	BLEU	NIST
Baseline system using GIZA++ with GDFA	1	10.92	4.13
PB-SMT system using Berkeley Aligner	2	11.42	4.16
Experiment 1 + root-root GIZA++ alignment	3	11.08	4.14
Experiment 2 + root-root Berkeley alignment	4	11.61	4.18
Union of all alignments	5	11.22	4.15
PB-SMT system with hybrid alignment by considering (a) GIZA++ as the standard alignment (b) Berkeley alignment as the standard alignment	6a[a]	15.77	4.34
	6b[a]	16.42	4.42
Single-tokenized NE + Experiment 3	7	11.84	4.18
Single-tokenized NE + Experiment 4	8	12.02	4.20
Single-tokenized NE + (a) Experiment 6a (b) Experiment 6b	9a[a]	16.98	4.47
	9b[a]	17.72	4.53
PB-SMT system with semi-supervised Berkeley Aligner + Single-tokenized NE	10[a]	21.17	4.74

[a]Systems produce statistically significant improvements on BLEU over the baseline system

141,821 chunks were identified from the source corpus, of which 96,438 (68 %) chunks were aligned by the system. 39,931 and 28,107 NEs were identified from the source and target sides of the parallel corpus respectively, of which 22,273 NEs are unique in English and 22,010 NEs in Bengali. A total of 14,023 NEs have been aligned through transliteration.

The experiments were carried out with various experimental settings: (1) single tokenization of NEs on both sides of the parallel corpus, (2) using Berkeley Aligner with unsupervised training, (3) union of the several alignment models: rule based, GIZA++ and Berkeley Alignment, root-to-root GIZA++ alignment, root-to-root Berkeley alignment, (4) hybridization of the three alignment models, and (5) supervised Berkeley Aligner. Extrinsic evaluation was carried out on the MT quality using BLEU (Papineni et al. 2002) and NIST (Doddington 2002).

In Table 4, the baseline system (experiment 1) is the state-of-art PB-SMT system where GIZA++ with grow-diag-final-and is used as the word alignment model. Experiment 2 provides better results than experiment 1 which signifies that Berkeley Aligner performs better than GIZA++ for the English-Bengali word alignment task. Experiments 3 and 4 are carried out with root-to-root alignment; i.e. both the source and the target words are stripped to their roots and alignments are established between source and target roots, as opposed to words as is done traditionally. Root-to-root alignment helps alleviate the data sparseness problem to certain extent. It is to be noted, however, that root-to-root alignments established at the sentence level are preserved back to the word-to-word alignments. The experiments with root-to-root alignment (i.e., experiment 3 and 4) also show the same trend, i.e., Berkeley Aligner performs better than GIZA++ on root-to-root alignment. The union of all alignments (Experiment 5) provides better scores than the baseline PB-SMT with GIZA++; however it cannot beat the results obtained with the Berkeley Aligner alone. Union of all three alignments results in improved word alignment recall; however it also introduces some noisy alignments yielding lower precision in word alignment.

In the rule based alignment table, each tuple or row provides a subset of word alignment such as NE alignment and chunk alignments in a parallel sentence. These alignments are directly incorporated into the hybrid word alignment model using Algorithm 1 (discussed in Sect. 3.4). Hybrid word alignment model with GIZA++ using root form of the source-target sentence aligned training corpus as the standard alignment (experiment 6a) and other alignments are incorporated using Algorithm 1. It produces statistically significant improvements over the baseline. Similarly, the use of Berkeley Aligner as the standard alignment of the same training data for Hybrid alignment model (experiment 6b) also results in statistically significant improvements over experiment 2 and 4. These two experiments (experiment 6a and 6b) demonstrate the effectiveness of the hybrid alignment model. It is to be noticed that the hybrid alignment model works better with the Berkeley Aligner than with GIZA++.

Single-tokenization of the NEs (experiment 7, 8, 9a and 9b) improves the system performance to some extent over the corresponding experiments without single-tokenization (experiment 3, 4, 6a and 6b); however, these improvements are not statistically significant. The Berkeley semi-supervised alignment method using a bootstrapping approach together with single-tokenization of NEs (experiment 10) provided the overall best performance in terms of both BLEU and NIST and the corresponding improvement is statistically significant on BLEU over the rest of the experiments.

6   Conclusions and Future Work

The paper proposes a hybrid word alignment model for PB-SMT. The paper also shows how effective pre-processing of NEs in the parallel corpus and direct incorporation of their alignment in the word alignment model can improve SMT system performance. In data driven approaches to MT, specifically for scarce resource language pairs, this approach can help to upgrade the state-of-the-art machine translation quality as well as the word alignment quality. The hybrid model with the use of the semi-supervised technique of the Berkeley word aligner in a bootstrapping manner, together with single tokenization of NEs, provides substantial improvements (10.25 BLEU points absolute, 93.86 % relative) over the baseline. On manual inspection of the output we found that our best system provides more accurate lexical choice as well as better word ordering than the baseline system.

As future work we would like to explore how to get the best out of multiple word alignments. We will explore other combination schemes such as majority voting for this purpose and the concept will be tested on different sizes of training data as well as for other language pairs. Furthermore, integrating the knowledge about multiword expressions into the word alignment models is another important future direction for this work.

Acknowledgements The research leading to these results has received funding from the EU project EXPERT –the People Programme (Marie Curie Actions) of the European Union's Seventh Framework Programme FP7/2007-2013<tel:2007-2013>/ under REA grant agreement no. [317471].

References

Ambati, Vamshi, Stephan Vogel, and Jaime Carbonell. 2010. *10th Proceedings of the NAACL HLT 2010 Workshop on Active Learning for Natural Language Processing (ALNLP-2010)*, 10–17.

Bouamor, Dhouha, Nasredine Semmar, and Pierre Zweigenbeaum. 2012. Automatic construction of a multiword expressions bilingual lexicon: A statistical machine translation evaluation perspective. In *Proceedings of the 3rd Workshop on Cognitive Aspects of the Lexicon (CogALex-III), COLING 2012*, 95–108. Mumbai.

Brown, Peter F., Stephen A. Della Pietra, Vincent J. Della Pietra, and Robert L. Mercer. 1993. The mathematics of statistical machine translation: parameter estimation. *Computational Linguistics* 19(2): 263–311.

Callison-Burch, Chris, David Talbot, and Miles Osborne. 2004. Statistical machine translation with word- and sentence-aligned parallel corpora. In *Association for Computational Linguistics 2004*, 175. Morristown, NJ: Association for Computational Linguistics.

Chapelle, O., B. Schölkopf, and A. Zien, ed. 2006. *Semi-supervised learning*. Cambridge, MA: MIT.

Doddington, George. 2002. Automatic evaluation of machine translation quality using n-gram cooccurrence statistics. In *Proceedings of the Second International Conference on Human Language Technology Research (HLT-2002)*, 128–132. San Diego, CA.

Duan, Xiangyu, Min Zhang, and Haizhou Li. 2010. Pseudo-word for phrase-based machine translation. In *Proceedings of the 48th Annual Meeting of the Association for Computational Linguistics*, 148–156. Uppsala.

Eck, Matthias, Stephan Vogel, and Alex Waibel. 2004. Improving statistical machine translation in the medical domain using the Unified Medical Language System. In *Proceedings of the 20th International Conference on Computational Linguistics (COLING 2004)*, 792–798. Geneva.

Ekbal, Asif, and Sivaji Bandyopadhyay. 2009. Voted NER system using appropriate unlabeled data. In *Proceedings of the ACL-IJCNLP-2009 Named Entities Workshop (NEWS 2009)*, 202–210. Singapore: Suntec.

Ekbal, Asif, Sudip Kumar Naskar, and Sivaji Bandyopadhyay. 2006. A modified joint source-channel model for transliteration. In *Proceedings of the COLING/ACL 2006 Main Conference Poster Sessions, (ACL-2006)*, 191–198. Sydney.

Feng, Donghui, Yajuan Lü, and Ming Zhou. 2004. A new approach for English-Chinese named entity alignment. In *Proceedings of the 2004 Conference on Empirical Methods in Natural Language Processing (EMNLP-2004)*, 372–379. Barcelona.

Fraser, Alexander, and Daniel Marcu. 2006. Semisupervised training for statistical word alignment. In *ACL-44: Proceedings of the 21st International Conference on Computational Linguistics and the 44th Annual Meeting of the Association for Computational Linguistics (ACL-2006)*, 769–776. Morristown, NJ

Kneser, Reinhard, and Hermann Ney. 1995. Improved backing-off for m-gram language modeling. In *Proceedings of the IEEE International Conference on Acoustics, Speech, and Signal Processing (ICASSP)*, vol. 1, pp. 181–184. Detroit, MI.

Koehn, Philipp. 2004. Statistical significance tests for machine translation evaluation. In *Proceedings of the 2004 Conference on Empirical Methods in Natural Language Processing (EMNLP-2004)*, 388–395. Barcelona.

Koehn, Philipp, Franz Josef Och, and Daniel Marcu. 2003. Statistical phrase-based translation. In *Proceedings of HLT-NAACL 2003: Conference Combining Human Language Technology Conference Series and The North American Chapter of the Association for Computational Linguistics Conference Series*, 48–54. Edmonton.

Koehn, Philipp, Hieu Hoang, Alexandra Birch, Chris Callison-Burch, Marcello Federico, Nicola Bertoldi, Brooke Cowan, Wade Shen, Christine Moran, Richard Zens, Chris Dyer, Ondřej Bojar, Alexandra Constantin, and Evan Herbst. 2007. Moses: open source toolkit for statistical machine translation. In *Proceedings of the 45th Annual Meeting of the Association for Computational Linguistics (ACL 2007): Proceedings of Demo and Poster Sessions*, 177–180. Prague.

Lambert, Patrik, and Rafael Banchs. 2005. Data inferred multiword expressions for statistical machine translation. In *Proceedings of Machine Translation Summit X*, 396–403. Phuket.

Liang, Percy, Ben Taskar, and Dan Klein. 2006. *6th Proceedings of the main conference on Human Language Technology Conference of the North American Chapter of the Association of Computational Linguistics, HLT-NAACL-2006*, 104–111.

Ma, Yanjun, Nicolas Stroppa, and Andy Way. 2007. *Proceedings of the 45th Annual Meeting of the Association of Computational Linguistics*, 304–311. Prague.

Moore, Robert C. 2003. Learning translations of named-entity phrases from parallel corpora. In *Proceedings of the 10th Conference of the European Chapter of the Association for Computational Linguistics (EACL 2003)*, 259–266. Budapest.

Och, Franz J. 2003. Minimum error rate training in statistical machine translation. In *Proceedings of the 41st Annual Meeting of the Association for Computational Linguistics (ACL-2003)*, 160–167. Sapporo.

Och, Franz Josef, and Hermann Ney. 2003. A systematic comparison of various statistical alignment models. *Computational Linguistics* 29: 19–51.

Pal, Santanu, and Sivaji Bandyopadhyay. 2012. Bootstrapping Chunk Alignment in Phrase-Based Statistical Machine Translation. In: *Joint Workshop on Exploiting Synergies between Information Retrieval and Machine Translation (ESIRMT) and Hybrid Approaches to Machine Translation (HyTra), EACL-2012*, 93–100, Avignon.

Pal, Santanu, Sudip Kumar Naskar, Pavel Pecina, Sivaji Bandyopadhyay, and Andy Way. 2010. Handling named entities and compound verbs in phrase-based statistical machine translation. In *Proceedings of the Workshop on Multiword Expression: From Theory to Application (MWE-2010), The 23rd International Conference of Computational Linguistics (Coling 2010)*, 46–54. Beijing.

Pal, Santanu, Tanmoy Chakraborty, and Sivaji Bandyopadhyay. 2011. Handling Multiword Expressions in Phrase-Based Statistical Machine Translation. Machine Translation Summit XIII (2011), 215–224. Xiamen

Papineni, Kishore, Salim Roukos, Todd Ward, and Wei-Jing Zhu. 2002. BLEU: a method for automatic evaluation of machine translation. In *Proceedings of the 40th Annual Meeting of the Association for Computational Linguistics (ACL-2002)*, 311–318. Philadelphia, PA.

Ren, Zhixiang, Yajuan Lü, Jie Cao, Qun Liu, and Yun Huang. 2009. Improving statistical machine translation using domain bilingual multiword expressions. In *Proceedings of the 2009 Workshop on Multiword Expressions, ACL-IJCNLP 2009*, 47–54. Singapore: Suntec.

Sag, Ivan A., Timothy Baldwin, Francis Bond, Ann Copestake, and Dan Flickinger. 2002. Multiword expressions: A pain in the neck for NLP. In *Proceedings of the 3rd International Conference on Intelligent Text Processing and Computational Linguistics (CICLing-2002)*, 1–15. Mexico City.

Stolcke, Andreas. 2002. SRILM—an extensible language modeling toolkit. In *Proceedings of the International Conference on Spoken Language Processing*, vol. 2, 901–904. Denver.

Vogel, Stephan, Hermann Ney, and Christoph Tillmann. 1996. HMM-based word alignment in statistical translation. In *Proceeding of the 16th International Conference on Computational Linguistics (COLING 1996)*, 836–841. Copenhagen.

Wu, Hua, Haifeng Wang, and Zhanyi Liu. 2006. Boosting statistical word alignment using labeled and unlabeled data. In *Proceedings of the COLING/ACL on Main Conference Poster Sessions*, 913–920. Morristown, NJ: Association for Computational Linguistics.

Wu, Hua, Haifeng Wang, and Chengqing Zong. 2008. Domain adaptation for statistical machine translation with domain dictionary and monolingual corpora. In *Proceedings of the 22nd International Conference on Computational Linguistics (COLING 2008)*, 993–1000. Manchester.

Zhu, Xiaojin. 2005. Semi-Supervised Learning Literature Survey. Technical Report 1530, Computer Sciences, University of Wisconsin-Madison. http://www.cs.wisc.edu/_jerryzhu/pub/ssl_survey.pdf

Syntax-Based Pre-reordering
for Chinese-to-Japanese Statistical Machine
Translation

Dan Han, Pascual Martínez-Gómez, and Yusuke Miyao

Abstract There are additional difficulties associated with the translation of language pairs that have different word orders. In this chapter, we introduce some of these difficulties and describe two syntax-based approaches to addressing these problems. First, we describe an approach that exploits regularities in the differences of phrase head locations between Chinese and Japanese and formalize rules that reorder branches of constituency trees. Second, we propose an approach that compensates the differences in typical locations of the Subject (S), the Verb (V), and the Object (O) between Chinese (SVO) and Japanese (SOV), and devise rules that reorder word blocks from dependency trees. These approaches are implemented in the form of pre-reordering methods, and we evaluate their impact on a phrase-based machine translation system in terms of translation quality in news and patent domains. These approaches rely on syntactic structures that are automatically extracted by means of parsers, and as such, they are sensitive to parse errors. We analyze the effect of these parse errors, and obtain upper bounds in translation performance that can be achieved with these syntax-based pre-reordering methods.

1 Introduction

Despite the political and economic importance of the relationship between China and Japan, translation between Chinese and Japanese has not received much attention within the machine translation community. There have been remarkable advances in machine translation in the past 20 years, but a straightforward

D. Han (✉) • P. Martínez-Gómez
National Institute of Advanced Industrial Science, Tokyo, Japan
e-mail: isdanhan@gmail.com; pascual.mg@aist.go.jp

Y. Miyao
The Graduate University for Advanced Studies, Hayama, Japan

National Institute of Informatics, Tokyo, Japan
e-mail: yusuke@nii.ac.jp

© Springer International Publishing Switzerland 2016
M.R. Costa-jussà et al. (eds.), *Hybrid Approaches to Machine Translation*,
Theory and Applications of Natural Language Processing,
DOI 10.1007/978-3-319-21311-8_4

application of these advances to this language pair provides an unsatisfactory translation performance.

Although Chinese and Japanese languages share many lexical similarities, their sentence structure is very different. Their having different sentence structures often leads to non-monotonic word alignments, which are more difficult to estimate correctly using automatic alignment methods (Brown et al. 1990) when compared to languages with similar sentence structures. Inaccurate word alignments affect both training and decoding stages in machine translation. During the training stage, poorly estimated word alignments are likely to produce illegitimate bilingual phrases, that is, phrase tables in which source phrases are not in good correspondence with target phrases. Moreover, wrong word alignments may also degrade the quality of lexicalized reordering models. Consequently, in the decoding stage, the machine will have fewer chances to select appropriate target phrases that are translations of their source phrases, and the order of the target phrases within the target sentence may also be inappropriate. Finally, the quality of machine translation between Chinese and Japanese also benefits from decoders that consider large distortion limits,[1] but computational performance is severely affected in exchange.

In Sect. 2.2, we describe several approaches that have been proposed to tackle the problem of translation between languages with different sentence structures. In this chapter, we focus on pre-reordering, which consists of changing the order of words in the source sentences to resemble the word order of the target sentences. Pre-reordering of words is typically performed using either automatically inferred rules, or by following linguistic intuitions. In this chapter, we introduce two mutually exclusive sets of linguistically motivated pre-reordering rules, inspired by two linguistic observations.

The first observation is that Chinese is a head-initial language (Gao 2008), whereas Japanese is a head-final language (Fukui 1992). That is, the head of Chinese phrases usually appears at the beginning of the phrase, whereas phrase heads usually appear at the end of the phrase in Japanese. For this reason, by moving phrase heads of Chinese sentences to the end of their constituents, we may obtain word orders of Chinese sentences that resemble the word orders of Japanese sentences.

The second observation is that Chinese is a Subject-Verb-Object (SVO) language (Gao 2008), whereas Japanese is a Subject-Object-Verb (SOV) language (Fukui 1992). That is, the object-argument of the verbs usually follows the verbal phrase in Chinese, but object-arguments usually precede verbal phrases in Japanese. Thus, by moving the verbal phrases ("V") of Chinese sentences to the right of their object-arguments ("O"), we may obtain word orders of Chinese sentences that resemble the word order of Japanese sentences.

Our contribution is the design of pre-reordering methods that implement these two linguistic observations in the form of well-defined pre-reordering rules. We test these methods in terms of several evaluation metrics that assess translation quality in two different domains when translating from Chinese to Japanese and compare their

---

[1]They produce target phrases that correspond to source phrases at a very different relative position.

performances with each other and to a phrase-based system with no pre-reordering stage.

The remainder of the present chapter is organized as follows. In Sect. 2, we introduce recent advances in constituent and dependency parsing for Chinese, which are essential tools to extract the structure of Chinese sentences, and then describe research related to reordering, and more specifically, to pre-reordering strategies. In Sect. 3, we present in detail pre-reordering rules inspired by the differences in head positions between Chinese and Japanese. In Sect. 4, we describe pre-reordering rules that are inspired by the differences in SVO and SOV structures between both languages. Section 5 contains a description of the experimental framework and comparison results in translation performance between the two pre-reordering strategies and a baseline phrase-based system. Experiments are followed by a discussion of the results, and we conclude the chapter with a section summarizing our findings.

2 Background

2.1 Chinese Parsing

Linguistically motivated pre-reordering models obtain syntactic information from source sentences using language parsers. In theoretical linguistics, parsing can be distinguished into several types in terms of the formal grammar, such as phrase structure grammars and dependency grammars.

In the first pre-reordering strategy, we adapt to Chinese an existing pre-reordering technique called head finalization (HF) (Isozaki et al. 2010b), which was originally designed to pre-reorder words in English sentences (head-initial) to resemble the word order of Japanese sentences (head-final). HF receives as input a constituency tree obtained using *Enju*[2] (Miyao and Tsujii 2008), a parser based on head-driven phrase structure grammars (HPSG) (Pollard and Sag 1994). For application to Chinese-to-Japanese translation, we use a Chinese HPSG parser called *Chinese Enju* (Yu et al. 2011). In Sect. 3, we describe the details of the adaptation of HF to reorder words in Chinese sentences based on the constituency parse trees obtained using *Chinese Enju*.

Figure 1 shows an example of the XML output of *Chinese Enju* for the sentence:
"我(wo3, I) 去(qu4, go to) 了(le0, -ed) 东京(dong1jing1, Tokyo) 和(he2, and) 京都(jing1du1, Kyoto)."[3]

---

[2]http://www.nactem.ac.uk/enju.

[3]In the text, we represent Chinese characters in Pinyin together with a tone number and its English translation in parentheses, e.g., 我(wo3, I). In total, there are 5 tones (i.e., 0, 1, 2, 3, and 4) in Chinese.

```
┌<cons id="c1" cat="N" head="t0">
│  <tok id="t0" cat="N" pos="PN">wo3 我 (I)</tok>
└</cons>
┌<cons id="c2" cat="V" head="c3" schema="head_mod">
│ ┌<cons id="c3" cat="V" head="c4" schema="head_comp">
│ │ ┌<cons id="c4" cat="V" head="c5" schema="head_marker">
│ │ │ ┌<cons id="c5" cat="V" head="t1">
│ │ │ │  <tok id="t1" cat="V" pos="VV" arg1="c1" arg2="c7">
│ │ │ │    qu4 去 (go to)
│ │ │ │  </tok>
│ │ │ └</cons>
│ │ │ ┌<cons id="c6" cat="MARK" head="t2">
│ │ │ │  <tok id="t2" cat="MARK" pos="AS" arg1="c5">
│ │ │ │    le0 了 (-ed)
│ │ │ │  </tok>
│ │ │ └</cons>
│ │ └</cons>
│ │ ┌<cons id="c7" cat="N" head="c8" schema="coord_left">
│ │ │ ┌<cons id="c8" cat="N" head="t3">
│ │ │ │  <tok id="t3" cat="N" pos="NR">dong1jing1 东京 (Tokyo)</tok>
│ │ │ └</cons>
│ │ │ ┌<cons id="c9" cat="COOD" head="c10" schema="coord_right">
│ │ │ │ ┌<cons id="c10" cat="CONJ" head="t4">
│ │ │ │ │  <tok id="t4" cat="CONJ" pos="CC" arg1="c8" arg2="c11">
│ │ │ │ │    he2 和 (and)
│ │ │ │ │  </tok>
│ │ │ │ └</cons>
│ │ │ │ ┌<cons id="c11" cat="N" head="t5">
│ │ │ │ │  <tok id="t5" cat="N" pos="NR">jing1du1 京都 (Kyoto)</tok>
│ │ │ │ └</cons>
│ │ │ └</cons>
│ │ └</cons>
│ └</cons>
└</cons>
┌<cons id="c12" cat="PU" head="t6">
│  <tok id="t6" cat="PU" pos="PU">。 </tok>
└</cons>
└</cons>
```

Fig. 1 XML format output of *Chinese Enju* for a Chinese sentence. For clarity, we only present information related to the phrase structure and heads

Labels <cons> and <tok> represent non-terminal and terminal nodes, respectively. Each node is identified by a unique "id" and may have several attributes. Among them, the attribute "head" indicates the identity of its syntactic head (within its subtree). As an example, the first line in Fig. 1 defines a non-terminal node, having the "c1" as its id and node "t0" as its syntactic head. Based on the binary tree structure and head information produced by the parser, a swapping tree operation can reorder a head-initial language such as Chinese to follow a head-final-word-order language such as Japanese.

In the second pre-reordering strategy, we use an unlabeled dependency parser for Chinese, *Corbit*[4] (Hatori et al. 2011) which is based on a dependency grammar. Compared to phrase structure grammars, dependency grammars have flatter structures because they are solely determined by the relation between a word and its dependents. Figure 2 presents an example of an unlabeled dependency parse tree.

---

[4]http://triplet.cc/software/corbit.

Fig. 2 Example of an unlabeled dependency parse tree of a Chinese sentence with words aligned to their Japanese counterparts. *Arrows* point from heads to their dependents

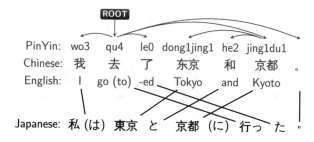

2.2   Related Research

Linguistically motivated pre-reordering methods usually rely on parsers that provide syntactic information of either the source or the target language, or both. This method has proved to be an effective auxiliary technique for traditional phrase-based statistical machine translation (SMT) systems to improve translation quality. It is especially effective when the source and target languages are structurally different, such as English-Arabic (Badr et al. 2009), English-Hindi (Ramanathan et al. 2009), English-Japanese (Isozaki et al. 2010b; Lee et al. 2010), and English to other SOV or VSO languages (Xu et al. 2009). As for Chinese-to-Japanese translation, research has been limited except in using pivot languages (Wu and Wang 2007; Tsunakawa et al. 2009), which involves a two-step translation, where each step may introduce inaccuracies. Linguistically, although Chinese and English are classified into the same group according to their sentence structure, language-specific characteristics of Chinese and English cause reordering issues when simply applying an existing English pre-reordering method to Chinese.

There are two main strategies to extract reordering rules from automatically generated parse trees. The first is to create handcrafted reordering rules based on linguistic analysis (Collins et al. 2005; Wang et al. 2007; Lee et al. 2010), and the other is to learn reordering rules from the data (Xia and McCord 2004; Li et al. 2007; Genzel 2010; Visweswariah et al. 2010; Wu et al. 2011).

The pre-reordering methods introduced in this chapter follow the first research approach, which consists of manually developing reordering rules for Chinese based on a detailed analysis of the order differences between Chinese and Japanese. This contrasts with the work on German and English in Collins et al. (2005) or English and Japanese in Lee et al. (2010). Wang et al. (2007) proposed several reordering rules to reorder Chinese sentences when translating into English, which is a relatively easier task than translating Chinese into Japanese, due to the similarities in sentence structure between Chinese and English.

Regarding the second line of research, Xia and McCord (2004) presented a method to automatically learn rewriting patterns from the combination of aligned phrases and their parse tree pairs. Therefore, their method requires both source and target side parse trees, which limits the application to other language pairs that do not count on parsers for the target language. In previous studies (Li et al. 2007; Visweswariah et al. 2010), reordering patterns were learned from constituent trees. Li et al. (2007) used tree operations to generate an N-best list of reordered candidates from which to produce the optimal translation, and Visweswariah et al. (2010) used maximum likelihood estimation to learn the probability of a reordering operation, and experimented on several language pairs. However, these methods have to contend with the problem of data sparseness when tree nodes have several children. Moreover, since the constituent tree structure is excessively restrictive, certain types of reorderings cannot be captured. In Genzel (2010), reorderings were carried out from shallow constituent trees, which were converted from dependency parse trees, and reordering rules were automatically extracted from aligned bitext. The authors used window heuristics to deal with data sparseness, which led to filtering out long-distance reordering patterns. Unlike in previous studies, Wu et al. (2011) automatically extracted reordering rules from predicate-argument structures. However, this method could only reorder words that were involved in a predicate-argument structure.

In the first pre-reordering method introduced in this chapter, we concentrate on the manual design of rules inspired by the HF pre-reordering method described in Isozaki et al. (2010b), which is one of the simplest methods that significantly improves word alignment and leads to better quality English-to-Japanese translations. A plausible explanation is the close match of the syntactic concept "head" in such language pairs. However, for the Chinese-to-Japanese language pair, differences in the definition of "head" lead to unexpected reordering problems while implementing HF. Moreover, we believe that such differences are also likely to be observed in other language pairs.

The refined application of the HF method (HFC) to reorder Chinese sentences showed gains in reordering quality, but it is impractical to increase the numbers of handcrafted rules to cover new reordering issues. Hence, we introduce a pre-reordering framework for Chinese that relies on unlabeled dependency parsing (DPC). A method similar to DPC was introduced in Xu et al. (2009), where the authors used an English dependency parser to formulate handcrafted reordering rules in the form of triplets that are composed of dependency labels, part-of-speech (POS) tags, and weights. The rules were operated recursively in a sentence during the reordering. The DPC approach introduced herein also uses dependency tree structures and POS tags,[5] but information on dependency labels is discarded because we did not find it informative to guide our reordering strategies in preliminary experiments, partly due to Chinese exhibiting fewer dependencies and a larger label variability (Chang et al. 2009).

Other approaches in pre-reordering include the development of reordering rules without using parsers (Costa-Jussà and Fonollosa 2006; Rottmann and Vogel 2007; Tromble and Eisner 2009; Visweswariah et al. 2011; Neubig et al. 2012). In Costa-Jussà and Fonollosa (2006), the task of reordering the source language was treated as a translation task in which statistical word classes were used. In Rottmann and Vogel

---

[5]We follow the POS tag guideline of the Penn Chinese Treebank v3.0 (Xia 2000). Table 6 in Appendix lists all POS tag definitions.

(2007), reordering rules were learned from POS tags instead of parse trees. Tromble and Eisner (2009) and Visweswariah et al. (2011) proposed methods based on binary classifications. Moreover, Neubig et al. (2012) presented context-free-grammar models for learning a discriminative parser which optimizes reordering accuracy as an extrinsic objective function.

Although the majority of efforts were dedicated to pre-reordering, other authors (Sudoh et al. 2011; Goto et al. 2012) examined the possibility of post-reordering on a Japanese-to-English translation task. The authors first translated Japanese to Japanese-ordered English, and then reordered this Japanese-ordered English to normal English using an existing reordering method. Compared to pre-reordering, post-reordering requires two types of reorderings: (1) reordering of common English to Japanese-ordered English for training and (2) reordering of Japanese-ordered English to common English for decoding. Thus, reordering errors may propagate in the translation pipeline, which may decrease the reordering accuracy and translation quality.

3   Head Finalization for Chinese (HFC)

Both Chinese and English are known to be head-initial languages.[6] Ideally, HF would reorder Chinese sentences to resemble their Japanese counterparts in word order, in the same fashion as it was conceived for English-to-Japanese machine translation. The essence of HF is to move syntactic heads to the right-hand side of their dependents by swapping child nodes in a binary phrase structure tree when the head child appears on the left of the dependent child. However, HF treats the coordination structure as an exception. See Fig. 3 for an example with its parse tree. In this example, although the syntactic heads are on the left-hand side branches

Fig. 3 English example of coordination structure

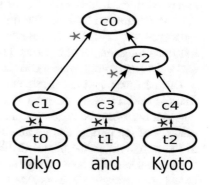

---

[6]However, it is still open for debate whether Chinese is a head-initial or a head-final language due to its flexible word order (Gao 2008). Nevertheless, the written form of Chinese behaves primarily as a head-initial language.

(i.e., "Tokyo" and "and" are the syntactic heads), HF will not swap them with their siblings and the phrase "Tokyo and Kyoto" will preserve the original word order. While applying HF to Chinese, we retained such an exception rule, because the coordination structure behaves similarly in Chinese as it does in English. From the XML output of *Chinese Enju*, the attributes of `cat` and `schema` are used to detect this case. Specifically, the attribute values `schema="coord-left/right"` and `cat="COOD"` signal a coordination structure.

HF does not prevent the swapping operation from crossing punctuation. However, the authors in Isozaki et al. (2010b) separated English sentences not only by periods, but also by colons and semicolons, which reduced the occurrence of reordering errors involving punctuation, at the expense of limitations in performing some long-distance reorderings. Unlike the English HPSG parser, the Chinese HPSG parser includes in the tree the periods that signal the end of sentences (see the example of a tree in Fig. 4a). Since the period branch is customarily not the syntactic head, we introduce (in HF and HFC) a punctuation exception rule that prevents all reorderings that involve any punctuation. Similarly to as done for the coordination exception rule, we monitor the attribute `cat="PU"` because it signals a punctuation node.

In order to motivate possible refinements in HF reordering, we first consider the straightforward application of HF to reorder words in Chinese sentences. Figure 4 displays the working mechanism of HF with the corresponding HPSG parse tree of the Chinese sentence in Fig. 1. The stars (∗) indicate the syntactic head branches. Figure 4a is the parse tree graph corresponding to the XML output in Fig. 1, whereas Fig. 4b is the reordered parse tree graph. As shown in Fig. 4a, nodes c2, c3, c4, c7, and c9 are candidates for performing a swapping operation on their children, because their head children are on the left-hand side of their dependents. However, since the attributes of nodes c7, c9, and c12 are `schema="coord-left/right"`, `cat="COOD"`, and `cat="PU"` (see Fig. 1), the child nodes of c2, c7, and c9 will not be swapped in consideration of the exception rules. In this example, as the result of applying HF, only child nodes of c3 and c4 are swapped (see Fig. 4b). Consequently, the verb "去(qu4, go to)" and aspect particle "了(le0, -ed)" have correctly been moved to the end of the sentence following the same word order as the Japanese translation. However, "去(qu4, go to)" and "了(le0, -ed)" were incorrectly swapped, producing a local misalignment.

Our best explanation for this unexpected local misalignment is that there are discrepancies in syntactic head definitions between Chinese and Japanese. In linguistics, a syntactic head of a phrase is the word that determines the syntactic category of the phrase, and its modifiers (also known as dependents) are the rest of the words within the phrase (Miller and Miller 2011). Based on the idea that head-dependent relation is consistent between English and Japanese, while the word orders are different, HF works well for reordering English to resemble Japanese in terms of word order. However, in Chinese, there has been significant debate on the definition of what constitutes a syntactic head, possibly because Chinese has fewer surface syntactic features than other languages like English or Japanese. This causes discrepancies between the definitions of syntactic head in Chinese

Fig. 4 Corresponding parse tree of the Chinese example in Fig. 1 illustrating the head finalization (HF) reordering method. In both figures, Chinese words are aligned with their Japanese translations. *Asterisk* indicates the syntactic head branch given by *Chinese Enju*. (**a**) Original HPSG tree. (**b**) Reordered HPSG tree

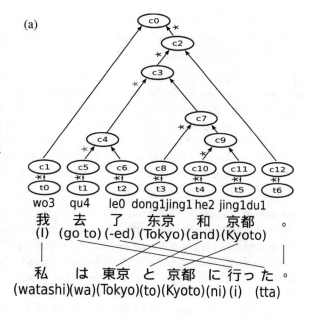

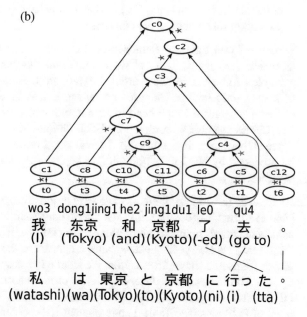

and Japanese, which leads to undesirable reorderings of Chinese sentences. In preliminary experiments, we observed several reordering problems that are caused by differences in syntactic head definitions:

Aspect Particle Since there is no tense marker in Chinese, three aspect particles express tense semantically by directly following the verbs they modify. These particles are "着(zhe0, -ing)", "了(le0, -ed)", and "过(guo4, -ed)". The last expresses the present perfect tense and appears in Figs. 1, 2, and 4. In Fig. 4, the Chinese parser treats the verb "去(qu4, go to)" as a phrase head, whereas the last word "た(-ed)" is the phrase head in Japanese and aligns to "了(le0, -ed)". Thus, HF produces an incorrect reordering (as indicated by the red box). In the refined model, an exception rule prevents this reordering from wrongly occurring.

Adverbial Modifier "不(bu4, not)" Chinese adverbial modifiers and their Japanese counterparts are usually in pre-verbal positions, and no reordering is necessary. However, there is an exceptional adverb in Chinese "不(bu4, not)" that translates into Japanese as "ない(not)". This Chinese adverb *precedes* the verb, but its Japanese translation *follows* the verb. Figure 5a shows a tree that illustrates this case. According to HF, the reordered sentence is "我(wo3, I) 电视(dian4shi4, TV) 不(bu4, don't) 看(kan4, watch) ." However, the ideal reordered sentence should be "我(wo3, I) 电视(dian4shi4, TV) 看(kan4, watch) 不(bu4, don't) ." We introduce an exception rule that considers this case.

Sentence-Final Particle Sentence-final particles are used to express a speaker's attitude in languages, such as "嗯(en0, uh)" and "啊(a0, ah)". Figure 5b shows an example of a sentence-final particle "啊(a0, ah)". Although it appears at the end of the sentence both in Chinese and Japanese, it is identified as the dependent in Chinese, whereas it is the head in Japanese due to differences of head definition. The Chinese sentence reordered by HF is "啊(a0, ah) 天气(tian1qi4, weather) 真好(zhen1hao3, good) 是(shi4, is) ." However, a more monotonic alignment could be produced by HFC if "啊(a0, ah)" is kept at the end of the reordered Chinese sentence.

Et Cetera In Chinese, there are two expressions that mean "and other things" or "and so forth": "等(deng3, etc.)" and "等等(deng3deng3, etc.)". Both are identified as dependents of nouns or noun phrases. In contrast, in Japanese, their translation "など(etc.)" is always the head because it appears as the right-most word of a noun phrase. Figure 5c shows an example. We handle this case as we did aspect particles.

Based on the previous observations, we propose a method by which to improve HF, referred to herein as HFC. The concept behind HFC is simple. We predefine a list of POS tags (see Table 1) and prevent HF reordering in a node if one of the child node's POS tags belongs to the list. Due to its particular nature, the adverbial modifier "不(bu4, not)" is taken as an exception. Note that rules for PU and CC are equivalent to the exception rules in Isozaki et al. (2012).

Unfortunately, there are more reordering problems that are difficult to solve by designing more exception rules. Examples include serial verb constructions, verbal nominalizations, nounal verbalizations, and complementizers. A more concrete

Fig. 5 Three examples demonstrating discrepancies in syntactic head definition between Chinese and Japanese. (**a**) Adverbial Modifier bu4 (not). (**b**) Sentence-final particle. (**c**) Et cetera

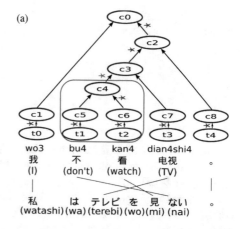

(a)

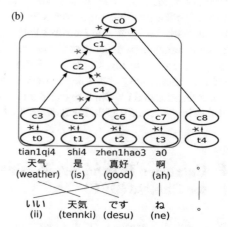

(b)

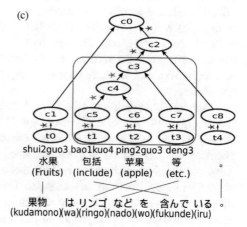

(c)

Table 1 List of POS tags for
exception reordering rules

AS	Aspect particle
SP	Sentence-final particle
ETC	*Et cetera*
IJ	Interjection
PU	Punctuation
CC	Coordinating conjunction

instance corresponds to the example shown in Fig. 5b. The ideal reordered Chinese sentence for the example is "真好(zhen1hao3, good) 天气(tian1qi4, weather) 是(shi4, is) 啊(a0, ah) ." However, neither HF nor HFC can obtain the word order "真好(zhen1hao3, good) 天气(tian1qi4, weather) 是(shi4, is)" by any possible combination of node swaps in the tree. This limitation does not arise from the lack of coverage of the rules, but rather from the hard constraints that binary tree structures impose on the possible word orders that can be reached. Moreover, HPSG parsers are currently not available for most languages, and the Chinese HPSG parser has lower accuracy than dependency parsers. It is also challenging to fix or compensate for parse errors during reordering. Parse errors, binary tree structure constraints, and low extensibility of reordering rules were our reasons for developing a new pre-reordering method for Chinese based on an unlabeled dependency parser in order to further improve the translation quality of Chinese-to-Japanese SMT.

4 Unlabeled Dependency Parsing Based Pre-reordering for Chinese (DPC)

Chinese and Japanese have different sentence structures. Reordering methods are effective but are sensitive to parse errors and require reliable parsers in order to extract the syntactic structure of the source sentences. However, Chinese has a loose word order, and Chinese parsers that extract the phrase structure do not perform well. Therefore, in this section we introduce a block-based pre-reordering framework where only POS tags and unlabeled dependency parse trees are necessary.

Linguistic knowledge of structural differences can be encoded in the form of reordering rules. As an SVO language, V (predicate) usually appears between its subject and its objects in Chinese sentences. In contrast, the location of V is switched with its objects in Japanese, since the language follows the SOV order. Thus, the reordering objective will be to move the V (predicate) to the right-hand side of its objects in Chinese sentences. There are two challenges associated with this reordering objective, namely determining the relevant words that need to be reordered and detecting the proper positions to which the words should be relocated. Evidently, in most sentences, V (predicate) consists not only of verbs, but also surrounding words (i.e., particles, adverbs, verbs in coordination structure, etc.).

Accordingly, there are mainly three stages in this reordering strategy. The first stage is to correctly identify reordering candidates (verbs and their accompanying words). We refer to candidates as *verbal blocks* (Vb), because they will be treated as a unit while reordering. The second stage is to determine the precise position to which Vb should be reordered. In a dependency relation, objects such as nouns and pronouns are dependents of their Vb and encode the potential reordering destination. Specifically, we are interested in finding the *right-most dependent* (RM-D). The third stage is to relocate reordering candidates, by moving Vb to the right-hand side of its RM-D (if it exists) and to reorder other particles if necessary.

Figure 6 demonstrates the reordering procedure. The original dependency tree is given in Fig. 2 for this example. In Fig. 6a, the rectangular box marks the Vb that needs to be reordered. The dependency tree shows that "京都(jing1du1, Kyoto)" is the right-most dependent of the Vb, and thus the Vb will be reordered to its right-hand side, as shown in Fig. 6b. The alignment between the reordered Chinese sentence and its Japanese reference becomes monotonic, and both follow SOV word order. In what follows, we describe in detail how to determine verbal blocks, in order to identify right-most dependents, and to perform reordering.

Identifying Verbal Block (Vb) A verbal block (Vb) is a reordering candidate and is composed of a head (Vb-H) and possibly accompanying dependents (Vb-D). In order to form a Vb, a Vb-H has to be confirmed first. According to our linguistic findings, prepositions behave in a manner similar to verbs in Chinese-to-Japanese translation, and are both potential Vb-Hs. The POS tags of verbs and

Fig. 6 A simple example of how to detect and reorder a verbal block (Vb) in a sentence. Figure 2 shows the dependency parse tree. In (a), the *rectangular box* marks the Vb. (b) presents the reordered Chinese sentence and the chunk-to-chunk alignment with its Japanese reference. (**a**) Vb in a rectangular box. (**b**) Reordered Vb

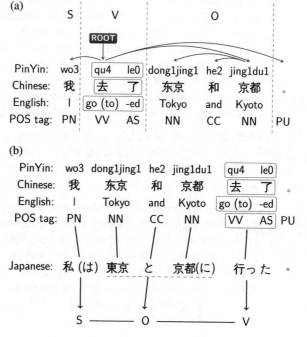

Table 2 List of Chinese POS tags for identifying words as different candidates

Category	POS tag
Vb-H	VV VE VC VA P
Vb-D	AD AS SP MSP CC VV VE VC VA
BEI	LB SB
RM-D	NN NR NT PN OD CD M FW CC
	ETC LC DEV DT JJ SP IJ ON
Oth-D	LB SB CS

The definition of each POS tag can be found in Table 6

prepositions are listed in the Vb-H entry of Table 2 and are used to identify Vb-H candidates. Syntactically, objects are dependents of their verb, and a Vb-H appears as the dependency head in a dependency tree. As an example, in Fig. 2, "去(qu4, go to)" is the main verb and its object is a noun coordination phrase "东京(dong1jing1, Tokyo) 和(he2, and) 京都(jing1du1, Kyoto)". According to the alignment to the Japanese reference, the verb "去(qu4, go to)" should be reordered to the right-hand side of the right-most word of its object (its dependent), i.e., "京都(jing1du1, Kyoto)".

In Chinese, there is a special sentence structure called bei-construction, which consists of a passive verb and one of the particles for which the POS tag is listed in the BEI entry of Table 2. The particle, which is the dependent of the verb, is used to compensate for the lack of verb inflection to produce a passive voice. Although the majority of Chinese sentences are SVO, similar to their Japanese counterparts, passive sentences that include a bei-construction in Chinese follow SOV word order. Therefore, a Vb-H candidate that involves a bei-construction should be excluded and not reordered. As an illustration, a bei-construction sentence is given in Fig. 7. In the example, the verb "割破(ge1po4, lacerate)" and its object "脚(jiao3, foot)" follow the same word order as the Japanese sentence, and thus there is no reordering required. Instead, the particle "被(bei4, passive voice)" should be relocated to the right-hand side of its verb to align to its Japanese counterpart.

In summary, there are three necessary conditions for a word to be a Vb-H:

1. the POS tag of the word must be in the Vb-H entry of Table 2;
2. the word must be a dependency head; and
3. the word must have no dependent for which the POS tag is in the BEI entry of Table 2.

Chinese does not have any inflection, conjugation, or case markers (Li and Thompson 1989). Particles (i.e., aspect particles, sentence-final particles, etc.) and adverbs are used to add aspectual value or signal modality or to indicate grammatical tense to verbs. For instance, in Fig. 2, the aspect particle "了(le0, -ed)" adds the past tense to the verb "去(qu4, go to)" by following it. Since Japanese verbs are inflected to express tense, the Chinese aspect particle should be reordered together with its verb, as shown in Fig. 6a, b. We refer to these tokens as Vb-Ds, because they are also dependents of the Vb-H.

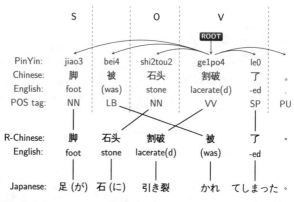

Fig. 7 Example of bei-construction

English Translation: (My) foot was lacerated by a stone.

There are also three conditions for a word to be considered a Vb-D:

1. the POS tag of the word must be in the Vb-D entry in Table 2;
2. the word must be a dependent of a token that is already in the Vb; and
3. the word must be next to its dependency head or be separated by only a coordination conjunction.

After the Vb-H is found, we search for Vb-Ds from its surrounding dependents to form a block Vb. A more complex Vb example is given in Fig. 8. Based on the dependency parse tree (see Fig. 8a), in accordance with the conditions of being a Vb-H, both "记录(ji4lu4, record)" and "发表(fa1biao3, publish)" are Vb-Hs, and thus two Vb will be initialized simultaneously. By examining the adjacent dependents of these two Vb-Hs with the Vb-D conditions, two Vbs are formed. Note that one Vb is embedded into the other, as shown in Fig. 8b. Nested Vbs will be merged as one and reordered together to the right-hand side of the right-most dependent of the Vb (see Fig. 8c).

Identifying the Right-Most Dependent (RM-D) After obtaining the reordering candidates, namely Vbs, another challenge is to find the precise location at which the Vb must be placed. Our objective is to reorder V to the right-hand side of O for an SVO sentence in order to follow the SOV word order. However, it is not trivial to recognize the object O in a sentence, due to the variety of words that may conform it, such as single words (e.g., noun, pronoun), noun phrases, or noun clauses. Since our main interest is finding the right-most boundary of the O, we simplify the task to identifying the right-most dependent (RM-D) of a Vb. We define an RM-D as a token that

1. has a POS tag that belongs to the RM-D entry of Table 2;
2. has its dependency head in the Vb; and
3. is located as the right-most object among all objects of the Vb.

Fig. 8 Example of how to detect and reorder nested Vbs in a sentence. (**a**) Original dependency tree. (**b**) Vbs in *rectangular boxes*. (**c**) Merged and reordered Vb

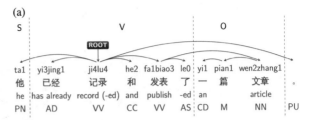

English Translation: He has already recorded and published an article.

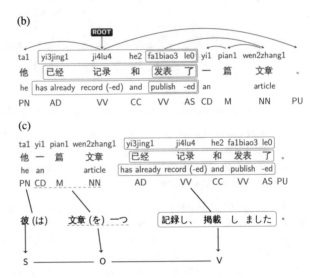

Consequently, in Figs. 6a and 8b, "京都(jing1du1, Kyoto)" and "文章(wen2zhang1, article)" are the RM-Ds of their respective Vbs.

Figure 9 shows two complex examples of determining the RM-D. The alignment lines between original Chinese sentences and reordered sentences indicate the reordering traces. The resulting monotonic alignment is evidenced by comparing the reordered sentences and the Japanese references. In Fig. 9a, two Vbs, "拿(na2, hold) 着(zhe0, -ing)" and "走进(zou3jin4, walk into)", are in a coordination structure, and their RM-Ds are different, namely "作业(zuo4ye4, homework)" and "教室(jiao4shi4, classroom)". Thus, these two Vbs are reordered separately to the right-hand side of their own RM-Ds. In Fig. 9b, a subordinate clause is the object of the main clause. In such a case, the Vb of the subordinate "发表(fa1biao3, voice)" is reordered to the right-hand side of its RM-D "意见(yi4jian4, opinion)", and the Vb of the main clause "鼓励(gu3li4, encourage)" is reordered to the end of the sentence. Such a sentence structure often appears in the news domain in the form of reported speech.

Identifying Other Dependent (Oth-D) There are other tokens that may need to be reordered apart from the Vb, such as the particle "被(bei4, passive voice)" in a

Fig. 9 Examples of complex RM-Ds. (**a**) Predicate consisting of a coordination of verb phrases. English Translation: The teacher walks into the classroom with homework. (**b**) Object consisting of a subordinate clause. English Translation: Teachers encourage students to voice their opinions

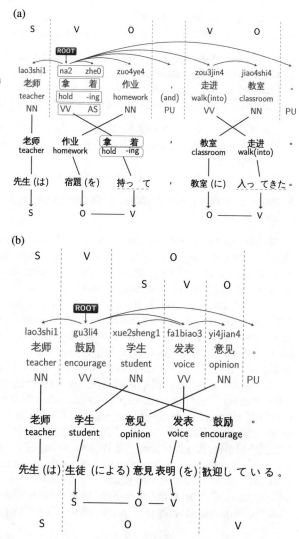

bei-construction (see the example in Fig. 7). These particles appear on the left-hand side of their dependency heads in Chinese, but on the right-hand side in Japanese. Therefore, we reorder them as follows:

1. find dependents of a Vb-H for which the POS tags are in the Oth-D entry of Table 2;
2. move such particles to the right-hand side of their (possibly reordered) heads; and
3. if there are several of these particles, keep the relative order between them during the reordering.

Reordering Procedure Based on the definitions given above, the unlabeled dependency parsing based pre-reordering framework proceeds as follows:

1. Obtain POS tags and an unlabeled dependency tree of the Chinese sentence.
2. Obtain reordering candidates: Vbs.
3. Obtain the right-most token in the object (RM-D) of each Vb.
4. Reorder each Vb in two exclusive cases by following the order:

    (a) If RM-D exists, reorder Vb to be the right-hand side of its RM-D.
    (b) If Vb-H is ROOT and its RM-D does not exist, reorder Vb to the end of the sentence.
    (c) If neither of the above two conditions is met, no reordering occurs.

5. Reorder grammatical particles (Oth-Ds) to the right-hand side of their corresponding Vbs.

   To illustrate this method, a more complex Chinese sentence example is given in Fig. 10. Given the dependency tree, the first step is to build up reordering candidates: Vbs. Based on the POS tag and dependencies, there are six tokens that qualify as Vb-Hs, namely, "报道(bao4dao4, report)", "随着(sui2zhe0, with)", "进入(jin4ru4, enter)", "成为(cheng2wei2, become)", "加强(jia1qiang2, strengthen)", and "力促(li4cu4, urge)". Vb-Ds are determined by examining these Vb-Hs' surrounding dependents. For instance, "逐渐(zhu2jian4, gradually)" and "了(le0, -ed)" are Vb-Ds of the Vb-H "进入(jin4ru4, enter)". Since the Vb-H "力促(li4cu4, urge)" is a qualified Vb-D of "加强(jia1qiang2, strengthen)", this nested Vb is merged with the larger one. Consequently, five Vbs are formed (marked with rectangular boxes). After finding Vbs, the next step is to identify RM-Ds for each Vb, if any. By checking all conditions, four Vbs, i.e., "随着(sui2zhe0, with)", "逐渐(zhu2jian4, gradually) 进入(jin4ru4, enter) 了(le0, -ed)", "成为(cheng2wei2, become)", and "加强(jia1qiang2, strengthen) 力促(li4cu4, urge)", have a corresponding RM-D: "发展(fa1zhan3, development)", "中国(zhong1guo2, China)", "节日(jie2ri4, festival)", and "节日(jie2ri4, festival)", respectively. During the reordering, we will relocate all Vbs to the right-hand side of their RM-Ds. Since the dependency root "报道(bao4dao4, report)" does not have an RM-D, it has been reordered to

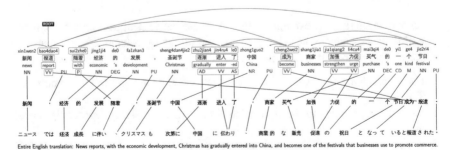

Fig. 10 Example of reordering a complex Chinese sentence by DPC

the end of the sentence. Finally, because there is no special particle (Oth-D) that must be reordered, the reordering procedure terminates. The resulting word-to-word alignment between the reordered Chinese sentence and the Japanese reference is almost monotonic.

Unlike HFC and other reordering methods for distant language pairs (Xu et al. 2009; Isozaki et al. 2010b), this method does not prevent chunks from crossing punctuation or coordination structures. However, in order to compare DPC with the original HF and HFC reordering methods, we insert artificial particles following the method as introduced in Isozaki et al. (2010b). The insertion of such artificial particles requires information (identity of the arguments) from an HPSG parser (i.e., *Chinese Enju*). Therefore, we cannot entirely disclaim the use of an HPSG parser at the present stage in DPC. However, we believe that dependency parsers can also provide sufficient information for inserting artificial particles, but this is beyond the scope of the present study.

5 Evaluation

5.1 Experimental Conditions

We used two corpora from the news domain and two corpora from the patent domain to evaluate the performance of both pre-reordering methods for Chinese-to-Japanese machine translation. For the news domain, we collected an in-house Chinese-Japanese parallel corpus of news articles that we refer to herein as "News" and used this corpus as a training set (Training 1). Then, we merged this corpus with the training corpus that was provided by the 7th China Workshop on Machine Translation (CWMT2011)[7] (Zhao et al. 2011) and used it as an extended training set (Training 2). For the patent domain, the corpora were extracted from patent applications filed from 2007 to 2010. The document alignment was based on the priority claims and the sentence alignment was performed using the Champollion Tool Kit (CTK)[8] (Ma 2006). We extracted sentence pairs for which the alignment score was higher than 0.95 and 0.9 in order to build Training 1 and Training 2, respectively. Therefore, Training 1 is a subset of Training 2. Finally, for every domain, we obtained a disjoint set of sentences for development and testing. Statistics on these corpora can be found in Table 3. Out-of-vocabulary words were computed with respect to Training 1 and Training 2, respectively.

---

[7]http://mt.xmu.edu.cn/cwmt2011/document/papers/e00.pdf.

[8]http://champollion.sourceforge.net/.

Table 3 Statistical characteristics of corpora

		News		Patent	
		Chinese	Japanese	Chinese	Japanese
Training 1	Sentences	342,050		2,559,581	
	Running words	7,414,749	9,361,867	64,028,414	78,624,671
	Avg. sent. len.	21.68	27.37	25.02	30.72
	Vocabulary	145,133	73,909	351,345	91,778
Training 2	Sentences	621,610		4,894,415	
	Running words	9,822,535	12,499,112	132,206,053	164,452,302
	Avg. sent. len.	15.80	20.11	27.01	33.60
	Vocabulary	214,085	98,333	526,545	124,512
Development	Sentences	1000		1144	
	Running words	46,042	56,748	31.57	39.71
	Avg. sent. len.	46.04	56.75	36,114	46,570
	Out of vocab.	301 and 262	67 and 57	112 and 73	26 and 20
Test	Sentences	2000		1144	
	Running words	51,534	65,721	37,145	47,750
	Avg. sent. len.	25.77	32.86	32.47	40.74
	Out of vocab.	594 and 546	310 and 278	100 and 53	23 and 9

Prior to carrying out pre-reordering, we pre-processed these parallel corpora using the following methods. For Japanese segmentation, we used the *MeCab*[9] (Kudo and Matsumoto 2000), while for Chinese segmentation, we used the *Stanford Chinese segmenter*[10] (Chang et al. 2008). Since both the Chinese HPSG parser *Chinese Enju* and the dependency parser *Corbit* require POS tag information, we extracted the information from the output of the *Berkeley parser*[11] (Petrov et al. 2006).

Our baseline system is the standard *Moses*[12] (Koehn et al. 2007). For comparison, we included the original *HF* system as well. Word-to-word alignments between paired Chinese sentences and their Japanese counterparts were estimated using *MGIZA++*[13] (Och and Ney 2003; Gao and Vogel 2008), and the scaling factors of the log-linear combination of models were tuned by applying *minimum error rate training (MERT)* (Och 2003).

---

[9]http://mecab.googlecode.com/svn/trunk/mecab/doc/index.html.

[10]http://nlp.stanford.edu/software/segmenter.shtml.

[11]http://nlp.cs.berkeley.edu/Software.shtml.

[12]http://www.statmt.org/moses.

[13]http://www.kyloo.net/software/doku.php/mgiza:overview.

For the purpose of generality, we used several evaluation metrics to assess the performance of the pre-reordering methods, namely *BLEU* (Papineni et al. 2002), *Rank-based Intuitive Bilingual Evaluation Score (RIBES)*[14] (Isozaki et al. 2010a), *WER, PER* (Tillmann et al. 1997), and *TER*[15] (Snover et al. 2006). *BLEU* and *RIBES* are precision metrics, and higher scores suggest higher performance. In contrast, *WER, PER*, and *TER* are error metrics, which means that lower scores are better.

5.2 Results

In phrase-based machine translation, the distortion limit is a parameter that governs the maximum distance at which a phrase can be translated. In SMT between language pairs having different sentence structures, large distortion limits might be appropriate in order to enable the translation of phrases that align at the beginning and at the end of Chinese and Japanese sentences, respectively.

In Tables 4 and 5, we present the results obtained using training data sets of different sizes for both news and patent corpora, respectively, and the results for the optimal distortion limit are shown in bold. In general, the patent domain requires larger distortion limits than the news domain, which might be due to sentences in the patent domain being longer (on average) than sentences in the news domain.

The DPC pre-reordering method exhibits consistently superior performance in terms of BLEU and RIBES (precision metrics), and WER, PER, and TER (error metrics), for all distortion limits in both domains. The proposed DPC achieves the best performance using distortion limits that range between 6 and 12 in the news domain and in the range between 9 and 12 in the patent domain.

Considering only the results of the methods for their optimal distortion limit, we find small or inconsistent differences in performance between the baseline, HF, and HFC methods in terms of the evaluation metrics. In the news domain, DPC provides small improvements in BLEU and RIBES over the second-best performing system, but slightly larger improvements in terms of WER, PER, and TER. In the patent domain, however, DPC obtains, on average (across all distortion limits), large improvements with respect to HFC in terms of BLEU (2.9 and 3.6 points in Training 1 and Training 2), RIBES (2.2 and 2.3 points), WER (5.3 and 5.5 points), PER (4.4 and 4.3 points), and TER (3.8 and 3.8 points).

---

[14]http://www.kecl.ntt.co.jp/icl/lirg/ribes.

[15]http://www.cs.umd.edu/~snover/tercom.

Table 4 Evaluation of translation quality for the news domain

	dl	0	1	2	3	4	5	6	7	9	12
Training 1											
BLEU	Baseline	38.29	38.58	38.55	38.72	38.91	39.11	39.16	39.21	**39.47**	39.44
	HF	39.09*	39.05*	39.22*	39.20*	39.34*	**39.59***	39.53	39.57	39.30	39.54
	HFC	39.55*	39.48*	39.00*	39.62*	39.70*	39.49	39.66*	**39.79***	39.66	39.66
	DPC	39.59*	39.66*	39.62*	39.77*	39.68*	39.43	39.94*	39.87*	**40.14***	39.85*
RIBES	Baseline	84.55	84.59	84.59	84.60	84.87	84.80	**85.07**	84.95	84.91	84.87
	HF	84.77	84.79	84.77	84.85	84.66	84.92	84.90	84.90	**84.95**	84.89
	HFC	84.86*	84.94*	84.91*	85.01*	84.98	84.77	85.08	84.99	**85.09**	85.04
	DPC	85.07*	85.12*	85.13*	85.22*	85.11	85.18*	**85.30**	85.25*	85.29*	85.29*
WER	Baseline	51.93	51.68	51.83	51.38	**51.08**	50.84	50.68	50.53	50.61	51.15
	HF	50.48	50.67	50.50	50.31	50.44	**50.01**	50.27	50.16	50.38	50.74
	HFC	50.00	50.03	50.20	49.91	49.79	50.23	49.72	**49.68**	49.70	49.92
	DPC	49.28	49.26	49.24	49.07	49.22	49.39	**48.74**	48.85	48.86	48.83
PER	Baseline	31.52	31.27	31.23	31.38	31.11	31.04	31.14	31.10	30.88	**30.81**
	HF	30.82	30.81	30.71	30.68	30.54	30.58	30.61	30.68	30.73	**30.34**
	HFC	30.65	30.65	31.00	30.52	**30.46**	30.92	30.51	30.66	30.54	30.59
	DPC	30.52	30.50	30.47	30.48	30.46	30.57	30.39	30.36	**30.25**	30.58
TER	Baseline	48.11	47.79	47.80	47.56	47.09	46.89	46.90	46.81	**46.65**	46.89
	HF	46.44	46.59	46.43	46.21	46.37	45.93	46.16	**46.12**	46.14	46.16
	HFC	45.99	46.02	46.16	45.89	45.67	46.21	45.71	45.75	**45.62**	45.73
	DPC	45.87	45.82	45.81	45.65	45.81	45.79	45.41	45.49	**45.34**	45.58
Training 2											
BLEU	Baseline	38.35	38.20	38.32	38.63	38.81	39.21	39.20	**39.43**	39.41	39.20
	HF	39.15*	39.48*	36.86	39.66*	39.41*	39.70*	39.55	36.29	**40.00***	39.85*
	HFC	39.54*	39.44*	39.61*	39.48*	37.39	39.65*	39.69*	39.79	39.91*	**39.94***
	DPC	39.62*	39.44*	39.56*	39.70*	39.66*	39.75*	39.82*	**40.01***	39.95*	39.81*
RIBES	Baseline	84.53	84.60	84.64	84.66	84.65	85.00	85.10	85.10	**85.12**	84.83
	HF	84.84*	84.78	84.06	84.85	84.80	84.96	84.80	82.62	**85.02**	84.71
	HFC	84.92*	84.77	84.99*	84.79	84.42	84.92	84.91	84.88	**85.10**	84.94
	DPC	85.17*	84.94*	85.19*	85.14*	85.23*	85.25*	85.26	85.18	85.21	**85.27***
WER	Baseline	52.07	52.15	52.02	51.59	51.39	50.85	50.75	50.42	**50.35**	51.00
	HF	50.59	50.46	52.62	50.18	50.19	50.04	50.10	53.93	**49.84**	51.02
	HFC	50.10	50.25	49.99	50.18	51.55	50.03	50.03	49.99	**49.64**	49.96
	DPC	49.18	49.66	49.17	49.32	49.00	49.15	**48.94**	48.99	48.99	48.95
PER	Baseline	31.39	31.48	31.40	31.00	31.31	30.85	30.87	30.83	**30.80**	30.91
	HF	30.59	30.48	31.31	30.45	30.47	30.45	30.45	30.73	**30.24**	30.37
	HFC	30.52	30.62	30.36	30.62	31.43	30.48	30.51	**30.34**	**30.34**	30.40
	DPC	30.50	30.55	30.51	30.35	30.30	30.46	30.31	30.21	**30.07**	30.28
TER	Baseline	48.09	48.12	47.97	47.40	47.60	46.94	46.84	46.74	**46.53**	46.73
	HF	46.42	46.35	48.22	46.09	46.00	45.92	45.94	49.10	**45.69**	46.24
	HFC	46.00	46.20	45.88	46.14	47.27	45.85	45.94	45.80	**45.63**	45.78
	DPC	45.83	46.29	45.80	45.92	45.56	45.88	45.61	45.70	45.54	**45.47**

Results are presented in terms of BLEU, RIBES, WER, PER, and TER for the baseline, HF, HFC, and DPC along with different values of the distortion limit (dl). Results significantly larger than the baseline with a confidence of over 95 % are indicated by an asterisk

Table 5 Evaluation of translation quality for the patent domain

Training 1

	dl	0	1	2	3	4	5	6	7	9	12
BLEU	Baseline	45.51	45.69	45.64	45.95	46.50	46.79	47.02	47.68	48.01	**48.03**
	HF	44.97	45.44	45.51	46.61	46.80	47.59*	48.00*	48.52*	**49.11***	48.25
	HFC	45.06	45.04	45.27	45.45	45.45	47.20	48.20*	48.49*	48.22	**48.84***
	DPC	48.06*	48.06*	48.23*	48.88*	49.23*	50.11*	50.20*	50.89*	51.31*	**51.44***
RIBES	Baseline	84.32	84.55	84.37	84.38	84.82	84.73	84.88	85.11	**85.41**	84.93
	HF	84.19	84.33	84.29	84.81	84.81	85.06	85.15	85.30	**85.51**	85.09
	HFC	84.16	84.17	84.21	84.19	84.19	84.82	85.18	**85.38**	85.18	85.20
	DPC	86.49*	86.46*	86.59*	86.65*	86.89*	86.92*	87.14*	87.14*	87.29*	**87.32***
WER	Baseline	49.03	48.80	49.01	48.58	47.92	47.87	47.90	47.36	**47.32**	48.85
	HF	50.70	50.04	50.41	48.93	49.17	48.36	47.88	47.42	**47.24**	49.42
	HFC	50.40	50.52	50.36	50.17	50.17	48.58	47.33	**47.09**	47.85	48.37
	DPC	44.79	44.98	44.66	44.20	43.83	43.31	43.22	42.84	**42.83**	43.30
PER	Baseline	26.41	26.37	26.30	26.02	25.74	25.37	25.06	24.93	24.61	**24.36**
	HF	27.97	27.39	27.89	26.71	26.99	26.67	26.26	**25.61**	**25.61**	26.63
	HFC	28.16	28.11	28.06	28.24	28.24	26.57	25.68	**25.29**	25.87	25.83
	DPC	22.88	23.36	22.95	22.97	22.99	22.52	22.35	22.16	21.93	**21.57**
TER	Baseline	41.67	41.72	41.68	41.09	40.57	40.10	40.11	39.65	**39.40**	40.08
	HF	42.34	41.82	42.19	40.93	40.93	40.18	39.68	39.07	**38.84**	40.18
	HFC	42.36	42.37	42.21	42.08	42.08	40.35	39.34	**38.97**	39.51	39.57
	DPC	38.15	38.49	37.95	37.83	37.44	36.66	36.53	36.12	36.04	**35.79**

Training 2

	dl	0	1	2	3	4	5	6	7	9	12
BLEU	Baseline	50.83	50.59	51.30	51.60	51.74	52.34	52.92	53.40	54.00	**54.51**
	HF	51.53	51.81*	51.74	52.38*	53.70*	54.05*	54.17*	54.82*	**55.28***	55.22
	HFC	51.77*	51.27	51.73	51.93	52.93*	53.75*	53.83*	54.05	55.03*	**56.13***
	DPC	54.76*	54.80*	54.93*	55.72*	56.48*	57.31*	57.91*	58.30*	59.01*	**59.18***
RIBES	Baseline	85.87	85.78	86.03	86.06	86.08	86.31	86.66	86.96	**87.18**	87.16
	HF	85.79	85.95	85.86	86.18	86.48	86.57	86.68	86.76	86.88	**86.92**
	HFC	86.03	85.85	86.04	85.91	86.30	86.55	86.62	86.55	86.98	**87.34**
	DPC	88.16*	88.21*	88.22*	88.34*	88.75*	88.88*	88.97*	88.93*	**89.25***	89.23*
WER	Baseline	45.37	45.26	44.68	44.51	44.39	43.49	43.03	42.49	42.40	**42.29**
	HF	45.59	45.09	45.45	44.76	43.67	43.40	43.46	42.95	**42.73**	43.58
	HFC	45.06	45.59	45.09	45.05	44.17	43.49	43.63	43.25	42.50	**41.63**
	DPC	40.17	40.14	39.90	39.32	38.43	38.01	37.46	37.46	**36.66**	37.24
PER	Baseline	23.71	24.00	23.54	23.24	23.17	22.91	22.77	22.43	21.96	**21.74**
	HF	24.78	24.38	24.82	24.71	23.51	23.66	23.94	23.44	**23.23**	23.31
	HFC	24.36	24.92	24.26	24.39	23.76	23.53	23.57	23.99	23.07	**21.52**
	DPC	20.11	20.01	20.06	19.98	19.94	19.18	18.98	18.90	18.55	**18.51**
TER	Baseline	37.74	37.67	37.32	37.03	36.86	36.20	35.93	35.45	35.04	**34.60**
	HF	37.58	37.23	37.50	37.13	35.72	35.53	35.55	35.06	**34.73**	35.08
	HFC	37.15	37.62	37.17	37.09	36.11	35.44	35.53	35.52	34.55	**33.31**
	DPC	33.57	33.49	33.47	33.10	32.32	31.78	31.18	31.31	**30.56**	30.65

The results are presented in terms of BLEU, RIBES, WER, PER, and TER for the baseline, HF, HFC, and DPC along with different values of the distortion limit (dl). Results significantly larger than the baseline with a confidence of over 95 % are indicated by an asterisk

5.3 Effects of Parse Errors

The pre-reordering methods that were introduced in this chapter require information on the structure of source sentences. This structure is extracted using automatic parsers, and, as such, is subject to parse errors. Thus, it is worthwhile to analyze the effects of parse errors on the pre-reordering methods. Such an analysis will assess the influence of parse errors on the performance of different reordering methods, and we also examine the upper bounds of the pre-reordering methods in the absence of parse errors. To this end, we first carried out pre-reordering using both erroneous and error-free parse trees, which were generated by parsers (automatic) and human annotations (gold), respectively, as indicated by the prefixes Auto- and Gold- (i.e., Auto-HFC/DPC, Gold-HFC/DPC). Then, we compared the resulting reordered Chinese sentences with two benchmarks in order to obtain the upper bounds of the pre-reordering methods.

Ideally, the benchmarks should consist of manually reordered Chinese sentences. However, building such manual benchmarks is time consuming and labor intensive. Therefore, we created a small data set of manually reordered Chinese sentences and a slightly larger data set of automatically reordered Chinese sentences derived from their Japanese references. For this purpose, we randomly selected 2643 human parse annotations from Chinese Penn Treebank ver. 7.0 (CTB-7)[16], and converted these annotations to both constituent trees and dependency trees. The parse trees of these sentences are the error-free input for HFC and DPC, which are used to produce Gold-HFC and Gold-DPC, respectively. We obtained the Japanese translations of these sentences from professional human translators. Then, a bilingual speaker of Chinese and Japanese manually reordered the first 517 Chinese sentences to resemble Japanese in word order according to the Japanese references. This small data set of manually reordered Chinese sentences is used in scenario-1 of the analysis. We also constructed a slightly larger data set of reordered Chinese sentences, by automatically aligning the 2643 Chinese sentences to their Japanese counterparts, by means of MGIZA++. Then, words from Chinese sentences were reordered to resemble Japanese in word order, given the output of MGIZA++. This second data set is used in scenario-2 of the analysis. However, due to parsing failures of the automatic parsers on some sentences, there were only 491 sentences available for scenario-1 and 2164 sentences available for scenario-2.

We calculated Kendall's tau (τ) rank correlation coefficient (Kendall 1938) to estimate the word-order similarity between benchmarks and automatically reordered Chinese sentences (i.e., Gold-HFC/DPC, Auto-HFC/DPC). Figures 11 and 12 present the distribution graphs of Kendall's tau values in the two scenarios. Baseline results correspond to the Kendall's tau distribution of word-order similarity between the original Chinese sentences and the benchmarks. In the figures, both Gold-HFC/DPC and Auto-HFC/DPC show higher average τ values as compared

---

[16]http://www.cis.upenn.edu/~chinese/.

Fig. 11 Scenario-1.
Distribution of Kendall's tau
values for 491 sentences pairs
of automatically reordered
sentences from the baseline,
Auto-HFC, Gold-HFC,
Auto-DPC, and Gold-DPC

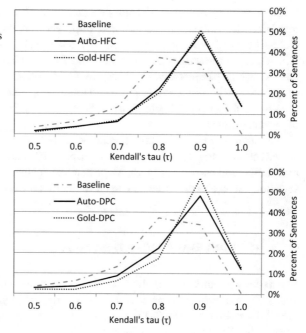

Fig. 12 Scenario-2.
Distribution of Kendall's tau
values for 2164 bilingual
sentences (Chinese-Japanese)
of automatically reordered
sentences from the baseline,
Auto-HFC, Gold-HFC,
Auto-DPC, and Gold-DPC

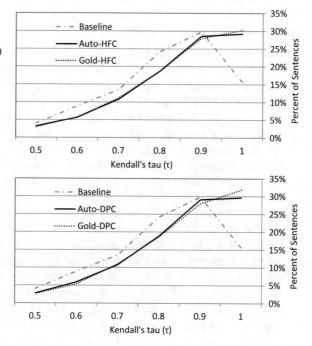

to the baseline system, which implies that both HFC and DPC have positively reordered the Chinese sentences and improved the word alignment. Moreover, Gold-HFC/DPC reduced the percentage of low τ sentences when compared to Auto-HFC/DPC, and revealed the upper bounds of these two pre-reordering methods in the absence of parse errors. Furthermore, Gold-DPC provides a higher percentage of sentences with higher values of Kendall's tau as compared to Gold-HFC, which suggests that DPC could potentially produce better reorderings as the performance of parsers improves.

Although the above preliminary analysis experiments provided a general idea of the effects of parse errors on pre-reordering performance, they do not reveal the most influential parse error types. More detailed analysis and description of the data selection and evaluation metrics can be found in the work of Han et al. (2013a).

6 Discussion and Future Research

Syntax-based reordering methods in a preprocessing stage have been developed and have been proved to be useful for extracting bilingual phrases and decoding. For Chinese-to-Japanese SMT, we carried out a detailed linguistic analysis on word-order differences of this language pair to improve the word alignment. We developed two linguistically motivated pre-reordering methods for Chinese to resemble Japanese in word order, and our experimental results revealed a significant improvement in translation quality.

1. Specifically, we first adapted an existing pre-reordering method called head finalization (HF) (Isozaki et al. 2010b) for Chinese (HFC) (Han et al. 2012) in order to improve the Chinese-to-Japanese translation quality of SMT systems. HF was originally designed to reorder English sentences for English-to-Japanese SMT and exhibited satisfactory performance. However, preliminary experimental results revealed disadvantages in reordering Chinese sentences due to the particular characteristic differences of the language pair. Thus, based on extensive linguistic research, we refined HF to obtain HFC. In order to obtain the required syntactic information, we used an HPSG parser for Chinese. However, an error analysis revealed that there are issues remaining that complicate the further refinement of HFC, such as constraints imposed by the binary structure of HPSG parse trees and inconsistencies in head definition for certain words.

2. We then introduced DPC (Han et al. 2013b), a new pre-reordering framework that uses unlabeled dependency parse trees and that achieved additional improvements in reordering Chinese sentences to resemble Japanese in word order. This method was inspired by the observation that Chinese is an SVO language, whereas Japanese is an SOV language. Thus, in order to achieve a monotonic alignment, we first needed to identify the word block that corresponds to the predicate V. Then, we showed how to identify the right-most boundary of the object-argument of the predicate V, which was useful for discovering the new

position to which it was necessary to move the word block V. Unlike other reordering systems, the boundaries of verbal blocks and their right-most object in DPC are defined only by the dependency tree and POS tags. In addition, not preventing reordering from occurring across punctuation was another benefit for the reordering of reported speech, a frequent phenomenon in the news domain. Experiments revealed the advantages of DPC over the SMT baseline (Moses) and the HFC systems. The important advantages of this method are the capability of transferring several reordering rules to other SVO and SOV language pairs, as well as the availability of dependency parsers and POS-taggers for many languages.

The pre-reordering methods introduced in this chapter are linguistically motivated and rely heavily on the output of HPSG or dependency parsers. As such, they are sensitive to parse errors. Therefore, a possible area for future study would be to design pre-reordering methods that are robust against parse errors. One possible solution to this problem would be to use N-best parse trees instead of 1-best parse trees, in order to compensate for parse errors. Moreover, while designing new pre-reordering methods, it would be meaningful to keep in mind the most frequently recurring parse errors and their potential impact.

Moreover, generalizing these linguistically motivated pre-reordering methods to other distant language pairs would be useful. Currently, the DPC model uses POS tags to categorize tokens, which poses some limitations for re-implementation with different POS tag sets. Thus, POS tag mappings and linguistic studies on source languages for new language pairs appear to be unavoidable. Therefore, in order to improve the extensibility of the DPC model, it would be useful to investigate methods of automatically learning reordering rules based on POS tags and dependencies from data.

7 Conclusion

In the present chapter, we described two hybrid state-of-the-art pre-reordering methods for Chinese-to-Japanese statistical machine translation. The first method relies on HPSG parsing and consists of swapping the head of phrases when certain conditions are met. The second method uses a dependency parser and a set of reordering rules. Both methods use parsing information to guide reordering decisions, and they are both sensitive to parse errors to different extents. We compared the performance of the two reordering methods for the same corpora with a baseline in terms of several metrics that account for different aspects of translation quality. The experimental results revealed that DPC provided significant improvements in translation quality and could potentially provide further improvements as parsing accuracy increases.

Appendix: Summary of Part-of-Speech Tag Set in Penn Chinese Treebank

See Table 6.

Table 6 POS tags defined in Penn Chinese Treebank v3.0 (Xia 2000)

POS tag	Category	Instance
AD	Adverb	还(yet)
AS	Aspect marker	了(-ed)
BA	ba3(把) in ba-construction	把(have sth. done)
CC	Coordinating conjunction	和(and)
CD	Cardinal number	一百(a hundred)
CS	Subordinating conjunction	虽然(although)
DEC	de0(的) in a relative-clause	的(as a complementizer or a nominalizer)
DEG	Associative de0(的)	的(as a genitive marker and an associative marker)
DER	de0(得) in V-de construction and V-de-R	得(resultative)
DEV	de0(地) before VP	地(manner)
DT	Determiner	这(the)
ETC	For words deng3(等), deng3deng3(等等)	等(et cetera)
FW	Foreign words	ISO
IJ	Interjection	啊(ah)
JJ	Other noun-modifier	共同(collective)
LB	bei4(被) in long bei-construction	被(passive voice)
LC	Localizer	里(inside)
M	Measure word	个(piece)
MSP	Other particle	所(that which)
NN	Common noun	书(book)
NR	Proper noun	美国(The United States)
NT	Temporal noun	今天(today)
OD	Ordinal number	第一(first)
ON	Onomatopoeia	哈哈(ahh)
P	Preposition excl. 被 and 把	从(from)
PN	Pronoun	他(he)
PU	Punctuation	。(.)
SB	bei4(被) in short bei-construction	被(passive voice)
SP	Sentence-final particle	吗(ma)
VA	Predicative adjective	红(red)
VC	shi4(是)	是(be)
VE	you3(有) as the main verb	有(have)
VV	Other verb	走(walk)

References

Badr, Ibrahim, Rabih Zbib, and James Glass. 2009. Syntactic phrase reordering for English-to-Arabic statistical machine translation. In *Proceedings of the 12th Conference of the European Chapter of the Association for Computational Linguistics*, 86–93. Association for Computational Linguistics.

Brown, Peter F, John Cocke, Stephen A Della Pietra, Vincent J Della Pietra, Fredrick Jelinek, John D Lafferty, Robert L Mercer, and Paul S Roossin. 1990. A statistical approach to machine translation. *Computational Linguistics* 16(2):79–85.

Chang, Pi-Chuan, Michel Galley, and Christopher D Manning. 2008. Optimizing Chinese word segmentation for machine translation performance. In *Proceedings of the Third Workshop on Statistical Machine Translation*, 224–232. Association for Computational Linguistics.

Chang, Pi-Chuan, Huihsin Tseng, Dan Jurafsky, and Christopher D Manning. 2009. Discriminative reordering with Chinese grammatical relations features. In *Proceedings of the Third Workshop on Syntax and Structure in Statistical Translation*, 51–59. Association for Computational Linguistics.

Collins, Michael, Philipp Koehn, and Ivona Kučerová. 2005. Clause restructuring for statistical machine translation. In *Proceedings of the 43rd Annual Meeting on Association for Computational Linguistics*, 531–540. Association for Computational Linguistics.

Costa-Jussà, Marta Ruiz, and José Adrián Rodríguez Fonollosa. 2006. Statistical machine reordering. In *Proceedings of the 2006 Conference on Empirical Methods in Natural Language Processing (EMNLP)*, 70–76. Association for Computational Linguistics.

Fukui, Naoki. 1992. *Theory of projection in syntax*. Stanford, CA/Tokyo: CSLI Publisher/Kuroshio Publisher.

Gao, Qian. 2008. Word order in mandarin: Reading and speaking. In *Proceedings of the 20th North American Conference on Chinese Linguistics (NACCL-20)*, vol. 2, pp. 611–626.

Gao, Qin, and Stephan Vogel. 2008. Parallel implementations of word alignment tool. In *Proceedings of Software Engineering, Testing, and Quality Assurance for Natural Language Processing*, 49–57. Association for Computational Linguistics.

Genzel, Dmitriy. 2010. Automatically learning source-side reordering rules for large scale machine translation. In *Proceedings of the 23rd International Conference on Computational Linguistics (COLING)*, 376–384. Association for Computational Linguistics.

Goto, Isao, Masao Utiyama, and Eiichiro Sumita. 2012. Post-ordering by parsing for Japanese-English statistical machine translation. In *Proceedings of the 50th Annual Meeting of the Association for Computational Linguistics: Short Papers - Volume 2*, 311–316. Association for Computational Linguistics.

Han, Dan, Katsuhito Sudoh, Xianchao Wu, Kevin Duh, Hajime Tsukada, and Masaaki Nagata. 2012. Head finalization reordering for Chinese-to-Japanese machine translation. In *Proceedings of the Sixth Workshop on Syntax, Semantics and Structure in Statistical Translation (SSST-6)*, 57–66. Association for Computational Linguistics.

Han, Dan, Pascual Martínez-Gómez, Yusuke Miyao, Katsuhito Sudoh, and Masaaki Nagata. 2013a. Effects of parsing errors on pre-reordering performance for Chinese-to-Japanese SMT. In *Proceedings of the 27th Pacific Asia Conference on Language Information and Computing (PACLIC)*. The PACLIC Steering Committee.

Han, Dan, Pascual Martínez-Gómez, Yusuke Miyao, Katsuhito Sudoh, and Masaaki Nagata. 2013b. Using unlabeled dependency parsing for pre-reordering for Chinese-to-Japanese statistical machine translation. In *Proceedings of the 2nd Workshop on Hybrid Approaches to Translation (HyTra)*, 25–33. Association for Computational Linguistics.

Hatori, Jun, Takuya Matsuzaki, Yusuke Miyao, and Jun'ichi Tsujii. 2011. Incremental joint POS tagging and dependency parsing in Chinese. In *Proceedings of the 5th International Joint Conference on Natural Language Processing (IJCNLP)*, 1216–1224. Asian Federation of Natural Language Processing.

Isozaki, Hideki, Tsutomu Hirao, Kevin Duh, Katsuhito Sudoh, and Hajime Tsukada. 2010a. Automatic evaluation of translation quality for distant language pairs. In *Proceedings of the 2010 Conference on Empirical Methods in Natural Language Processing*, 944–952. Association for Computational Linguistics.

Isozaki, Hideki, Katsuhito Sudoh, Hajime Tsukada, and Kevin Duh. 2010b. Head finalization: A simple reordering rule for SOV languages. In *Proceedings of the Joint Fifth Workshop on Statistical Machine Translation and Metrics MATR*, 244–251. Association for Computational Linguistics.

Isozaki, Hideki, Katsuhito Sudoh, Hajime Tsukada, and Kevin Duh. 2012. HPSG-based preprocessing for English-to-Japanese translation. *ACM Transactions on Asian Language Information Processing (TALIP)* 11(3):8:1–8:16.

Kendall, Maurice G. 1938. A new measure of rank correlation. *Biometrika* 30(1/2):81–93.

Koehn, Philipp, Hieu Hoang, Alexandra Birch, Chris Callison-Burch, Marcello Federico, Nicola Bertoldi, Brooke Cowan, Wade Shen, Christine Moran, and Richard Zens, et al. 2007. Moses: Open source toolkit for statistical machine translation. In *Proceedings of the 45th Annual Meeting of the Association for Computational Linguistics on Interactive Poster and Demonstration Sessions*, 177–180. Association for Computational Linguistics.

Kudo, Taku, and Yuji Matsumoto. 2000. Japanese dependency structure analysis based on support vector machines. In *Proceedings of the 2000 Joint SIGDAT Conference on Empirical Methods in Natural Language Processing and Very Large Corpora: Held in Conjunction with the 38th Annual Meeting of the Association for Computational Linguistics-Volume 13*, 18–25. Association for Computational Linguistics.

Lee, Young-Suk, Bing Zhao, and Xiaoqiang Luo. 2010. Constituent reordering and syntax models for English-to-Japanese statistical machine translation. In *Proceedings of the 23rd International Conference on Computational Linguistics (COLING)*, 626–634. Association for Computational Linguistics.

Li, Charles N., and Sandra Annear Thompson. 1989. *Mandarin Chinese: A functional reference grammar*. Linguistics-Asian studies. Berkeley, CA: University of California Press.

Li, Chi-Ho, Minghui Li, Dongdong Zhang, Mu Li, Ming Zhou, and Yi Guan. 2007. A probabilistic approach to syntax-based reordering for statistical machine translation. In *Proceedings of the 45th Annual Meeting on Association for Computational Linguistics (ACL)*, vol. 45(1), pp. 720–727. Association for Computational Linguistics.

Ma, Xiaoyi. 2006. Champollion: A robust parallel text sentence aligner. In *Proceedings of 5th International Conference on Language Resources and Evaluation (LREC-5)*, 489–492. Citeseer.

Miller, James Edward, and Jim Miller. 2011. *A critical introduction to syntax*. New York: Continuum International Publishing Group.

Miyao, Yusuke, and Jun'ichi Tsujii. 2008. Feature forest models for probabilistic HPSG parsing. *Computational Linguistics* 34(1):35–80.

Neubig, Graham, Taro Watanabe, and Shinsuke Mori. 2012. Inducing a discriminative parser to optimize machine translation reordering. In *Proceedings of the 2012 Joint Conference on Empirical Methods in Natural Language Processing and Computational Natural Language Learning*, 843–853. Association for Computational Linguistics.

Och, Franz Josef. 2003. Minimum error rate training in statistical machine translation. In *Proceedings of the 41st Annual Meeting on Association for Computational Linguistics-Volume 1*, 160–167. Association for Computational Linguistics.

Och, Franz Josef, and Hermann Ney. 2003. A systematic comparison of various statistical alignment models. *Computational Linguistics* 29(1):19–51.

Papineni, Kishore, Salim Roukos, Todd Ward, and Wei-Jing Zhu. 2002. Bleu: a method for automatic evaluation of machine translation. In *Proceedings of the 40th Annual Meeting on Association for Computational Linguistics*, 311–318. Association for Computational Linguistics.

Petrov, Slav, Leon Barrett, Romain Thibaux, and Dan Klein. 2006. Learning accurate, compact, and interpretable tree annotation. In *Proceedings of the 21st International Conference on Computational Linguistics and the 44th Annual Meeting of the Association for Computational Linguistics*, 433–440. Association for Computational Linguistics.

Pollard, Carl Jesse, and Ivan Andrew Sag. 1994. *Head-driven phrase structure grammar*. Chicago and Stanford, CA: The University of Chicago Press and CSLI Publications.

Ramanathan, Ananthakrishnan, Hansraj Choudhary, Avishek Ghosh, and Pushpak Bhattacharyya. 2009. Case markers and morphology: Addressing the crux of the fluency problem in English-Hindi SMT. In *Proceedings of the Joint Conference of the 47th Annual Meeting of the ACL and the 4th International Joint Conference on Natural Language Processing*, 800–808. Association for Computational Linguistics.

Rottmann, Kay, and Stephan Vogel. 2007. Word reordering in statistical machine translation with a pos-based distortion model. In *Proceedings of the 11th International Conference on Theoretical and Methodological Issues in Machine Translation (TMI)*, 171–180.

Snover, Matthew, Bonnie Dorr, Richard Schwartz, Linnea Micciulla, and John Makhoul. 2006. A study of translation edit rate with targeted human annotation. In *Proceedings of Association for Machine Translation in the Americas (AMTA)*, 223–231. The Association for Machine Translation in the Americas.

Sudoh, Katsuhito, Xianchao Wu, Kevin Duh, Hajime Tsukada, and Masaaki Nagata. 2011. Post-ordering in statistical machine translation. In *Proceedings of the 13th Machine Translation Summit*, 316–323. The International Association for Machine Translation (IAMT).

Tillmann, Christoph, Stephan Vogel, Hermann Ney, Alex Zubiaga, and Hassan Sawaf. 1997. Accelerated dp based search for statistical translation. In *Proceedings of the 5th European Conference on Speech Communication and Technology*, 2667–2670.

Tromble, Roy, and Jason Eisner. 2009. Learning linear ordering problems for better translation. In *Proceedings of the 2009 Conference on Empirical Methods in Natural Language Processing*, vol. 2, pp. 1007–1016. Association for Computational Linguistics.

Tsunakawa, Takashi, Naoaki Okazaki, Xiao Liu, and Jun'ichi Tsujii. 2009. A Chinese-Japanese lexical machine translation through a pivot language. *ACM Transactions on Asian Language Information Processing* 8(2):9:1–9:21.

Visweswariah, Karthik, Jiri Navratil, Jeffrey Sorensen, Vijil Chenthamarakshan, and Nanda Kambhatla. 2010. Syntax based reordering with automatically derived rules for improved statistical machine translation. In *Proceedings of the 23rd International Conference on Computational Linguistics (COLING)*, 1119–1127. Association for Computational Linguistics.

Visweswariah, Karthik, Rajakrishnan Rajkumar, Ankur Gandhe, Ananthakrishnan Ramanathan, and Jiri Navratil. 2011. A word reordering model for improved machine translation. In *Proceedings of Empirical Methods in Natural Language Processing*, 486–496. Association for Computational Linguistics.

Wang, Chao, Michael Collins, and Philipp Koehn. 2007. Chinese syntactic reordering for statistical machine translation. In *Proceedings of the 2007 Joint Conference on Empirical Methods in Natural Language Processing and Computational Natural Language Learning (EMNLP-CoNLL)*, 737–745. Association for Computational Linguistics.

Wu, Hua, and Haifeng Wang. 2007. Pivot language approach for phrase-based statistical machine translation. *Machine Translation* 21(3):165–181.

Wu, Xianchao, Katsuhito Sudoh, Kevin Duh, Hajime Tsukada, and Masaaki Nagata. 2011. Extracting pre-ordering rules from predicate-argument structures. In *Proceedings of 5th International Joint Conference on Natural Language Processing (IJCNLP)*, November 2011, 29–37. Chiang Mai: Asian Federation of Natural Language Processing. http://www.aclweb.org/anthology/I111004.

Xia, Fei. 2000. *The part-of-speech tagging guidelines for the Penn Chinese Treebank 3.0*. Technical Report IRCS0007 (October 2000). Institute of Research and Cognitive Science (IRCS). Pennsylvania: University of Pennsylvania. http://repository.upenn.edu/ircs_reports/38/.

Xia, Fei, and Michael McCord. 2004. Improving a statistical MT system with automatically learned rewrite patterns. In *Proceedings of the 20th International Conference on Computational Linguistics (COLING)*, 508–514. Association for Computational Linguistics.

Xu, Peng, Jaeho Kang, Michael Ringgaard, and Franz Och. 2009. Using a dependency parser to improve SMT for subject-object-verb languages. In *Proceedings of Human Language*

Technologies: The 2009 Annual Conference of the North American Chapter of the Association for Computational Linguistics, 245–253. Association for Computational Linguistics.

Yu, Kun, Yusuke Miyao, Takuya Matsuzaki, Xiangli Wang, and Junichi Tsujii. 2011. Analysis of the difficulties in Chinese deep parsing. In *Proceedings of the 12th International Conference on Parsing Technologies*, 48–57. Association for Computational Linguistics.

Zhao, Hong-Mei, Ya-Juan Lv, Guo-Sheng Ben, Yun Huang, and Qun Liu. 2011. Evaluation report for the 7th China workshop on machine translation (CWMT2011). In *The 7th China Workshop on Machine Translation (CWMT2011)*. http://mt.xmu.edu.cn/cwmt2011/document/papers/e00.pdf.

Part II
Using Machine Learning in MT

Machine Learning Applied to Rule-Based Machine Translation

Annette Rios and Anne Göhring

Abstract Lexical and morphological ambiguities present a serious challenge in rule-based machine translation (RBMT). This chapter describes an approach to resolve morphologically ambiguous verb forms if a rule-based decision is not possible due to parsing or tagging errors. The rule-based core system has a set of rules to decide, based on context information, which verb form should be generated in the target language. However, if the parse tree is not correct, part of the context information might be missing and the rules cannot make a safe decision. In this case, we use a classifier to assign a verb form. We tested the classifier on a set of four texts, increasing the correct verb forms in the translation from 78.68 %, with the purely rule-based disambiguation, to 95.11 % with the hybrid approach.

1 Introduction

The term hybrid machine translation refers to any combination of statistical MT with rule-based MT (España-Bonet et al. 2011) or example-based MT (Smith and Clark 2009), or a mixture of all three approaches (Alegria et al. 2008).

A statistical translation system may be improved by rule-based pre-editing, such as reordering, or by the addition of linguistic features, for instance through a morphological analysis of the words in the source sentence. Furthermore, statistical methods may enhance a rule-based system on different levels: A common type of hybrid systems uses statistical ranking of translation alternatives of one rule-based system (Oepen et al. 2007) or of several rule-based systems (Eisele et al. 2008). Sawaf (2010) outlines yet another hybrid approach for the 'translation' of different Arabic dialect into the normalized Modern Standard Arabic: A rule-based system handles rare word combinations or phrasal structures, whereas statistical methods are used in situations where word combinations and phrasal structures occur frequently enough to estimate reliable statistics.

A. Rios (✉) • A. Göhring
Institute of Computational Linguistics, University of Zurich, Zurich, Switzerland
e-mail: rios@cl.uzh.ch; arios@ifi.uzh.ch; goehring@cl.uzh.ch

© Springer International Publishing Switzerland 2016
M.R. Costa-jussà et al. (eds.), *Hybrid Approaches to Machine Translation*,
Theory and Applications of Natural Language Processing,
DOI 10.1007/978-3-319-21311-8_5

The hybrid architecture that we describe in this chapter consists of a rule-based core system that uses statistical modules for certain disambiguation tasks. As for the language pair in question, Spanish-Quechua, the amount of parallel text is too small to train a statistical MT system, we use a rule-based approach that relies on linguistic information and transfer rules. Nevertheless, certain ambiguities are extremely difficult to handle in a purely rule-based setting. For instance, if a word has more than one translation in the dictionary, a device for lexical selection is necessary in order to output the correct translation in the given context. This procedure presents a great challenge for a rule-based architecture, as it is not feasible to cover all possible contexts with rules. A possible solution can be to use a statistical MT system to fill in the template of the target sentence generated by the rule-based system (España-Bonet et al. 2011; Hunsicker et al. 2012). If no MT system is available, another option is to use a machine learning approach, e.g. sequence labeling (Rudnick and Gasser 2013) or to generate all possible translations and use a statistical language model to score the alternatives (Melero et al. 2007).

Words may not only have different lexical translations, there can also be morphological ambiguities: a word may have more than one translation with the same lemma, but different morphology. A set of rules that match the context of the verb decides which verb form should be generated in the target language. However, due to parsing or tagging errors, these rules might not be applicable in all cases. In this chapter, we will present an approach to disambiguate such morphological ambiguities with machine learning.

2   SQUOIA Spanish to Quechua MT System

As part of our research project SQUOIA,[1] we have implemented a mostly rule-based machine translation system that translates text from Spanish to Quechua. The system uses a classical transfer approach, where several modules are joined in a processing chain: each module relies on the output of the previous module for further processing, see Fig. 1 for an overview. One of the most difficult parts during the translation is the disambiguation of subordinated Spanish verbs in order to generate the correct Quechua forms, as the grammatical features encoded in verbs differ considerably between these two languages. To a certain extent, subordinated verb forms can easily be disambiguated with a set of rules, but this strategy is not practical in all cases. In this chapter, we will present an approach that uses machine learning to resolve verb forms in contexts that cannot be safely disambiguated by rules.

There are two kinds of subordinated clauses that we need to disambiguate: clauses with a verbal head (complement clauses, final clauses, etc.) and clauses with a nominal head (relative clauses). In both cases, we use a set of rules to determine which Quechua verb form should be generated in the given context.

---

[1]http://tiny.uzh.ch/xc.

Fig. 1 SQUOIA translation
pipeline Spanish-Quechua

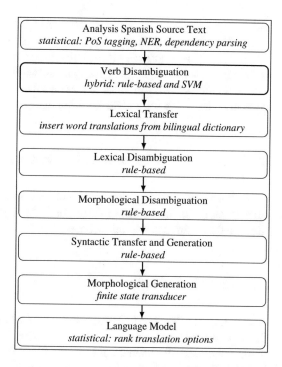

| Analysis Spanish Source Text |
| *statistical: PoS tagging, NER, dependency parsing* |

↓

| Verb Disambiguation |
| *hybrid: rule-based and SVM* |

↓

| Lexical Transfer |
| *insert word translations from bilingual dictionary* |

↓

| Lexical Disambiguation |
| *rule-based* |

↓

| Morphological Disambiguation |
| *rule-based* |

↓

| Syntactic Transfer and Generation |
| *rule-based* |

↓

| Morphological Generation |
| *finite state transducer* |

↓

| Language Model |
| *statistical: rank translation options* |

For relative clauses, we have to rely on semantic information about the head and the subcategorization frames of the verb, whereas for other subordinated clauses, we need the conjunction and the semantics of the main verb to determine the correct Quechua verb form. In a real application scenario however, we might not have access to all the information we need to make a rule-based decision, due to tagging or parsing errors.

In the case of relative clauses, it is important to note that the syntactic structure alone does not always allow for a safe decision, as Spanish relative clauses can be highly ambiguous. In this case, the rule-based module guesses the correct form based on semantic information.

In a previous experiment, we extracted context information about subordinated clauses with verbal heads from two treebanks and trained different classifiers on this data (Rios and Göhring 2013). In this first setup, we used the lemmas of the main and the subordinated verb as attributes. However, as the decision relies on lemmas, we might have a problem with sparse data, as the classifier has only information about the lemmas seen in training. Therefore, we will present an alternative approach in this chapter that relies on semantic information about verbs[2] and verb frames.[3] In

---

[2]Extracted from the Spanish part of Multilingual Central Repository 3.0 (Gonzalez-Agirre et al. 2012).

[3]Extracted from the AnCora verb lexicon (Taulé et al. 2008).

the previous setting, Naïve Bayes achieved the best results, with 81 % in tenfold cross-validation and 84 % on a separate test set. With the new set of features, the independence assumption may not always be true anymore. As a consequence, Naïve Bayes is no longer an option, and so we decided to use libsvm (Chang and Lin 2011) instead. We were able to increase the accuracy with this new approach to 92 % in cross-validation and 86 % on the same test set.

3   Subordinated Quechua Verb Forms

Subordinated clauses in Quechua are often non-finite, nominal forms. There are several nominalizing suffixes that are used for different clause types that will be illustrated in more detail in this section.

3.1   Switch-Reference

A common type of subordination in Quechua is the so-called switch-reference: the subordinated, non-finite verb bears a suffix that indicates whether its subject is the same as in the main clause or not. If the subject in the subordinated clause is different, the non-finite verb bears a possessive suffix that indicates the subject person. Consider the following examples[4]:

(1)   Same subject: *Mikhuspa hamuni.*

    Mikhu **-spa** *hamu* *-ni.*

    eat   **-SS**   come -1.Sg

    "When I finished eating, I'll come."
    (lit. "My eating, I come.")

---

[4]Abbreviations used:

Acc: accusative	Add: additive ('too,also')
Ag: agentive	Ben: benefactive ('for')
Con: connective ('and')	Dir: directional
DirE: direct evidentiality	DS: different subject
Gen: genitive	Imp: imperative
Inch: inchoative	Loc: locative
Neg: negation	Obl: obligative
Perf: perfect	Poss: possessive
Prog: progressive	Pst: past
Rflx: reflexive	Sg: singular
SS: same subject	Top: topic

(2)   Different subject: *Mikhuchkaptiy pasakura.*

    Mikhu -chka **-pti** -y   *pasa* -ku   -ra -ø.

    eat   -Prog **-DS** -1.Sg.Poss leave -Rflx -Pst -3.Sg

"While I was eating, he left."
(lit. "my being-eating, he left.")

(Dedenbach-Salazar Sáenz et al. 2002, p. 168)

In the source language, Spanish, subordinated verbs are usually finite. An overt subject is not necessary, as personal pronouns are used only for emphasis ("pro-drop"). In order to generate the correct verb form, we need to find the subject of the subordinated verb and compare it to the main verb. For this reason, we included a module that performs coreference resolution on subjects. So far, the procedure is based on the simple assumption that an elided subject is coreferential with the previous explicit subject, if this subject agrees in number and person with the current verb. However, some exceptions have to be considered, e.g. the subject of a verb in direct speech is not a good antecedent.

3.2   Other Types of Subordination

Generally, the relation of the subordinated clause to the main clause is expressed through different conjunctions in Spanish. In Quechua, on the other hand, a specific verb form in combination with a case suffix indicates the type of subordination. For instance, Spanish *para que* - "in order to" has to be translated with a nominal verb form with the suffix *-na* ('obligative') and the case suffix *-paq* (usually called benefactive, "for"):

(3)
    Ventanata kichay wayraq haykurimunanpaq.

    Ventana -ta   *kicha* -y   *wayra* -q   *hayku* -ri   -mu **-na** -n

    window -Acc open -2.Sg.Imp wind -Gen enter -Inch -Dir **-Obl** -3.Sg.Poss

    -paq.

    -Ben

"Open the window, so the air comes in."
(lit. "Open the window for his entering of the wind")

(Cusihuamán 2001, p. 210)

Finite verb forms are also possible in subordinated clauses; in this case, the relation of the subordinated and the main clause is indicated through a "linker". A linker often consists of a demonstrative pronoun combined with case suffixes or so-called independent suffixes; these are special suffixes that can be attached to any word class and their position is usually at the end of the suffix sequence. The functions of the independent suffixes include data source, polar question marking and topic or contrast, amongst others (Adelaar and Muysken 2004, p. 209). In combination with demonstrative pronouns, the independent suffixes are used for linking clauses, similar to Spanish or English conjunctions. For instance, the combination of demonstrative *chay* - "this" with the topic marker -*qa*, *chayqa*, is used in the sense of "if, in case that":

(4)   *Munanki **chayqa**, Arekipatapis rinki makinapi.*

       *Muna -nki   **chay -qa**,   Arekipa   -ta   -pis   ri   -nki   makina   -pi.*

       want   -2.Sg   **this   -Top**   Arequipa   -Acc   -Add   go   -2.Sg   machine   -Loc

     "If you like, you can also go to Arequipa by train (machine)."

                                           (Cusihuamán 2001, p. 264)

Indirect speech in the Spanish source text is a special case, as the Quechua equivalence of indirect speech is direct speech. The conversion from indirect to direct speech is not trivial, because coreference resolution for the subject is required: if the subject of the main verb is the same as the subject of the indirect speech clause, the verb has to be generated as first person form in direct speech. Consider this English example:

(5)   "John said he wanted to go fishing."

    a.   *if John = he:* "I want to go fishing", John said.

    b.   *if John ≠ he:* "He wants to go fishing", John said.

In this case, we naively consider both subjects as being equal and mark the direct speech Quechua verb as a first person form, as the current rule-based approach is not good enough to distinguish these two cases. However, we plan to integrate a statistical means for coreference resolution in order to make better decisions as to which form should be generated.

Furthermore, the form of the subordinated verb may also depend on the semantics of the main verb, e.g. complement clauses of control verbs usually require -*na* ('obligative'), whereas with other verbs, the nominalizer -*sqa* ('nominal perfect') is used[5]:

(6)   a.   *Ri **-na**   -yki   -ta   muna -ni.*

          go   **-Obl**   -2.Sg.Poss   -Acc   want   -1.Sg

          "I want you to leave."

          (lit. "I want your going.")

---

[5]Double marking of negation in (6.b): *ama:* negation particle in imperative clauses ('don't'), -*chu*: negation suffix, attached to the constituent in focus.

b. *Ama -n   chay yacha **-sqa** -yki   -ta   qunqa -nki -chu.*
   don't -DirE this know **-Perf** -2.Sg.Poss -Acc forget -2.Sg -Neg

"Don't forget what you learned."
(lit. "Don't forget those your learned-ones.")

(Cusihuamán 2001, p. 125)

For all of these cases, the translation system has a set of rules to match the given context, so that the correct form can be assigned to each verb.

4   Verb Form Disambiguation with Machine Learning

4.1   Training Data

In order to generate the correct Quechua verb form in a subordinated clause, we need to extract the following information from the Spanish source sentence:

- semantics of the main verb
- the conjunction
- tense and mood of the subordinated verb (in some cases needed to distinguish between 'obligative' *-na* and 'perfect' *-sqa*)

Based on these features, the rule-based verb disambiguation module of the translation system assigns the Quechua verb form. Given a correct dependency tree, this rule-based approach achieves a high precision, but it is bound to fail if the parse tree is erroneous. In order to obtain instances of main and subordinated clauses for training a classifier, we pre-translated two manually annotated dependency treebanks: the Spanish AnCora dependency treebank[6] (Taulé et al. 2008) and the IULA Spanish LSP Treebank[7] (Marimon et al. 2012). As these are correctly annotated, the rule-based module can disambiguate the subordinated verbs with great reliability, and we can extract these clauses as instances for training. With this approach, we collected 8579 instances from AnCora and 5704 from IULA,[8] which results in a total of 14,283 instances for training.

4.2   Features

Instead of lemmas we use the semantic categories from the Spanish wordnet (Gonzalez-Agirre et al. 2012) and the AnCora verb frames (Taulé et al. 2008) to describe the main verb. For the subordinated verb, only tense and mood are relevant

---

[6]http://clic.ub.edu/corpus/en/ancora.

[7]http://www.iula.upf.edu/recurs01_tbk_uk.htm.

[8]Note that, although IULA contains more than twice as many sentences as AnCora, the sentences in IULA are mostly short, simple sentences, without subordinated clauses.

Table 1 Evaluation[a]

Features	libsvm C-SVC, RBF, c=32, g=0.0078125		Naïve Bayes with semantic/ syntactic feat		Naïve Bayes with lemmas	
	10× cv	Test set	10× cv	Test set	10× cv	Test set
Main verb, sub. verb, conjunction	92.08	86	81.47	75	84.28	78
Sub. verb, conjunction	87.97	81	85.07	75	74.02	72

[a]C-support vector classification (C-SVC) with RBF kernel parameters c (cost) and g (gamma) obtained through search grid on tenfold cross-validation (10× cv)

(extracted from the PoS tag in the treebank). For the conjunctions, we use the lexical forms, as there is no good way to describe them semantically. All features are binarized for training.

In our previous pipeline (Rios and Göhring 2013) we relied on the lemmas of main and subordinated verb instead of semantic and syntactic features. In this setting, Naïve Bayes achieved the best results, yet as with the new set of features, the independence assumption might not always be given, we switched to support vector machines.

4.3 Classification

We decided to use libsvm for the classification, as it provides a simple way of optimizing the parameters c (cost) and g (gamma) via grid search. Table 1 shows the accuracy of libsvm in tenfold cross validation and on a manually annotated test set of 100 instances. This is the same test set that we used before with Naïve Bayes (Rios and Göhring 2013). For comparison, Table 1 also contains the results obtained with Naïve Bayes, once trained on the exactly same data set as libsvm, and once trained on the same data, but with verb lemmas instead of semantic and syntactic features. The results in Table 1 indicate that libsvm achieves the best accuracy, with 92.07 % in cross-validation and 86 % on the test set.[9]

The classification is slightly worse if only the conjunction and the subordinated verb are set, but the main verb is unknown (second line in Table 1). The third option, that the classifier has only information about the main and the subordinated verb while the conjunction is unknown, is not relevant: In case no conjunction has been found, the module assumes that the verb form in question must be either a main verb, a relative clause or a coordination. All of these options are set by rules, not by the SVM classifier.

---

[9]In our previous setting with Naïve Bayes, we achieved only 81 % accuracy, but we had a smaller training set of only ∼7300 instances.

4.4 RBMT System with SVM Verb Disambiguation

Figure 2 illustrates how the SVM module is integrated into the translation pipeline: The rule-based verb disambiguation module tries to assign a Quechua form to all

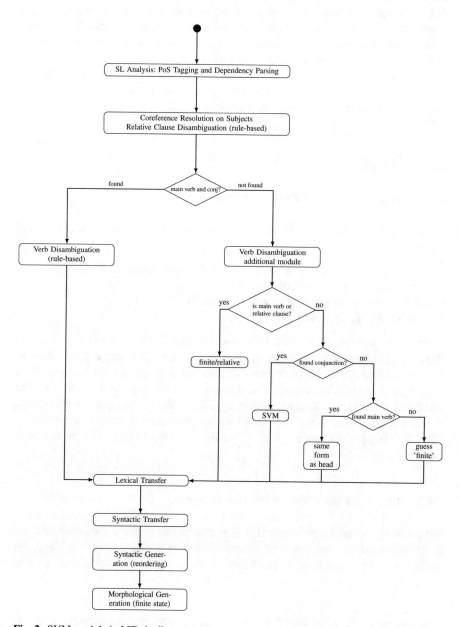

Fig. 2 SVM module in MT pipeline

verbs in the Spanish tree. If the main verb or the conjunction is not found during this rule-based disambiguation, the verb form is marked as ambiguous and passed to the additional module for further disambiguation. This additional module checks in a first step if a given ambiguous verb form could be the actual main verb of the sentence or a relative clause that the parser attached to a non-nominal head. If this is the case, it assigns the verb form *finite* or *rel* for main or relative clauses respectively, and the disambiguation is done. Otherwise, it checks if there is a conjunction, if so, it looks for the main verb in the linear sequence of the tokens,[10] and then invokes the SVM model to assign a verb form. If there was no conjunction, the module assumes that this must be a coordination and assigns the same verb form as the preceding verb. If there is no preceding verb, this might be a tagging error, in this case the module assigns the verb form *finite*, as this is the most common form.

4.5 Evaluation

4.5.1 Whole Verb Disambiguation Pipeline

We used the same four texts for the evaluation as in the previous setup (Rios and Göhring 2013):

- *La catarata de la sirena*—'the waterfall of the siren' (Andean story)
- first two chapters of 'The Little Prince'
- article from the Peruvian newspaper 'El Diario'
- Spanish Wikipedia article about Peru

Since our previous publication (Rios and Göhring 2013), we have improved our tagger, and therefore the number of recognized verbs is slightly higher than in the version from 2013. The rule-based module disambiguates only 78.67 % of all verb forms correctly, as it marks many verbs as ambiguous. In the next step, the additional disambiguation module with the SVM classifier assigns a verb form to all the ambiguous forms and thus increases the proportion of correct verb forms to 95.11 %. The previous module, with Naïve Bayes, achieved only 89 % accuracy on these texts, see Table 2.

4.5.2 Additional Verb Disambiguation Module

Furthermore, we used three larger texts to test the performance of the rule-based and the SVM part of the additional verb disambiguation module. As shown in Fig. 2, the additional module relies on a set of rules to decide if the 'subordinated' verb in

---

[10]The first verb to the left or right that is not an auxiliary and with no conjunction or relative pronoun between them.

Table 2 Evaluation of the complete disambiguation pipeline

		Correct	Incorrect
Rule based:	186	177	9
		78.67 %	4 %
With additional module (includes SVM) :	39	37	2
Total "verb" chunks:	225	214	11
		95.11 %	4.89 %
Old version, with Naïve Bayes:		89 %	11 %

Table 3 Evaluation of the additional verb disambiguation module

	Rule-based decision (main verb, relative clause or coordination)	SVM	Total
Total ambiguous verb forms	73	19	92
Total correct	64	15	79
			85.87 %
Total wrong	9	4	13
		14.13 %	
Total tagging errors (no verbs)	4	1	5
Total disambiguated (actual verbs)	69	18	87
Correct	64	15	79
			90.8 %
Wrong	5	3	8
			9.2 %

question is the actual main verb, a relative clause or a coordinated clause. If this is not the case, but the clause is clearly subordinated (indicated through a conjunction), the verb form is determined via SVM.

The texts that we used for this evaluation are:

- Festschrift 40th anniversary of the Peruvian-German chamber of commerce and industry (322 sentences)[11]
- Memoria 2009, Peruvian-German chamber of commerce and industry (314 sentences)[12]
- *La papa y el cambio climático*—'potatoes and climate change', inforesources 2008 (development aid, 456 sentences)[13]

---

[11]http://www.camara-alemana.org.pe/Publicaciones/MIGEdiciones/2010MEMORIA2009.pdf.

[12]http://www.camara-alemana.org.pe/Publicaciones/MIGEdiciones/2010MEMORIA-JAHRESBE RICHT2009x.pdf.

[13]http://www.inforesources.ch/pdf/focus08_1_s.pdf.

Table 3 illustrates the performance of the additional verb disambiguation module. Most of the potential ambiguous verbs (73 out of 92) are either main verbs, relative clauses or coordinations that had been attached to the wrong head and could therefore not be disambiguated by the rule-based module, but by the rule-based decision part of the additional verb disambiguation module. Not all ambiguous verb form candidates are actual verbs: the middle part of Table 3 shows five cases where nouns have been erroneously tagged as verbs. In total, the additional module assigned 79 out of 87 actual verb forms correctly, which results in 90.8 % accuracy.

5 Relative Clauses

5.1 Quechua Relativization

Relative clauses in Quechua are nominal forms that are either agentive or non-agentive. For non-agentive relative clauses, there are two nominalizing suffixes available: *-sqa* ('perfect') is used for actions that have been completed, whereas *-na* ('obligative') occurs in contexts where the action has not been completed or indicates an intention, obligation or purpose. Consider the following examples:

(7) a.   agentive:
            Wasi ruwaq runa hamuchkan.
            Wasi   ruwa -q   runa hamu -chka -n.
            house make **-Ag** man come -Prog -3.Sg

            'The man who builds houses is coming.'
            (lit. 'the house-making man is coming')

     b.   non-agentive:
            yachasqayki llaqta
            yacha -sqa -yki   llaqta
            live   **-Perf** -2.Sg.Poss village

            'the village where you live'
                                              (Dedenbach-Salazar Sáenz et al. 2002, p. 141)

     c.   non-agentive:
            Qantaq, Gregorio, montanay caballoyta hap'iy!
            *Qan -taq, Gregorio, monta **-na** -y   caballo -y*
            you -Con Gregorio ride   **-Obl** -1.Sg.Poss horse   -1.Sg.Poss

            -ta   hap'i -y!
            -Acc grab -2.Imp

            'And you, Gregorio, grab my riding horse!'
            (lit. 'grab the horse that I will ride/intend to ride')
                                              (Valderrama Fernández and Escalante Gutiérrez 1982)

In order to generate the correct verb form for a Quechua relative clause, it is necessary to automatically distinguish between relativization on subjects and relativization on obliques. The latter are always translated with the non-agentive forms, but relative clauses where the head noun is the subject need to be further disambiguated: If the subject is a semantic agent, the verb in the relative clause has to be rendered in the agentive form (-*q*), if the subject is not agentive, either -*sqa* or -*na* is the correct form.

Relative clauses in the source language Spanish can be very ambiguous, consider the following examples:

(8) a. agentive:

la   mujer   que   comió la   manzana
the woman REL ate   the apple

'the woman who ate the apple'

b. non-agentive:

la   manzana que   comió la   mujer
the apple   REL ate   the woman

'the apple that the woman ate'

The only difference between sentence (8a) and (8b) is the semantic class of the head noun: The verb *comer* - 'to eat' requires an animate, agentive subject like *mujer*. An inanimate noun like *manzana* can therefore not be the subject of *comer*. The correct translation of example (8a) uses the verb form with -*q*, whereas the verb in (8b) should be translated with -*sqa*:

(9) a. agentive:

mansana mikhu -q   warmi
apple   eat   **-Ag** woman

'the woman who eats/ate the apple'

b. non-agentive:

warmi -p   mikhu -sqa -n   mansana
woman -Gen eat   **-Perf** -3.Sg.Poss apple

'the apple that the woman eats/ate'

Not every Spanish relative clause is as ambiguous as the examples in (8a) and (8b). In the following cases, the head noun cannot be the subject of the relative clause, and therefore the agentive form can be discarded for the translation:

1. if the relative pronoun is preceded by a preposition (*el hombre a quien vió*),
2. if the relative pronoun is something other than *que, quien* or *cual*
3. if the verb in the relative clause is not congruent with the head noun
4. if the relative clause contains a subject noun or pronoun

Note that case 4 is not a reliable feature in the translation process, as the parser frequently labels subjects as objects and vice versa, therefore, even if the parser detected a subject in the relative clause, the following disambiguation steps will still be applied. The rule-based module uses a lexicon of Spanish verb frames (Taulé et al. 2008): If the verb has only one frame, and the frame is intransitive, the head noun must be the subject. The semantic role indicated in the lexicon (agent, patient, impersonal, causer etc.) is the key to the correct translation: the Quechua verb should be rendered with the *-q* form, if the semantic role is agentive. In all other cases, the verb form in Quechua should be generated with either *-sqa* or *-na*. Whether to use the obligative or the perfect form has to be decided based on tense, aspect and mood of the Spanish verb.

If the frame retrieved from the semantic lexicon is transitive or ditransitive, the head noun is either the subject or object, but never the indirect object, as in this case the relative pronoun is preceded by the preposition *a*:

(10)   indirect object as head of a relative clause:
       *el   vecino   **a** quien la   mujer   muestra el   libro*
       the neighbor to REL   the woman shows   the book

       'the neighbor, to whom the woman shows the book'

If the verb frame is transitive or ditransitive with an agentive subject, we cannot know whether the head noun is the subject or the object (see examples (8a) and (8b)). In case the verb lexicon contains more than one possible frame for a given verb, the module tries to delete all inapplicable frames with some additional context checks. If the frames cannot be reduced to one semantic role for the subject, the module takes a guess based on the semantics of the head noun. In this case, the disambiguation module retrieves the semantic information of the head noun from a semantic noun lexicon (Marimon et al. 2007): if the head noun is a likely agent (e.g. animate, human, a social group, an instrument), it assumes the agentive form, but if the head noun is an unlikely agent (e.g. an inanimate or an abstract noun, a plant) it assigns one of the non-agentive verb forms.

The basic assumption is that only nouns of certain semantic groups are plausible agents, while others are not (e.g. plants, abstract nouns, inanimates). This premise is of course not always correct, therefore we tested a machine learning approach to disambiguate relative clauses.

5.2   Relative Clause Disambiguation with Machine Learning

The disambiguation of relative clauses with machine learning differs substantially from the disambiguation of other subordinated verb forms. Section 4 illustrates how the MT system relies on a classifier to determine the Quechua verb form in cases where the analysis of the Spanish source sentence went wrong. In the experiments with relative clauses, on the other hand, we try to use a classifier to assign the correct form instead of guessing the form based on semantic information in highly ambiguous cases.

5.3 Training Data

The training material consists of automatically annotated relative clauses from the AnCora and IULA treebanks. Most relative clauses are not ambiguous: As AnCora and IULA are manually annotated, the annotation of subjects in relative clauses is reliable, as opposed to automatically parsed texts. Therefore, relative clauses that contain a subject in the treebanks are always non-agentive. Furthermore, if the verb has only intransitive frames with either agentive or non-agentive subjects, we need no further disambiguation, as we can fully rely on the semantic role of the subject given in the verb frame lexicon. The ambiguous cases in AnCora and IULA that the module had to guess were manually checked and corrected.

Note that not all relative clauses are interesting for training, as we want to use the classifier only on ambiguous forms that cannot be determined by considering only the syntactic context. With this approach, we extracted 5018 instances from AnCora and 3201 instances from IULA to train the classifier.

5.4 Features

In addition to the verb frames (Taulé et al. 2008) and the semantic noun classes (Marimon et al. 2007) used by the rule-based module, we integrated semantic information about the verb and the head noun from the Spanish wordnet (Gonzalez-Agirre et al. 2012) to the classification with libsvm. The semantic noun classes of the Spanish Resource Grammar include e.g. *human*, *body part*, *plant*, *abstract noun*, etc. The classes from the Spanish wordnet overlap with these in part, but are more fine-grained for abstract nouns, they include e.g. *feeling*, *event*, *phenomenon*, *motive*, *process* and some more.

Furthermore, we included some syntactic information, or more specifically whether the relative clause contains:

- the reflexive *se*[14]
- an indirect object
- a prepositional object
- an adjunct
- the demoted subject of a passive clause
- a predicative element (in equational clauses)

---

[14]The Spanish reflexive *se* is a device to render a transitive verb intransitive.

Note that we did not include the presence of a subject or direct object in the relative clause as features, as we cannot safely rely on the parser for this distinction.

Furthermore, we included an additional binary feature that indicates whether the lemma of the verb in Quechua is the copula *ka-*. The reason behind this feature is that relative clauses with *ka-* use the agentive form, although the head noun is not a semantic agent. Relative clauses with the copula thus do not follow the general rule, see Example (11).

(11) *urqu*   *-kuna -pi   ka -q   ayllu   -kuna*
      mountain -Pl   -Loc be -Ag village -Pl

      'mountain villages'
      (lit. the villages that are in the mountains)

5.5 *Evaluation*

The test set consists of 106 ambiguous relative clauses extracted from Spanish Wikipedia articles about three authors: Gabriel García Márquez, Mario Vargas Llosa and Pablo Neruda.[15]

The baseline in Table 4 is the performance of the rule-based module that guesses the form based on semantic information about the head. This simple guess was correct in 88 out of 106 cases, which results in 83.02 % accuracy. As Table 4 shows, the SVM classifier does not achieve the accuracy of the rule-based method: Even in the best setting, with all features, the classifier assigns the correct form only in 83 out of 106 cases. This results in an accuracy of 78.3 %, which is slightly worse than the performance of the rule-based module.

Table 4 Evaluation of the SVM classifier on relative clauses

	10× cv	Test set
libsvm:	(C-SVC, RBF, c=8, g=0.03125)	
All features	77.81	78.30
No wordnet	75.46	75.47
No verb frames	72.89	64.15
No resource grammar noun classes	77.17	77.36
No syntactic features	76.10	75.47
Baseline (rule-based)	–	83.02

----

[15]http://es.wikipedia.org/wiki/ retrieved 11.01.2014.

A possible explanation is the relatively small number of training instances: although we exploited two treebanks, the training set consists of only 8219 instances, as opposed to the 14,283 instances used to train the classifier for the subordinated verbs. Furthermore, the training material is probably not as clean as the instances used for the disambiguation of the subordinated verbs: Only the highly ambiguous (guessed) cases were manually checked, but there might as well be a number of errors in the remaining relative clauses.

6 Conclusions

We enhanced a purely rule-based machine translation system for the language pair Spanish-Quechua with an SVM module that predicts the form of subordinated verbs in the target language Quechua, based on information collected from the Spanish input text. The MT system has rules to match the context of the subordinated verb and assign a Quechua verb form for generation. Due to parsing and tagging errors, the information needed for this rule-based disambiguation cannot always be retrieved. In order to disambiguate these forms, we use a classifier that predicts the verb form even if all of the context information is not accessible.

We use two Spanish dependency treebanks to generate the training instances for the classifier: We let the rule-based part of the MT system assign a verb form to the subordinated clauses in the treebanks, and then extract these clauses for training. As the trees in the treebanks are annotated correctly, the rules assign the correct verb form reliably.

In a previous version of the verb disambiguation module, we used Naïve Bayes to decide the ambiguous cases, based on the lemmas of the main and the subordinated verb, as well as the conjunction. With this approach, the decision relies on lemmas, and we might have a problem with sparse data, as the classifier has only information about the lemmas seen in training.

In order to avoid this problem, we decided to use the semantic classes from the Spanish wordnet (Gonzalez-Agirre et al. 2012) and the verb frames from the AnCora Verbframe Lexicon (Taulé et al. 2008) instead of lemmas. Due to the introduction of semantic classes and verb frames as features instead of lexical forms, the independence assumption may no longer be true, and therefore, we decided to use libsvm instead. Additionally, we enlarged the training set by exploiting not only AnCora (Taulé et al. 2008), but also IULA (Marimon et al. 2012).

Previously, Naïve Bayes achieved 81 % in tenfold cross-validation and 84 % on a separate test set. We were able to increase the accuracy with the new feature set and libsvm to 92 % in cross-validation and 86 % on the same test set. As for now, only verb forms marked as ambiguous by the preceding rule-based module are disambiguated by the SVM module. Nevertheless, quite a large proportion of these verbs were identified as the actual main verb of the sentence. This implies that the verb that appears as head of the sentence in the parse tree should actually be a subordinated verb. In the future, we will use the SVM classifier to reassign the correct verb form to these verbs and thus increase the number of correct forms in the translation.

Furthermore, we tested if a similar approach would be suitable for the disambiguation of relative clauses, as opposed to a rule-based approach where, in ambiguous cases, the module guesses the form of the verb based on semantic information. As with the subordinated verbs, we used the rule-based module to assign a form to the relative clauses in both AnCora and IULA, and then extracted these relative clauses as instances for training, after manually checking the ambiguous forms. However, the rule-based approach still outperforms the classifier with 83.02% to 78.3%, respectively. A possible reason for the poor performance might be the relatively small number of training instances: we extracted only 8219 relative clauses from the treebanks, as opposed to 14,283 instances of subordinated verbs.

Acknowledgements This research is funded by the Swiss National Science Foundation under grant 100015_132219/1.

References

Adelaar, W.F.H., and P. Muysken. 2004. *The languages of the Andes*. Cambridge language surveys. Cambridge: Cambridge University Press.

Alegria, I., A. Casillas, A. Díaz de Ilarraza, J. Iguartua, G. Labaka, M. Lersundi, A. Mayor, and K. Sarasola. 2008. Mixing approaches to MT for Basque: Selecting the best output from RBMT, EBMT and SMT. In *Proceedings of the MATMT2008 Workshop: Mixing Approaches to Machine Translation*.

Chang, C.C., and C.J. Lin. 2011. LIBSVM: A library for support vector machines. *ACM Transactions on Intelligent Systems and Technology* 2(3):27:1–27:27.

Cusihuamán, A.G. 2001. *Gramática Quechua: Cuzco-Collao*, 2nd ed. Serie Saber Andino. Lima: Ministerio de Educación.

Dedenbach-Salazar Sáenz, S., U. von Gleich, R. Hartmann, P. Masson, and C. Soto Ruiz. 2002. *Rimaykullayki - Unterrichtsmaterialien zum Quechua Ayacuchano*, 4th ed. Berlin: Dietrich Reimer Verlag GmbH.

Eisele, A., C. Federmann, H. Uszkoreit, H. Saint-Amand, M. Kay, M. Jellinghaus, S. Hunsicker, T. Herrmann, and Y. Chen. 2008. Hybrid machine translation architectures within and beyond the EuroMatrix project. In *Proceedings of the European Machine Translation Conference EAMT*, European Association for Machine Translation, 27–34.

España-Bonet, C., G. Labaka, A. Díaz de Ilarraza, L. Màrquez, and K. Sarasola. 2011. Hybrid machine translation guided by a rule-based system. In *Proceedings of the 13th Machine Translation Summit*, Xiamen, 554–561.

Gonzalez-Agirre, A., E. Laparra, and G. Rigau. 2012. Multilingual central repository version 3.0: Upgrading a very large lexical knowledge base. In *Proceedings of the Sixth International Global WordNet Conference (GWC'12)*, Matsue.

Hunsicker, S., Y. Chen, and C. Federmann. 2012. Machine learning for hybrid machine translation. In *Proceedings of the Seventh Workshop on Statistical Machine Translation*, Montreal, 312–316.

Marimon, M., N. Seghezzi, and N. Bel. 2007. An open-source Lexicon for Spanish. *Procesamiento del Lenguaje Natural* 39:131–137.

Marimon, M., B. Fisas, N. Bel, B. Arias, S. Vázquez, J. Vivaldi, S. Torner, M. Villegas, and M. Lorente. 2012. The IULA treebank. In *Proceedings of the Eight International Conference on Language Resources and Evaluation (LREC'12)*, Istanbul.

Melero, M., A. Oliver, T. Badia, and T. Suñol. 2007. Dealing with bilingual divergences in MT using target language N-gram models. In *Proceedings of the METIS-II Workshop: New Approaches to Machine Translation*, Leuven, 19–26.

Oepen, S., E. Velldal, J.T. Lønning, P. Meurer, V. Rosén, and D. Flickinger. 2007. Towards hybrid quality-oriented machine translation. On linguistics and probabilities in MT. In *Proceedings of Theoretical and Methodological Issues in Machine Translation*, Skövde.

Rios, A., and A. Göhring. 2013. Machine learning disambiguation of Quechua verb morphology. In *Proceedings of the Second Workshop on Hybrid Approaches to Translation*, Sofia, 13–18.

Rudnick, A., and M. Gasser. 2013. Lexical selection for hybrid MT with sequence labeling. In *Proceedings of the Second Workshop on Hybrid Approaches to Translation*, Sofia, 102–108.

Sawaf. H. 2010. Arabic dialect handling in hybrid machine translation. In *Proceedings of the 9th Conference of the Association for Machine Translation in the Americas*.

Smith, J., and S. Clark. 2009. EBMT for SMT: A new EBMT-SMT hybrid. In *Proceedings of the 3rd Workshop on ExampleBased Machine Translation*, 3–10.

Taulé, M., M.A. Martí, and M. Recasens. 2008. AnCora: Multilevel annotated corpora for Catalan and Spanish. In *Proceedings of the Sixth International Language Resources and Evaluation (LREC'08)*, Marrakech.

Valderrama Fernández, R., and C. Escalante Gutiérrez. 1982. *Gregorio Condori Mamani: Autobiografía*. Cuzco: Centro Bartolomé de las Casas.

Language-Independent Hybrid MT: Comparative Evaluation of Translation Quality

George Tambouratzis, Marina Vassiliou, and Sokratis Sofianopoulos

Abstract The present chapter reviews the development of a hybrid Machine Translation (MT) methodology, which is readily portable to new language pairs. This MT methodology (which has been developed within the PRESEMT project) is based on sampling mainly monolingual corpora, with very limited use of parallel corpora, thus supporting portability to new language pairs. In designing this methodology, no assumptions are made regarding the availability of extensive and expensive-to-create linguistic resources. In addition, the general-purpose NLP tools used can be chosen interchangeably. Thus PRESEMT circumvents the requirement for specialised resources and tools so as to further support the creation of MT systems for diverse language pairs.

In the current chapter, the proposed hybrid MT methodology is compared to established MT systems, both in terms of design concept and in terms of output quality. More specifically, the translation performance of the proposed methodology is evaluated against that of existing MT systems. The chapter summarises implementation decisions, using the Greek-to-English language pair as a test case. In addition, the detailed comparison of PRESEMT to other established MT systems provides insight on their relative advantages and disadvantages, focusing on specific translation tasks and addressing both translation quality as well as translation consistency and stability. Finally, directions are discussed for improving the performance of PRESEMT. This will allow PRESEMT to move beyond the original requirements for an MT system for gisting, towards a high-performing general-purpose MT system.

1 Introduction

Rule-based machine translation (RBMT) is one of the oldest MT paradigms and still has a substantial influence over modern MT systems. An RBMT system relies on

G. Tambouratzis (✉) • M. Vassiliou • S. Sofianopoulos
ILSP, Athens R.C., 6 Artemidos & Epidavrou Str., Paradissos Amaroussiou, 151 25, Marousi, Greece
e-mail: giorg_t@ilsp.gr; mvas@ilsp.gr; s_sofian@ilsp.gr

© Springer International Publishing Switzerland 2016   131
M.R. Costa-jussà et al. (eds.), *Hybrid Approaches to Machine Translation*,
Theory and Applications of Natural Language Processing,
DOI 10.1007/978-3-319-21311-8_6

creating a comprehensive set of rules at various levels e.g. in syntax, semantics etc. for translating between two languages.

RBMT systems have been developed for over 50 years and still remain one of the most popular paradigms because of their superior translation quality. However, the main disadvantage of this paradigm is that in most cases it is impossible to use directly the rules and expertise of an existing RBMT system to create a translation system for new language pairs. In addition, progress in RBMT is hindered mainly by inadequate grammar resources for most languages and absence of appropriate lexical resources and methods that would enable correct disambiguation and lexical choice.

The alternative approach is the development of Corpus-based (CBMT) approaches for MT. The advantage of corpus-based approaches lies in the hypothesis that language-specific information can be induced rather than being hand-written explicitly as was done in RBMT. In CBMT linguistic rules denoting the syntactic and semantic preferences of words, as well as word order, constitute a large part of the implicit information provided by the corpus. As a result, much of the linguistic knowledge is retrieved directly from the corpora, while rules are minimised. The two major approaches within CBMT are Example-Based MT (EBMT) and Statistical MT (SMT).

In terms of research activity, the most important representative of CBMT is the SMT paradigm. SMT has been introduced by Brown et al. (1993), while the most recent developments are summarised in Koehn (2010). A main benefit of SMT is that it is directly amenable to new language pairs using the same set of algorithms. However, an SMT system requires appropriate training data in the form of parallel corpora for extracting the relevant translation models. Thus, to develop an SMT system from a source language (SL) to a target language (TL), SL-TL parallel corpora of the order of millions of tokens are required to allow the extraction of meaningful models for translation. Such corpora are hard to obtain, particularly for less resourced languages and are frequently restricted to a specific domain (or a narrow range of domains), and thus are not suitable for creating general-purpose MT systems that focus on other domains. For this reason, in SMT, researchers are increasingly using syntax-based models as well as investigating the extraction of information from monolingual corpora, including lexical translation probabilities (Klementiev et al. 2012) and topic-specific information (Su et al. 2012).

The third MT paradigm is EBMT (Gough and Way 2004; Hutchins 2005), which is based on having a set of known pairs of input sentence (in SL) and corresponding translation (in TL) and translations are generated by analogy, by appropriately utilising the information within this set.

In a bid to achieve higher translation quality, researchers have studied the combination of principles from more than one MT paradigm, leading to what is termed as Hybrid MT (HMT). Examples of HMT include the systems by Eisele et al. (2008) and Quirk and Menezes (2006). The general convergence of MT systems towards the combination of the most promising characteristics of each paradigm has been documented by Wu (2005, 2009), having started from pure MT systems belonging to one of the main paradigms (RBMT, SMT, EBMT) and increasingly progressing towards systems that combine characteristics from multiple paradigms. A comprehensive survey of the latest HMT activity is provided by Costa-Jussa et al. (2013).

Alternative techniques have been studied for creating MT systems requiring resources which may be less informative but are also less expensive to collect or to create from scratch. The approach adopted has been to eliminate the parallel corpus needed in SMT (or drastically reduce its size), employing instead monolingual corpora. Monolingual resources can be readily assembled for any language, for instance by harvesting the web with relatively low effort. Methods following this approach had been proposed by Carbonell et al. (2006), Dologlou et al. (2003), Carl et al. (2008) and Markantonatou et al. (2009). Though these methods do not provide a translation quality as high as SMT, their ability to develop MT systems with a very limited amount of specialised resources represents an important starting point.

It is on the basis of the aforementioned works that the PRESEMT methodology (Tambouratzis et al. 2013) has been established. In PRESEMT, the design decision is to use a large monolingual corpus, supplemented by a small parallel corpus (whose size is only a few hundred sentences) to provide information on the mapping of sentence structures from SL to TL. The design brief for PRESEMT has been to create a language-independent methodology that -with limited resources- can translate unconstrained texts giving a quality suitable for gisting purposes. According to the preceding review of MT systems, PRESEMT can be classified within Hybrid MT, based on the argumentation of Quirk and Menezes (2006) and Wu (2005) for cross-fertilisation between SMT and EBMT.

The reader may visit the project's website[1] to either download the PRESEMT package and some limited resources for the German-to-English and Greek-to-English language pairs or run the fully functional online system that currently supports 13 language pairs. The website also provides detailed technical documentation and links to the standalone versions of the major PRESEMT modules hosted at Google Code.

2   Description of the PRESEMT Methodology

The MT methodology has been developed within the PRESEMT (Pattern REcognition-based Statistically Enhanced MT) project, funded by the European Commission. The MT methodology encompasses three stages:

Stage 1: Pre-processing of the input sentence. This involves tagging, lemmatising and grouping the tokens into phrases, in preparation for the actual transformation from SL to TL.

---

[1] www.presemt.eu

Stage 2: Main translation, where the actual translation output is generated. The main translation process can in turn be divided into two phases, namely:

Phase A: the establishment of the translation structure in terms of phrase order
Phase B: the definition of word order and resolution of lexical ambiguities at an intra-phrase level

Stage 3: Post-processing. The tokens in TL are generated from lemmas.
In terms of resources, PRESEMT employs the following:

- A bilingual lemma dictionary providing SL—TL lexical correspondences
- An extensive TL monolingual corpus, compiled via web crawling, to generate a language model
- A very small bilingual corpus

The bilingual corpus only numbers a few hundred sentences, which provide samples of the structural transformation when moving from SL to TL. The use of a small corpus reduces substantially the need for locating parallel corpora, whose procurement or development can be extremely expensive. Instead, in PRESEMT due to its small size the parallel corpus can be assembled with limited recourse to costly human resources. More specifically, in the present chapter such corpora are assembled from available parallel corpora which are extracted from multilingual websites. These corpora are only processed by replacing free translations with more literal ones, to allow the accurate extraction of structural modifications. According to the specifications of the methodology, the parallel corpus coverage is not studied prior to integration in PRESEMT.

3   Processing the Parallel Corpus

The present section describes how the parallel corpus is analysed, to extract information supporting the MT process. Initially, the bilingual corpus is annotated with lemma and Part-of-Speech (PoS) information and other language-specific morphological features (e.g. case, number, tense etc.). Furthermore, the TL side is chunked into phrases. As the PRESEMT methodology has been developed to maximise the use of publicly-available software, the user is free to select any desired parser for the TL language. For the implementation reported here, TreeTagger (Schmid 1994) has been used for the English (TL) text processing and the FBT PoS tagger (Prokopidis et al. 2011) has been employed for the processing of the Greek (SL) text.

3.1 Aligning the SL and TL Tokens

To determine the optimal transfer of phrases from SL to TL, it is essential to have the sentences of the parallel corpus split into corresponding phrases in both SL and TL. Development work in earlier systems revealed that the establishment of equivalent phrasing schemes for SL and TL is very time-consuming, and thus cannot form the basis for an MT methodology which is readily portable to new language pairs with minimal effort. To avoid either (a) having to locate an additional SL side parser or (b) resolving (most likely by hand-written rules) the inconsistencies of two separate parsers in different languages, in PRESEMT the Phrase aligner module (PAM) (Tambouratzis et al. 2011) is implemented. This module is dedicated to transferring to the SL side the TL side parsing scheme, which encompasses lemma, tag and parsing information. The information being transferred encompasses phrase boundaries and phrase type, where the TL-phrase type is used to characterise the SL phrase.

PAM establishes the SL-side phrasing automatically, based on the TL phrasing, by (a) identifying SL-to-TL token alignments and (b) extracting probabilistic information of SL-tag to TL-tag correspondences. In this process the types of allowed alignment from SL-to-TL are n-to-m (where $n \geq 1$ and $m \geq 1$).

The information used to perform the alignments includes lexical information as well as statistical data on PoS tag correspondences extracted from the lexicon. More specifically, PAM follows a 3-step process, where in each subsequent step tokens that remain unaligned are processed. Each step has a lower likelihood of producing the correct alignment, as it uses more general information to achieve alignment. In the first step alignments are performed on the basis of the bilingual lexicon entries. In the second step, existing alignments are discovered based on similarity of grammatical features between adjoining tokens and PoS tag correspondences. Finally, in the third step, alignments are performed based on the established alignments of their neighbouring words. This process is described in more detail in Tambouratzis et al. (2012).

Following this step, phases in SL are established, by grouping together all tokens from SL that correspond to the same single TL phrase. In the case of split phrases, the constituents are merged into a single phrase.

3.2 Phrasing the Input Text

Following the transfer of the phrasing scheme to SL, training examples have been prepared which describe the appropriate phrasing of SL texts according to the TL parser. Now, the aim is to construct a linguistic tool (termed Phrasing model generator) that can accurately segment arbitrary input text into phrases which are compatible with the TL phrasing scheme. If this is achieved, the aligned parallel corpus can be used to transform the structure from SL to TL.

When initiating the work on the Phrasing model generator (PMG), a survey of the literature was undertaken for appropriate methods. It was established that among the statistical-based models used, Conditional Random Fields (CRF) provides the most promising avenue, due to the considerable representation capabilities of this model (Lafferty et al. 2001). CRF is a statistical modelling method that takes context into account to predict labels for sequences of input samples. Within PRESEMT, the open-source implementation of CRF has been employed. In addition, comparative experiments have shown that it provides a performance superior to that of other approaches, both statistical (based on Hidden Markov models) and rule-based ones.

A recent development has involved the implementation of an alternative phrasing methodology (termed PMG-simple) based on template-matching principles. PMG-simple is trained with the parallel corpus, similarly to CRF. However, the PMG-simple learning method is different. The wide acceptance of CRF is based on its use of complex mathematical models, which require a wealth of training data. Since the small PRESEMT parallel corpus is the sole source for training data, it is likely that the data available for CRF to learn the phrasing scheme is limited.

PMG-simple locates phrases that match exactly what it has seen before, based on a simple template-matching algorithm (Duda et al. 2001). In contrast to CRF, which constructs an elaborate mathematical model, PMG-simple implements a greedy search (Black 2005) without backtracking. In PMG-simple, initially all phrases from the SL side of the parallel corpus are recorded and are then inserted into a list, ordered according to their likelihood of being accurately detected. The aim is then to determine the most likely phrases to which the sentence can be split, starting with no phrases being defined in the sentence to be segmented. At each turn, the phrase with the highest likelihood is chosen, and for this phrase PMG-simple examines if the corresponding sequence of tokens occurs at any point in the input sentence (taking into account word tag and case information). If it does and none of the constituent words in the sentence form part of an already established phrase, the constituent words are marked as parts of this phrase and are no longer considered in the phrase-matching process. On the other hand, if the phrase sequence does not exist, or if at least one of the required constituent tokens is already allocated to another phrase, no match is attained. In this case, the next phrase from the ordered list is considered, until either the ordered phrase list is exhausted, or all sentence tokens are assigned into phrases. In order to improve the performance of PMG-simple, a generalisation step is added to the PMG-simple mechanism (for more details cf. Tambouratzis 2014), which provides equivalence information between PoS types, to enrich the variety of phrasal templates that may be established from the parallel corpus. Comparative results for CRF and PMG-simple are reported in the evaluation section (Sect. 7.2).

4 Main Translation Engine

Local and long distance reordering is one of the most challenging aspects of any machine translation system. In phrase-based SMT, numerous approaches have used pre-processing techniques that perform word reordering in the source side based on the syntactic properties of the target side (Rottmann and Vogel 2007; Popovic and Ney 2006; Collins et al. 2005) in order to overcome the long distance word reordering problem. Short range reorderings are captured by the phrase table and the target side language model. Of course, in order for the statistical approaches to be effective, a sizeable amount of parallel training data needs to be available.

In PRESEMT, translation is performed in two steps, each step challenging different aspects of the translation process making use of syntactic knowledge. The first step performs structural transformation of the source side in accordance with the syntactic phrases of the target side, trying to capture long range reordering, while the second step makes lexical choices and performs local word reordering within each phrase. Because of the modular nature of PRESEMT each one of the steps is performed by a separate module: structural transformations are executed by the structure selection module (SSM), while local word reordering and disambiguation by the translation equivalent selection module (TES).

5 Structure Selection Module (SSM)

The objective of the Structure selection module is to transform the structure of the input text using the limited bilingual corpus as a structural knowledge base, closely resembling the "translation by analogy" aspect of EBMT systems. Using available structural information, namely the type of syntactic phrases, the part-of-speech tag of the head token of each phrase and the case of the head token (if available) we retrieve the most similar source side sentence from the parallel corpus. Using the stored alignment information from the corpus between the source and target side, we then perform all necessary actions in order to transform the structure of the input sentence to the structure of the target side of the corpus sentence pair.

Figure 1 depicts the functionality of the structure selection module. The input is a source sentence that has been annotated with PoS-tag and lemma information and segmented in clauses and chunks by the Phrasing model generator; the output is the same sentence with a target language structure.

For the retrieval of the most similar source side sentence, we selected an algorithm from the dynamic programming paradigm, treating the structure selection process as a sequence alignment, aligning the input sentence to a source side sentence from the aligned parallel corpus and assigning a similarity score. The implemented algorithm is based on the Smith-Waterman algorithm (Smith and Waterman 1981), initially proposed for performing local sequence alignment for determining similar regions between two protein or DNA sequences, structural

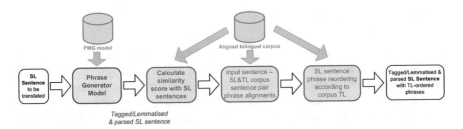

Fig. 1 Data flow in the structure selection module

alignment and RNA structure prediction. The algorithm is guaranteed to find the optimal local alignment between the two input sequences at clause level.

The similarity of two clauses is calculated using intra-clause information by taking into account the edit operations (replacement, insertion or removal) needed to be performed to the input sentence in order to transform it to a source side sentence from the corpus. Each of these operations has an associated cost, considered as a system parameter. The aligned corpus sentence that achieves the highest similarity score is the most similar one to the input source sentence.

5.1 Calculating Similarity Using a Dynamic Programming Algorithm

The source sentence is parsed in accordance to the phrasing model extracted from the Phrasing model generator (PMG). The first step of the algorithm is to compare each input source sentence (ISS) of the SL text to all the source side sentences of the parallel corpus in terms of structure. A two-dimensional table is built with each of the ISS phrases occupying one column (the corresponding phrases being shown at the top of the table) and the candidate corpus sentence (CCS) phrases each occupying one row (the corresponding CCS phrases being shown along the left side of the table). A cell (i, j) represents the similarity of the subsequence of elements up to the mapping of elements E_i of CCS and E'_j of ISS. Elements refer to syntactic phrases, represented by their type and the Part-of-speech (PoS) tag and case (where available) of each phrase head word.

The value of cell (i, j) is filled by taking into account the cells directly to the left $(i, j-1)$, directly above $(i-1, j)$ and directly above-left $(i-1, j-1)$, these containing values V1, V2 and V3 respectively, and is calculated as the maximum of the three numbers {V1, V2, V3 + ElementSimilarity(Ei, E'j)}. While calculating the value of each cell, the algorithm also keeps tracking information so as to allow the construction of the actual alignment vector.

The similarity of two phrases (**PhrSim**) is calculated as the weighted sum of the phrase type similarity (**PhrTypSim**), the phrase head PoS tag similarity (denoted as **PhrHPosSim**), the phrase head case similarity (**PhrHCasSim**) and the functional phrase head PoS tag similarity (**PhrfHPosSim**):

$$\text{PhrSim}\left(E_i,\ E'_j\right)$$

$$= W_{\text{phraseType}} * \text{PhrTypSim}\left(E_i,\ E'_j\right) + W_{\text{headPoS}} * \text{PhrHPosSim}\left(E_i,\ E'_j\right)$$

$$+ W_{\text{headCase}} * \text{PhrHCasSim}\left(E_i,\ E'_j\right) + W_{\text{fheadPoS}} * \text{PhrfHPosSim}\left(E_i,\ E'_j\right)$$

In the current implementation of the algorithm, the weights have been given the following initial values, yet the optimal values are to be determined during an optimisation phase:

- $W_{\text{phraseType}} = 0.6$
- $W_{\text{headPoS}} = 0.1$
- $W_{\text{fheadPoS}} = 0.1$
- $W_{\text{headCase}} = 0.2$

For normalisation purposes, the sum of the four aforementioned weights is equal to **1**.

The similarity score range is from **100** to **0**, denoting exact match and total dissimilarity between two elements E_i and E'_j respectively. In case of a zero similarity score, a penalty weight (-50) is employed, to further discourage selection of such correspondences.

When the algorithm has reached the jth element of the ISS, the similarity score between the two SL clauses is calculated as the value of the maximum-scoring j^{th} cell. The CCS that achieves the highest similarity score is the one closest to the input SL clause in terms of phrase structure information.

Apart from the final similarity score, the comparison table of the algorithm is used for finding the actual alignment of phrases between the two SL clauses. By combining the SL clause alignment from the algorithm with the alignment information between the CCS and the attached TL sentence, the ISS phrases are reordered according to the TL structure. The algorithm has been extended to tackle the subject pronoun drop phenomenon in languages like Greek, using the same alignment information. In the parallel corpus when a subject is dropped from either side of a given corpus sentence, then the phrase containing the subject on the other side will be mapped to an "empty phrase". This allows the algorithm to exploit this information during translation in order to add or remove the subject phrase accordingly in TL.

If more than one CCS achieve the same similarity score, and they lead to different structural transformations, then the module returns both results as equivalent TL structures. Moreover, if the highest similarity score is lower than a threshold, the input sentence structure is maintained, to prevent transformation towards an ill-fitting prototype. For most of our experiments an indicative threshold value is between 85 and 90 %. For a better understanding of this approach an example is provided next with Greek as the source language and English as the target.

5.2   Structural Similarity Example

The input source sentence is the following:

Με τον όρο Μηχανική Μετάφραση αναφερόμαστε σε μια αυτοματοποιημένη διαδικασία.

Exact translation: *with the term Machine Translation refer (1st pl) to an automated procedure*

Correct translation: *The term Machine Translation denotes an automated procedure*

The ISS phrase structure representation, after applying the parsing scheme using the Phrase aligner module, is the following:

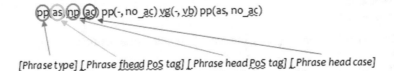

[Phrase type] [Phrase fhead PoS tag] [Phrase head PoS tag] [Phrase head case]

One of the retrieved candidate sentence pairs from the aligned bilingual corpus is the following:

(Greek) Οι ιστορικές ρίζες της Ευρωπαϊκής Ένωσης ανάγονται στο Δεύτερο Παγκόσμιο Πόλεμο .

(Lexicon-based translation) *the historical roots the$_{gen}$ European$_{gen}$ Union$_{gen}$ lie (3rd pl) in-the Second World War*

(English) "The historical roots of the European Union lie in the Second World War"

Its structural information being:

pp(no_nm) pp(no_ge) vg(vb) pp(no_ac)

After calculating the similarity scores for each phrase pair of the above sentences (the input sentence ISS and the SL-side sentence from the bilingual corpus, hereafter denoted as Aligned Corpus Sentence—ACS) the dynamic programming table (depicted in Fig. 2) is filled out (the arrows denoting the longest aligned subsequence):

When an arrow moves diagonally from cell A to cell B, this denotes that the phrases mapped at cell A are aligned. When an arrow moves horizontally, the ISS phrase is aligned with a space, and when an arrow moves vertically the ACS phrase is aligned with a space.

Figure 2 forms then the base for calculating the transformation cost (being 340 in this case), on the basis of which the ISS is modified in accordance to the attached TL structure.

			Input source sentence (ISS)			
			pp(as, np_ac)	pp(-, no_ac)	vg(-, vb)	pp(-, no_ac)
		0	0	0	0	0
Aligned corpus sentence (ACS)	pp(-, no_nm)	0	60	80	-20	60
	pp(-, no_ge)	0	60	140	40	40
	vg(vb)	0	-50	10	240	140
	pp(as, no_ac)	0	100	30	-40	**340**

Fig. 2 Example of a dynamic programming table

6 Translation Equivalent Selection Module (TES)

The second step of the PRESEMT translation process is the translation equivalent selection module, which performs word translation disambiguation, local word reordering within each syntactic phrase as well as addition and/or deletion of auxiliary verbs, articles and prepositions. In the default settings of PRESEMT, all of the above are performed by only using a syntactic phrase model extracted from a large TL monolingual corpus. The final translation is produced by the token generation component, since all processing during the translation process is lemma-based.

The module input is the output of the structure selection module, augmented with the TL lemmata of the source words provided by the bilingual lexicon. Each sentence contained within the text to be translated is processed separately, so there is no exploitation of inter-sentential information. The first task is to select the correct TL translation of each word. In the PRESEMT methodology, alternative methods for the word translation disambiguation have also been integrated and can be used instead of the default. These include Self-Organising Maps, n-gram vector space models or SRI n-gram models extracted from the TL monolingual corpus, though none of these is used in the PRESEMT configuration reported here. The second task involves establishing the correct word order within each phrase. With the default settings of the PRESEMT system this step is performed simultaneously with the translation disambiguation step, using the same TL phrase model. In the case of selecting one of the alternative methods for disambiguation, the phrase model is used only for local word reordering, within the boundaries of the phrases. During word reordering the algorithm also resolves issues regarding the insertion or deletion of words such as articles and other auxiliary tokens. Finally, token generation is applied to the lemmas of the translated sentence together with their morphological features. In that way, the final tokens are generated.

The token generator used constitutes a simple mapping from lemmas and morphological features to tokens. This mapping has been extracted from morphological and lemma information contained in the monolingual corpus. Due to data sparseness, such a mapping will always contain gaps particularly in the case of rather infrequent words. A more sophisticated approach would therefore try to close

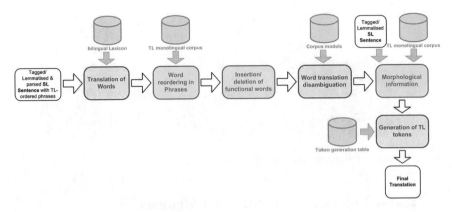

Fig. 3 Data flow in the translation equivalent selection module

the gaps in the inflectional paradigms of the lemmas. This could for instance be done by inferring inflectional paradigms of infrequent words from those of more frequent words.

Figure 3 provides an overview of the translation equivalent selection module, which receives as input the output of the first phase of the main translation engine, i.e. a source sentence with its constituent phrases reordered in accordance to the target language. The output is the final translation generated by the system.

It should be noted that the two instances of the TL monolingual corpus depicted in the diagram are actually two different TL models: the first instance refers to the indexed model of TL phrases (see Sect. 6.1), whereas the second one refers to a table of lemma-token pairs, which is also extracted from the TL corpus.

6.1   Description of the Phrase Model

The phrase model used in the translation equivalent selection module is in essence a language model, but instead of n-grams of words such as used in most SMT systems, the words here are grouped together based on the syntactic phrases extracted from the chunked TL monolingual corpus. The extracted phrases are then organised in a hash map, using as a key the following 3 criteria: (1) type of the syntactic phrase (i.e. whether it is a noun phrase or a verb phrase), (2) lemma of the phrase head word and (3) PoS tag of the phrase head word. For each TL phrase we store its frequency of occurrence in the corpus. However, it is likely that a slightly different modelling scheme may prove more effective. For instance, the environment of the phrase may also be required to be used (i.e. the type of the previous and next phrases within the sentence may be of use in the translation equivalent selection, and in this case the phrase organisation may be modified) either in the current model or in a complimentary model for the structural context.

Finally, each map is serialized and stored in a separate file in the file system, with an appropriate name for easy retrieval. For example, for the English monolingual corpus, all verb phrases with the lemma of the head token being "read" (verb) and the PoS tag "VV", are stored in a file named "read_VV".

For example, let us assume a very small TL-side monolingual corpus consisting only of the following sentence: "A typical scheme would have eight electrodes penetrating human brain tissue; wireless electrodes would be much more practical and could be conformal to several different areas of the brain." The syntactic phrases extracted from this small corpus are shown in Table 1, while the files created for the model are shown in Fig. 4. Because all phrases only appear once in the corpus, the frequencies are omitted in the specific example.

It should be noted that, with respect to large corpora, in order to reduce the number of files created, if a sub-group file remains very small (based on the definition of a small threshold value), it is not stored independently but is grouped with all other phrases from very small files. This allows (1) the reduction in the number of files, in order to prevent the creation of an excessive number of groups but also (2) allows the system to process phrases with heads for which no groups have been created from the monolingual corpus. Another step towards reducing the number of produced files is to altogether skip the creation of files for phrases that only contain a single word, as these would not be of use for word reordering.

One issue that has been studied during the implementation of the translation equivalent selection is the sheer size of the monolingual corpus, which necessitates special techniques to organise and process it, so that during run-time the required intermediate results are readily available, to minimise the computational load. To obtain a more precise understanding of the task, it is essential to have a quantitative view of the corpora involved. The monolingual corpora for two of the PRESEMT target languages, namely English and German, are summarised in Table 2.

Table 1 Syntactic phrases extracted from the TL monolingual corpus

Phrase id.	Phrase type	Phrase content	Phrase head lemma/PoS
1	PC	A typical scheme	Scheme/NN
2	VC	Would have	Have/VH
3	PC	Eight electrodes	Electrode/NN
4	VC	Penetrating	Penetrate/VV
5	PC	Human brain tissue	Tissue/NN
6	PC	Wireless electrodes	Electrode/NN
7	VC	Would be	Is/VB
8	PC	Much more practical	Practical/JJ
9	VC	Could be	Is/VB
10	PC	Conformal	Conformal/JJ
11	PC	To several different areas	Area/NN
12	PC	Of the brain	Brain/NN

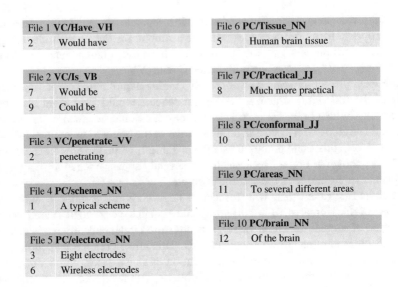

Fig. 4 Example of monolingual corpus phrases split into files

Table 2 Characteristics of monolingual corpora

	English	German
Size in tokens	3,658,726,327	3,076,812,674
Number of raw text files (*each containing a block of ca. 1 Mbyte*)	87,000	96,000
Number of sentences[a]	1.0×10^8	9.5×10^7
Number of phrases[a]	8.0×10^8	6.0×10^8
Number of extracted phrase files	380,000	478,000

[a]Indicates the inclusion of an estimate rather than an exact value

6.2 Applying the Phrase Model to the Tasks of the Translation Equivalent Selection Module

When initiating the translation equivalent selection module, a matching algorithm accesses the TL phrase model to retrieve similar phrases and select the most similar one through a comparison process with the aim of performing word sense disambiguation and establishing the correct word order within each phrase. The comparison process is viewed as an assignment problem that can be solved by using either exact algorithms guaranteeing the identification of the optimal solution or algorithms which yield sub-optimal solutions. In the current implementation we have opted for the Gale-Shapley algorithm (Gale and Shapley 1962 and Mairson 1992), a non-exact algorithm, over the Kuhn-Munkres algorithm (Kuhn 1955 and Munkres 1957) that computes an exact solution of the assignment problem. This has been decided upon after experimentation with the Kuhn-Munkres algorithm in the METIS-2 project Markantonatou et al. (2009), where it has been found that the exact solution of the assignment problem was responsible for a large fraction of the required computation effort.

On the contrary, the Gale-Shapley algorithm solves the assignment problem by separating the items into two distinct sets with different properties. In this approach, the two sets are termed (1) suitors and (2) reviewers. In the present MT application, the aim is to create assignments between tokens of the SL (which are assigned the role of suitors) and tokens of the TL (which undertake the roles of reviewers). In the Gale-Shapley algorithm, the two groups have different roles. More specifically, the suitors have the responsibility of defining their order of preference of being assigned to a specific reviewer, giving an ordered list of their preferences. Based on these lists, the reviewers can select one of the suitors by evaluating them based on their ordered lists of preference, in subsequent steps revising their selection so that the resulting assignment is optimised. As a consequence, this process provides a solution which is suitor-optimal but potentially non-optimal from the reviewers' viewpoint. However, the complexity of the algorithm is substantially lower to that of Kuhn-Munkres and thus it is used in the translation equivalent selection process as the algorithm of choice, so as to reduce the computation time required. Any errors due to using this sub-optimal approach are limited to the reordering of phrases on the TL-side, with no lexical selection changes (since these are decided upon by sampling the files of phrases).

The main issue at this stage is to be able to reorder appropriately any items within each phrase, while at the same time selecting the most appropriate translation for each word that the bilingual lexicon has provided. This entails that tokens from (a) a given phrase of the input sentence, call it ISP (Input Sentence Phrase), and from (b) a TL phrase extracted from the TL phrase model and denoted as MCP (Monolingual Corpus Phrase), are close to each other in terms of number of tokens and type. More specifically, the number and identity of items in a given MCP being used as a template is at least equal to (or larger than) the number of elements in ISP (since it is required to be in a position to handle all tokens of ISP, it is safer to delete existing MCP elements from their existing locations rather than introduce new ones). In principle, the number of ISP tokens should be equal to or very close to that of MCP. This means that a search needs to be performed, which is algorithmically described by the following steps:

Step 1: For each phrase (ISP) a decoder creates a vector containing all translation equivalents using the bilingual lexicon. The number of vectors created is the same as the number of translation equivalents of the phrase head words. The word order does not change.

Step 2: Iteratively process each vector; retrieve for each one the corresponding set of phrases of MCP from the phrase model, based on the phrase type, the lemma and PoS tag of the phrase head token.

Step 3: For each ISP in the vector apply the Gale-Shapley algorithm for aligning the tokens of the ISP to those of the retrieved MCPs. The word alignment provides a guideline for reordering the ISP according to the MCP word order and also provides a similarity score through a comparison formula applied to each one of the aligned word pairs (see the equation below). The similarity score is calculated as the weighted sum of the comparison scores of four types of information, namely (a) phrase types (**PTypeCmp**), (b) phrase head word lemma (**LemCmp**), (c) phrase head word PoS tag (**TgCmp**) and (d) phrase case (**CsCmp**), if this latter information is available.

$$Score = w_{ptype} \times PTypeCmp + w_{lem} \times LemCmp + w_{tag} \times TgCmp + w_{case} \times CsCmp$$

where all weights are real positive-valued parameters that sum up to one.

Step 4: After performing all comparisons the best matching ISP-MCP pair is selected taking into account the similarity score as well as the MCP frequency of occurrence in the TL corpus. Similarity scores are not compared as absolute values but as a ratio, so as to allow the insertion and/or deletion of words such as articles and other functional words. If the similarity scores of two or more MCPs are close according to the ratio score, then we compare their frequencies in order to select one, and only if the frequencies are also close, we use the absolute comparison values to select the most appropriate ISP-MCP.

Step 5: By selecting the most appropriate ISP-MCP pair, the algorithm performs lexical disambiguation by rejecting all other equivalent ISPs in the vector. Words are also reordered based on the MCP using the word alignment produced by the Gale-Shapley algorithm. After applying the previous steps for all phrases in the input sentence, the final sentence translation is produced. It should be noted that the order of phrases has already been established in the structure selection module.

Step 6: A token generator component is applied to the lemmas of the TL sentence together with their morphological features. In that way, the final tokens are generated and the final translation is produced.

6.3   Example of Translation Equivalent Selection

To illustrate the Translation equivalent selection, the handling of the final phrase from the example sentence of Sect. 5.2 is discussed here. This specific phrase comprises four tokens as shown in Table 3, where for reasons of simplicity abbreviated SL tags are used, including PoS tag and case only:

Table 3 Phrase tokens and their tags in SL and TL respectively

Token id.	SL token (lemma)	SL PoS tag	Lemmas from bilingual lexicon	TL PoS tag
1	σε(σε)	AsPpSp	[at, in, into, on, to, upon]	IN
2	μια (ένας)	At_Ac	[1, a, an, one]	CD
3	αυτοματοποιημένη (αυτοματοποιημένος)	VbPv_Ac	[automate, automated]	VVN
4	διαδικασία (διαδικασία)	No_Ac	[procedure, process]	NN

Table 4 Candidates of phrase translation retrieved from TL model

Candidates	Sequence of tokens (lemmatised)	Originating indexed file	TL corpus frequency	Matching score (%)
1	To a store procedure	PC/procedure_NN	3	92.5
2	To an automate procedure	PC/procedure_NN	1	92.5
3	In an ongoing process	PC/process_NN	12	92.5

In this phrase, the fourth token ("διαδικασία") is the phrase head. Thus, when searching for the best phrase translation, the indexed files for each of the two candidate translations ("procedure" and "process") are searched using as an additional constraint the phrase type (in this case "PC") and the head PoS type (here "NN"). Hence, following the annotation introduced in Sect. 6.1, files "PC/procedure_NN" and "PC/process_NN", which contain 21,939 and 35,402 distinct entries, respectively, are searched for matching phrase occurrences. Since all four tokens have multiple translations suggested by the lexicon, a number of possible combinations ($6 \times 4 \times 2 \times 2 = 96$) of lemma sequences need to be matched to the phrase instances contained in the two indexed files. The best-matching phrase instances retrieved from the indexed files are shown in Table 4 in order of retrieval.

As can be seen, the first two entries are retrieved from the file containing PC-type phrases with "procedure" as their head while the third one from the file containing PC phrases with head "process". An exhaustive search of the two indexed files has shown that no exact matches to the input phrase exist. The highest matching score is 92.5%, as for all three examined phrases the lemma of the third token is not matched. Still, the 92.5% score is sufficiently high to form a sound basis for the translation (on the contrary if it was below a user-defined threshold typically chosen from the range of 75 to 90%, this translation would be rejected and the SL order of tokens in the phrase would be adopted). In addition, the frequencies of candidates 2 and 3 are comparable, differing by less than an order of magnitude. As all retrieved phrases have equal matching scores, the winning phrase is selected to be the one with the highest frequency of occurrence in the TL monolingual corpus. In this specific example, based on the contents of the 4th column, the chosen phrase is the third phrase of Table 4. This phrase is then used as the basis for translating the respective SL-side phrase, by replacing the token "ongoing" (which is not an appropriate translation, based on the bilingual lexicon) with the token "automated" that is suggested by the lexicon. The sequence obtained with this replacement (namely "in an automated process") represents the translation of this phrase, which forms part of the final sentence translation.

7   Evaluation of the PRESEMT MT System

The current section provides an account of the evaluation conducted in order to assess the performance of PRESEMT both individually and against other MT systems with respect to the Greek-to-English language pair.

MT systems are normally evaluated via automatic metrics, which compare the MT system output to one (or more) human-produced reference translation(s) and calculate their similarity. Such metrics, pretty much established and widely used in the field, include BLEU, NIST, Meteor and TER.

BLEU (Papineni et al. 2002) and NIST (NIST 2002) measure the common n-grams between the system output and the reference translation. The BLEU score may range between [0, 1], with 1 denoting a perfect match, i.e. a perfect translation, while the NIST score range is [0, ∞), where a higher score signifies a better translation quality. Meteor (Denkowski and Lavie 2011) calculates similarity against each reference translation and produces in the end the highest score. Its score range is [0, 1], with 1 signifying a perfect translation. Finally TER (Snover et al. 2006) resembles the philosophy of the Levenshtein distance (Levenshtein 1966), in that it calculates the minimum number of edits needed to change a candidate translation so that it exactly matches one of the reference translations, normalised by the average length of the references (Snover et al. 2006, p. 3).

The translation output of MT systems can also be evaluated by humans, usually in terms of adequacy, referring to how much information of the source language text has been retained in the translation, and fluency, which measures the degree to which the translation is grammatically well-formed according to the grammar of the target language.

For PRESEMT both types of evaluation were employed. The present section describes the results of the automatic evaluation only for the Greek to English language pair. The interested reader is referred to the project deliverable D9.2,[2] which additionally reports on the human evaluation process and contains the results of the evaluation for the other language pairs that PRESEMT handles.

7.1   Dataset

The test dataset, which was used for the evaluation, was collected over the web in accordance to appropriately defined specifications. More specifically, the web was crawled over for retrieving a corpus of 1000 sentences, the length of which ranged between 7 and 40 tokens. Subsequently, 200 sentences were randomly chosen out of the given corpus, these sentences constituting the test dataset. Since the specific dataset was intended to be used for development, its size was purposely kept small.

---

[2]http://www.presemt.eu/files/Dels/PRESEMT_D9.2_supplement.pdf

Table 5 Description of the test dataset

Source language	Greek
Target language	English
Sentence size	7–40 tokens
Number of tokens	2758
Test dataset size for automatic evaluation	200 sentences
Number of reference translations	1

Then, these sentences were manually translated by native speakers of Greek into English. The correctness of the translations, which would serve as reference ones, was next checked by target language-native speakers, who were independent to the ones that originally created the data. Table 5 illustrates the profile of the test dataset.

7.2 Evaluation Results

Our goal during evaluation was not only to evaluate the translation output of PRESEMT but also to examine how it performs in comparison to other MT systems. Therefore, the test dataset was translated by three other MT systems as well: Google Translate, Bing Translator and WorldLingo.

Our experiments (cf. results in Table 6) span two different time periods, namely mid-2012 (as reported in Sofianopoulos et al. (2012)) and beginning of 2014, thus allowing the reader to form a view of how those MT systems evolve over time. Especially as far as PRESEMT is concerned, two sets of results are provided, reflecting the utilisation of a different module for the segmentation of the SL input in phrases (based on CRF and PMG-simple respectively, as discussed in Sect. 3.2). For each system, the scores obtained in 2012 and 2014 are provided, together with a measure of the improvement in each metric, expressed as a percentage. Since PMG-simple is a recent enhancement to the PRESEMT system, the improvement in performance is reported over the 2012 PRESEMT system employing CRF.

From the evaluation results it is evident that PRESEMT has exhibited a remarkable improvement, which is the outcome of various factors such as the modifications in the Structure selection algorithm, the fine-tuning of the Phrase aligner and the PMG, the enhancement of the token generation module through the expansion of the TL monolingual corpus, lexicon corrections, and the improved handling of syntactic phenomena.

PRESEMT is outperformed by 215 % and by 162 % by Google and Bing respectively in the first period (for the BLEU metric), indicating a very large difference in translation quality, this difference being markedly reduced (to 51 % and to 43 %) in the second period. This indicates a substantial improvement in the quality of the translation generated by PRESEMT. In addition, the improvement in PRESEMT is quite high (always being in absolute values more than 15 %),

Table 6 Evaluation results for PRESEMT and other MT systems for Greek-to-English

	PRESEMT				
	CRF	PMG-simple	Google	Bing	WL
BLEU					
2012	0.1756	–	0.5544	0.4600	0.2659
2014	*0.3060*	*0.3462*	*0.5259*	*0.4974*	–
	+74%	*+97%*	*−5%*	*+8%*	–
NIST					
2012	5.7907	–	8.8051	7.9409	5.9978
2014	*6.6915*	*6.9736*	*8.5377*	*8.2791*	–
	+16%	*+20%*	*−3%*	*+4%*	–
Meteor					
2012	0.3364	–	0.4665	0.4281	0.3666
2014	*0.3776*	*0.3947*	*0.4609*	*0.4524*	–
	+12%	*+17%*	*−1%*	*+6%*	–
TER					
2012	61.862	–	29.791	37.631	50.627
2014	54.564	51.045	42.230	34.181	–
	−12%	*−18%*	*+42%*	*−9%*	–

WorldLingo translations are not included for 2014, since they could not be obtained via the corresponding website (www.worldlingo.com)

while the corresponding improvement in Bing is much smaller (typically less than 10%). Finally, though Google Translate still remains the system with the highest scores, its actual performance over time seems to be deteriorating as measured by the metrics. Therefore, as PRESEMT is maturing, its performance can be seen to be improving substantially in terms of translation accuracy. On the other hand, PRESEMT expectedly sacrifices the top-end of translation quality due to a number of design factors including (1) the easy portability to new language pairs and (2) the use of publicly-available linguistic tools, without enhancements and adaptation to the specific MT methodology.

One final point concerns the margin over which Google Translate and Bing Translator exceed the PRESEMT performance. This is quite sizeable, as evidenced by Table 6. However, it is widely accepted that automatic metrics such as BLEU and NIST tend to favour statistical MT approaches. Thus, it is plausible that the performance advantages of Google and Bing are not as sizeable as suggested by Table 6. The human evaluation did confirm the higher performance of Bing/Google over the PRESEMT version which was current in December 2012, and thus it would be useful to perform a new human evaluation comparing the more recent versions of the MT systems.

As a further indication of the proposed methodology characteristics, results of building an MT system for the Greek-to-German language pair are summarised in Table 7, for lemmatised output. For comparison purposes, the metric values obtained for Bing Translator and Google Translate are also included in this table. PRESEMT

Table 7 Evaluation results for PRESEMT and other MT systems for Greek-to-German

	PRESEMT				
	CRF	PMG-simple	Google	Bing	WL
BLEU					
2014	0.0853	0.0804	0.3135	0.2764	–
NIST					
2014	4.1542	4.1306	6.4894	6.1931	–
Meteor					
2014	0.2214	0.2250	0.2994	0.2872	–
TER					
2014	82.568	83.321	54.575	56.934	–

WorldLingo translations are not available for 2014, since they could not be obtained via the corresponding website (www.worldlingo.com)

is clearly outperformed by both Bing and Google. The reason for this is that the Greek-to-German system has been much less extensively developed, which has resulted in substantial improvements in the metric scores being achieved with a limited number of actions. Several areas still exist for improvements in the MT translation. For instance, the bilingual dictionary adopted for reasons of availability is quite fragmentary and has been developed by scanning a printed version, without any editing of entries by a native speaker. In addition, even chunking for the TL-side (German) corpora has been performed using the TreeTagger package for German, which however has not been as accurate as the English-language version of TreeTagger, and which does not currently generate adverbial or adjectival chunks (ADVC and ADJC respectively). This indicates one of the weaknesses of the proposed method, namely that by adopting resources and tools from third parties there is a risk that these are not fully compatible or have inconsistencies which can affect the translation accuracy. At present, efforts are continuing towards improving this language pair. In addition, due to the highly-inflectional nature of German, and its more complex syntax, further work is needed to bring the performance to levels comparable to those of Greek-to-English. A final note that should be made is that for this language pair, the CRF-based variant is more effective than PMG-simple. However, as more work is needed for this specific language pair, these results need to be revisited for more reliable conclusions to be drawn. These developments are to be reported in future publications.

7.3 Comparison to Other MT Systems

Leaving aside the numerical results it is worth looking at individual cases, to gain an insight on the behaviour of the different MT systems. In the following examples we take a look at the translation output provided by PRESEMT, Bing and Google at the two evaluation periods, which show that PRESEMT, although still outperformed, exhibits a consistent performance against that of the other systems in certain cases. The following examples are not intended to degrade the good translation quality achieved by either Bing or Google but they are rather an attempt to highlight the fact that the mere alignment of SL-TL segments without any information about the syntactic structure fails to handle grammatical phenomena successfully. In each example the SL sentence is initially provided together with its translation in English (placed in brackets). Then, the translations of the 3 systems are listed in tabular form. Missing tokens in the translation are indicated by the symbol 'Ø'.

Examples 1 and 2 illustrate that Bing or Google sometimes omit the translations of some source words. In Example 1, this concerns the adverb 'mainly', while in Example 2, it is the possessive clitic 'her' that is missing. Furthermore, Example 3 shows that the handling of gender is not always successful.

Of course, PRESEMT does not produce perfect translations (cf. the placement of the possessive clitic in the second example or the choice of the adjective 'mysterious' for translating 'σκοτεινό' in the third example). The argument placed here is that since PRESEMT is aware of grammatical features, then it is expected to have a consistent behaviour when translating.

Example 1 SL sentence: Πρώτον, αυτή είναι μια **κυρίως** πολιτική πρόκληση. *[= Firstly, this is a **mainly** political challenge]*

	2012	2014
PRESEMT	First, she are an especially civil challenge	First, this is an especially political challenge
Bing	Firstly, this is a Ø political challenge	Firstly, this is primarily a political challenge
Google	First, this is primarily a political challenge	First, this is primarily a political challenge

Example 2 SL sentence: Ο πατέρας της προσπαθεί μάταια να τη μεταπείσει. *[= Her father tries in vain to dissuade her]*

	2012	2014
PRESEMT	Her father tries vain to her coax	Her father tries in vain to her dissuade
Bing	Her father tries in vain to dissuade Ø	Her father tries in vain to dissuade Ø
Google	Her father tries in vain to convince **the** Ø	Her father tries in vain to persuade her

Example 3 SL sentence: Έχω ζήσει μ' **αυτήν** σ' ένα σκοτεινό, κρύο και υγρό δωμάτιο. *[= I have lived with **her** in a dark, cold and damp room]*

	2012	2014
PRESEMT	Have lived in she in mysterious , wet and room cold	Have lived to her in a dark, cold and wet room
Bing	I have experienced **it** in a dark, cold and wet room.	I've lived with **it** in a dark, cold and wet room.
Google	I've lived with **it** in a dark, cold and damp room.	I've lived with **it** in a dark, cold and wet room .

Other grammatical features such as subject-verb agreement (example 4) or verb (non-)finiteness (example 5) can also be mishandled by Bing and Google.

Example 4 SL sentence: Αν διαβάσουμε ιστορία θα καταλάβουμε γιατί δεν έχει γίνει Εθνικό Κτηματολόγιο. *[=If **we** read history **we** will understand why there has been no National Cadastre.]*

	2012	2014
PRESEMT	If the book read history because not will understand has become the ethnic register land	If we read history we will understand because has not been national land register
Bing	If **you** read history **you** will understand why there has been no National Register	If **you** read history **you** will understand why **he** has not become a national cadastre
Google	If we read history Ø will understand why there has been no National	If **you** read history **you** will understand why **he** has become National Cadastre

Example 5 SL sentence: Την εκπαίδευση **έχουν αναλάβει** οι επιχειρήσεις. *[= Companies **have undertaken** the training]*

	2012	2014
PRESEMT	Operations have undertaken education	The teaching have undertaken the companies
Bing	Education Ø responsible businesses	The training Ø undertaken by businesses
Google	The training Ø undertaken by companies	The training Ø undertaken by businesses

8 Future Extensions and Potential Improvements on PRESEMT

Within the work reviewed in the present chapter, a number of potential directions for further improving the PRESEMT system have been identified. These have been based on the experiments performed and the corresponding observations, as summarised above.

An obvious avenue for improvements concerns revising the two translation phases. Experimentation with the PRESEMT prototype has indicated scope for improving in particular the structure selection algorithm. More elaborate metrics and methods for measuring the matching of sentence structures may be introduced. In addition, a more elaborate process for combining sub-sentential parts from different clauses can be employed to define the structure of the entire sentence.

Regarding the Translation equivalent selection step, improvements in the target language model may also be achieved. To that end, the indexing scheme employed in PRESEMT for phrases will be expanded to include—apart from frequency of occurrence—information regarding the context in which the phrase appears. Such information will support the search for a more appropriate match, conforming to the environment of each phrase.

In a similar vein, it is possible to augment the language model, to include a combination of models. Currently, the PRESEMT TL model relies on phrases indexed on the basis of head lemma and phrase type information. Experiments have shown that errors in the resulting translations can in some cases be corrected by resorting to simple n-gram information. Even a sequential application of the n-gram information for correction purposes leads to improvements in the translation accuracy. The issue then becomes to optimally combine the two language models by applying them concurrently, so as to achieve the best possible translation performance. This would allow the more appropriate treatment of cases where less than accurate matches in terms of sentence structure are achieved (for instance when very long sentences need to be translated). This approach can notably address errors at the phrasal boundaries (i.e. between the last tokens of a phrase and the first tokens of the following phrase).

All aforementioned improvements relate to the existing resources, and thus should not affect the portability of PRESEMT to new language pairs. One of the shortcomings of the system has been the establishment of an effective disambiguation module. At present, both the disambiguation and intra-phrase token sequencing tasks are established by a single search in the language model of indexed phrases. However, this arrangement potentially results in interference between the two tasks, as a single solution is chosen in one step. If a reliable disambiguation module can be established, which samples the same corpus as the indexed phrases, this may lead to more consistency in the translations, by decoupling the disambiguation between multiple translations and the token order within each phrase.

It should be noted that all disambiguation modules could be constructed with monolingual data (using solely TL-side corpora), or with bilingual data. In the latter case, the requirement for more corpora to develop a new language pair becomes evident. On the other hand, the benefits of combining SL and TL corpora can be much greater in terms of translation quality.

A further addition could be the introduction of linguistic knowledge in the translation process. For instance, PRESEMT is agnostic regarding the role of subject and object, leading to less than optimal translations. The introduction of such knowledge is expected to improve the structure selection performance, though in part this contradicts the requirement for minimal specialised linguistic tools. Nonetheless, it appears that, short of providing a much larger parallel corpus, this is the main way to a much more natural translation. This is one of the main issues being researched by the PRESEMT research group, in pursuit of a breakthrough in translation quality.

Closing Note

Please visit the project's website (www.presemt.eu) to download and experiment with the PRESEMT package or just play around with the fully functional online system. Detailed technical documentation for even creating a new language pair is provided.

References

Black, P.E. 2005. *Dictionary of algorithms and data structures.* U.S. National Institute of Standards and Technology (NIST)

Brown, P.F., S.A. Della Pietra, V.J. Della Pietra, and R.L. Mercer. 1993. The mathematics of statistical machine translation: Parameter estimation. *Computational Linguistics* 19(2): 263–311.

Carbonell, J., S. Steve Klein, D. Miller, M. Steinbaum, T. Grassiany, and J. Frey. 2006. Context-based machine translation. In *Proceedings of the 7th AMTA Conference*, 19–28. Cambridge, MA.

Carl, M., M. Melero, T. Badia, V. Vandeghinste, P. Dirix, I. Schuurman, S. Markantonatou, S. Sofianopoulos, M. Vassiliou, and O. Yannoutsou. 2008. METIS-II: Low resources machine translation: background, implementation, results and potentials. *Machine Translation* 22(1–2): 67–99.

Collins, M., P. Koehn, and I. Kucerova. 2005. Clause re-structuring for statistical machine translation. In *Proceedings of the Annual Meeting of the Association for Computational Linguistics*, vol. 43, 531.

Costa-jussà, M. Ruiz, R. Banchs, R. Rapp, P. Lambert, K. Eberle, and B. Babych. 2013. Workshop on hybrid approaches to translation: overview and developments. In *Proceedings of the 2nd HYTRA Workshop, held within ACL-2013*, 1–6. Sofia.

Denkowski, M., and A. Lavie. 2011. Meteor 1.3: Automatic metric for reliable optimization and evaluation of machine translation systems. In: *Proceedings of the EMNLP 2011 Workshop on Statistical Machine Translation*, 85–91. Edinburgh.

Dologlou, I., S. Markantonatou, G. Tambouratzis, O. Yannoutsou, A. Fourla, and N. Ioannou. 2003. Using monolingual corpora for statistical machine translation: the METIS system. In *Proceedings of the EAMT-CLAW 2003 Workshop*. 61–68. Dublin.

Duda, R.O., P.E. Hart, and D.G. Stork. 2001. *Pattern classification*, 2nd edn. New York: Wiley.

Eisele, A., C. Federmann, H. Uszkoreit, H. Saint-Amand, M. Kay, M. Jellinghaus, S. Hunsicker, T. Herrmann, and Y. Chen. 2008. Hybrid machine translation architectures within and beyond the EuroMatrix project. In *European Machine Translation Conference*. Hamburg.

Gale, D., and L.S. Shapley. 1962. College admissions and the stability of marriage. *American Mathematical Monthly* 69: 9–14.

Gough, N., and A. Way. 2004. Robust large-scale EBMT with marker-based segmentation. In *Proceedings of the 10th Conference on Theoretical and Methodological Issues in Machine Translation (TMI-04)*, 95–104. Baltimore, MD.

Hutchins, J. 2005. Example-based machine translation: A review and commentary. *Machine Translation* 19: 197–211.

Klementiev, A., A. Irvine, C. Callison-Burch, and D. Yarowsky. 2012. Toward statistical machine translation without parallel corpora. In *Proceedings of EACL 2012*, 130–140. Avignon

Koehn, P. 2010. *Statistical machine translation*. Cambridge: Cambridge University Press.

Kuhn, H.W. 1955. The Hungarian method for the assignment problem. *Naval Research Logistics Quarterly* 2: 83–97.

Lafferty, J., A. McCallum, and F.C.N. Pereira. 2001. Conditional random fields: probabilistic models for segmenting and labeling sequence data. In *Proceedings of the Eighteenth International Conference on Machine Learning (ICML '01)*, 282–289. San Francisco: Morgan Kaufmann.

Levenshtein, V.I. 1966. Binary codes capable of correcting deletions, insertions, and reversals. *Soviet Physics Doklady* 10: 707–710.

Mairson, H. 1992. The stable marriage problem. *The Brandeis Review* 12: 1. Available at: http://www.cs.columbia.edu/~evs/intro/stable/writeup.html.

Markantonatou, S., S. Sofianopoulos, O. Giannoutsou, and M. Vassiliou 2009. Hybrid machine translation for low- and middle- density languages. In *Language engineering for lesser-studied languages*, eds. S. Nirenburg, 243–274. Amsterdam: IOS Press.

Munkres, J. 1957. Algorithms for the assignment and transportation problems. *Journal of the Society for Industrial and Applied Mathematics* 5: 32–38.

NIST. 2002. Automatic Evaluation of Machine Translation Quality Using n-gram Co-occurrences Statistics (Report). Available at: http://www.itl.nist.gov/iad/mig/tests/mt/doc/ngram-study.pdf

Papineni, K., S. Roukos, T. Ward, and W.J. Zhu 2002. BLEU: a method for automatic evaluation of machine translation. In *Proceedings of the 40th Annual Meeting of the Association for Computational Linguistics*, 311–318. Philadelphia.

Popovic, M., and H. Ney 2006. POS-based word reorderings for statistical machine translation. In *Proceedings of the 5th International Conference on Language Resources and Evaluation (LREC2006)*, 1278–1283. Genoa.

Prokopidis, P., B. Georgantopoulos, and H. Papageorgiou 2011. A suite of NLP tools for Greek. In *Proceedings of the 10th ICGL Conference*, 373–383. Komotini.

Quirk, C., and A. Menezes. 2006. Dependency Treelet translation: The convergence of statistical and example-based machine translation? *Machine Translation* 20: 43–65.

Rottmann, K., and S. Vogel .2007. Word reordering in statistical machine translation with a POS-based distortion model. In *Proceedings of the 11th International Conference on Theoretical and Methodological Issues in Machine Translation (TMI 2007)*, 171–180. Skövde.

Schmid, H. 1994. Probabilistic part-of-speech tagging using decision trees. In *Proceedings of International Conference on New Methods in Language Processing*, 44–49. Manchester.

Smith, T.F., and M.S. Waterman. 1981. Identification of common molecular subsequences. *Journal of Molecular Biology* 147: 195–197.

Snover, M., B. Dorr, R. Schwartz, L. Micciulla, and J. Makhoul. 2006. A study of translation edit rate with targeted human annotation. In *Proceedings of the 7th AMTA Conference*, 223–231. Cambridge, MA.

Sofianopoulos, S., M. Vassiliou, and G. Tambouratzis. 2012. Implementing a language-independent MT methodology. In *Proceedings of the 1st Workshop on Multilingual Modeling (held within ACL-2012)*, 1–10. Jeju

Su, J., H. Wu, H. Wang, Y. Chen, X. Shi, H. Dong, and Q. Liu. 2012. Translation model adaptation for statistical machine translation with monolingual topic information. In *Proceedings of the ACL2012*, 459–468. Jeju.

Tambouratzis, G., F. Simistira, S. Sofianopoulos, N. Tsimboukakis, and M. Vassiliou. 2011. A resource-light phrase scheme for language-portable MT. In *Proceedings of the 15th International Conference of the European Association For Machine Translation*, eds. M. L. Forcada, H. Depraetere, and V. Vandeghinste, 185–192. Leuven.

Tambouratzis, G., M. Troullinos, S. Sofianopoulos, and M. Vassiliou. 2012. Accurate phrase alignment in a bilingual corpus for EBMT systems. In *Proceedings of the 5th BUCC Workshop, held within the LREC2012 Conference*, 104–111. Istanbul.

Tambouratzis, G., S. Sofianopoulos, and M. Vassiliou. 2013. Language-independent hybrid MT with PRESEMT. In *Proceedings of HYTRA-2013 Workshop, held within the ACL-2013 Conference*, 123–130. Sofia (ISBN 978-1-937284-53-4).

Tambouratzis, G. 2014. Comparing CRF and template-matching in phrasing tasks within a Hybrid MT system. In *Proceedings of the 3rd Workshop on Hybrid Approaches to Translation (held within the EACL-2014 Conference)*, 7–14. Gothenburg.

Wu, D. 2005. MT model space: statistical versus compositional versus example-based machine translation. *Machine Translation* 19: 213–227.

Wu, D. 2009. Toward machine translation with statistics and syntax and semantics. In *Proceedings of the IEEE Workshop On Automatic Speech Recognition & Understanding*, 12–21. Merano.

Part III
Hybrid NLP Tools Useful for MT

Creating Hybrid Dependency Parsers
for Syntax-Based MT

Nathan David Green and Zdeněk Žabokrtský

Abstract Dependency parsers are almost ubiquitously evaluated on their accuracy scores, these scores say nothing of the complexity and usefulness of the resulting structures. As dependency parses are basic structures in which other systems are built upon, it would seem more reasonable to judge these parsers down the NLP pipeline. In this chapter, we will discuss how different forms and different hybrid combinations of dependency parses effect the overall output of Syntax-Based machine translation both through automatic and manual evaluation. We show results from a variety of individual parsers, including dependency and constituent parsers, and describe multiple ensemble parsing techniques with their overall effect on the Machine Translation system. We show that parsers' UAS scores are more correlated to the NIST evaluation metric than to the BLEU Metric, however we see increases in both metrics. To truly see the effect of hybrid dependency parsers on machine translation, we will describe and evaluate a combined resource we have released, that contains gold standard dependency trees along with gold standard translations.

1 Introduction

Dependency parsing is an integral part of Natural Language Processing (NLP) research for many languages. However, research in dependency parsing has mainly dealt with improving accuracy for a limited number of languages. Current dependency parsing algorithms have developed mainly for languages with an ample amount of training data. Most of this data has been collected from shared tasks at conferences and are available mainly for European and resource-rich languages. New researchers into the area may not know which algorithm and techniques work best with a new, untested, language.

N.D. Green (✉)
Westfield State University, Westfield, MA, USA
e-mail: nathan@nathangreen.com; nathangreen@nathangreen.com

Z. Žabokrtský
Charles University in Prague, Prague, Czech Republic
e-mail: zabokrtsky@ufal.mff.cuni.cz

© Springer International Publishing Switzerland 2016
M.R. Costa-jussà et al. (eds.), *Hybrid Approaches to Machine Translation*,
Theory and Applications of Natural Language Processing,
DOI 10.1007/978-3-319-21311-8_7

161

To address this issue, we will look at hybrid ensemble approaches to dependency parsing. More specifically, we look at three methods. First, stacking parsers' outputs into a weighted graph and extracting a tree structure using simple voting. Second, analyzing each parsers' errors distribution and using that as an input into the weighted graph through fuzzy clustering methods. Third, using a meta-classifier to choose the best parser for each and every word in our input. The parsers in each situation may come from a variety of techniques such as graph-based, transition-based, and constituent conversion. Using a variety of parsers allows us to study the errors associated with the parsers and choose the best combination or individual parser for each situation.

Even though many tools exist for these European and resource-rich languages, dependency parsing techniques are most commonly tested using accuracy scores, both unlabeled (UAS) and labeled (LAS). If a new technique is developed for a high accuracy languages such as English or Japanese, the results are often equivalent to existing techniques or sometimes worse. Due to this, research is often only concerned with a very specific linguistic construction, domain, or localized feature. This often leads to a scenario, where one size does not fit all, particularly for under-resourced languages. To make sure our techniques are useful for most languages, we analyzed them on large and small language data sets from a variety of language families. Whether under-resourced or resource-rich, we feel that limiting the analysis to accuracy scores does not fully determine whether a technique is useful or not. To test our techniques down a typical NLP pipeline, we turn to machine translation.

Machine translation is often the first task people want solved for their language but often the last step in the process. Many components go into a successful system. These systems come in a variety of forms, whether rule-based or statistically based. One concern for machine translation is whether the early components of the pipeline are accurate. A 2 % error in part-of-speech tagging may lead to a much higher percentage of parsing errors which in turn ends up in a double figure error rate in the final translation. Reducing the errors in early pipeline components is a prime concern so that researchers in machine translation can focus on the actual translation and not generalize earlier errors.

We take a hybrid approach to machine translation by using our hybrid parsers for source text analysis. Each technique described within this chapter is statistically based and can be recreated regardless of language of component making up the hybrid source analysis. To examine the effects of dependency parsing down the NLP pipeline, our hybrid dependency models will be evaluated using the Treex system and TectoMT translation system. This system, as opposed to other popular machine translation systems, makes direct use of the dependency structure during the conversion from source to target languages via a tectogrammatical tree translation approach. We will compare UAS accuracy to corresponding NIST and BLEU score from the start to finish of the machine translation pipeline. BLEU and NIST are automated metrics for machine translation that do not need human evaluation.

Unfortunately any current approach to test dependency parsing's effect on machine translation is going to run into one major road block. There is no gold data for English dependency trees that has a corresponding gold standard translation. For the vast majority of English dependency parsers, the status quo is to train with data automatically converted from constituent trees. This leads to a final parse with at least an 8 % error rate in UAS. This is too high of a rate to truly test the dependency's effect on the final output of the NLP pipeline. To address this issue we have hand annotated dependency trees for the WMT 2012 data set, commonly used to judge machine translation systems.

Within this chapter, we aim to show both improvements to dependency parsing using hybrid methods for a variety of languages including under-resourced and resource-rich and show how these new dependency parsers effect the overall result in a machine translation pipeline. In addition to these results, we have developed new gold standard dependency trees for the purpose of machine translation.

2 Background and Related Work

2.1 Dependency Parsing

Dependency parsing has been shown to be an important part of many NLP applications. Dependency techniques, however, vary greatly. In Kübler et al. (2009), the authors confirm that two parsers, MSTParser and MaltParser, give similar accuracy results but with very different errors. MSTParser, a maximum spanning tree graph-based algorithm, has evenly distributed errors in terms of sentence length while MaltParser, a transition based parser, has errors on mainly longer sentences. This result comes from the approaches themselves. MSTParser is globally trained so the best mean solution should be found, this is why errors on the longer sentences are about the same as the shorter sentences. MaltParser on the other hand uses a greedy algorithm with a classifier that chooses a particular transition at each vertex. This leads to the possibility of the propagation of errors further in a sentence (McDonald and Nivre 2007).

2.1.1 Parsers

For all our experiments we will be working with a hybrid or ensemble of the following three types of parsers:

- **Graph-Based:** A dependency tree is a special case of a weighted edge graph that spawns from an artificial root and is acyclic. Because of this we can look at a large history of work in graph theory to address finding the best spanning tree for each dependency graph. In this section we use MST Parser (McDonald et al. 2005a) as an input to our ensemble parser.
- **Transition-Based:** Transition-based parsing creates a dependency structure that is parametrized over the transitions used to create a dependency tree. This is

closely related to shift-reduce constituency parsing algorithms. The benefit of transition-based parsing is the use of greedy algorithms which have a linear time complexity. However, due to the greedy algorithms, longer arc parses can cause error propagation across each transition (Kübler et al. 2009). We make use of Malt Parser (Nivre et al. 2007), which in the shared tasks was often tied with the best performing systems. Additionally we use Zpar (Zhang and Clark 2011) which is based on Malt Parser but with a different set of non-local features.

- **Constituent Transformation:** While not a true dependency parser, one technique often applied is to take a state-of-the-art constituent parser and transform its phrase based output into dependency relations. This has been shown to also be state-of-the-art in accuracy for dependency parsing in English. In this section we transformed the constituency structure into dependencies using the Penn Converter conversion tool (Johansson and Nugues 2007). A version of this converter was used in the CoNLL shared task to create dependency treebanks as well. For the following ensemble experiments we make use of both (Charniak and Johnson 2005) and Stanford's (Klein and Manning 2003) constituent parsers.

We also address parsing with two smaller language sets, Tamil and Indonesian.

Tamil Parsing In later experiments, we will make use of two different treebanks for dependency parsing, Tamil and Indonesian. Previous parsing experiments in Tamil were done using a rule based approach which utilized morphological tagging and identification of clause boundaries to parse the sentences (Ramasamy and Žabokrtský 2011). The results were also reported for MaltParser and MSTParser. When the morphological tags were available during both training and testing, the rule based approach performed better than Malt and MST parsers. We will be examining the combination of both MST and Malt parsers.

Indonesian Parsing There was research done on developing a rule based Indonesian constituency parser applying syntactic structure to Indonesian sentences. It uses a rule based approach by defining the grammar using PC-PATR (Joice 2002). There was also research that applied the above constituency parser to create a probabilistic parser (Gusmita and Manurung 2008). To the best of our knowledge, no dependency parser has been created and publicly released for Indonesian.

2.2   Hybrid Dependency Parsing

Ensemble learning (Dietterich 2000) has been used for a variety of machine learning tasks and recently has been applied to dependency parsing in various ways and with different levels of success. Surdeanu and Manning (2010) and Haffari et al. (2011) showed a successful combination of parse trees through a combination of trees with various weighting formulations. To keep their tree constraint, they applied Eisner's algorithm for reparsing (Eisner 1996).

Parser combination with dependency trees have been examined in terms of accuracy (Sagae and Lavie 2006; Sagae and Tsujii 2007; Zeman and Žabokrtský 2005). However, the various techniques have generally examined similar parsers or parsers which have generated various different models. Our experiments look deeper and compare the accuracy and part-of-speech error distribution when combining constituent and dependency parsers of many different techniques together.

Other methods of parse combinations have shown to be successful such using one parser to generate features for another parser. This was shown in Nivre and McDonald (2008), in which MaltParser was used as a feature to MSTParser. The result was a successful combination of a transition-based and graph-based parser, but did not address adding other types of parsers into the framework. While this chapter focuses on statistical approaches to parsing, rule based parsing has been successfully used to correct parsers trained via machine learning, creating a hybrid approach (Bick 2007).

2.2.1 Parsing Data Sets

CoNLL Data

Throughout this document we use the English CoNLL data. This data comes from the Wall Street Journal (WSJ) section of the Penn treebank (Marcus et al. 1993). All parsers are trained on sections 02–21 of the WSJ except for the Stanford parser which uses sections 01–21. Charniak, Stanford and Zpar use pre-trained models *ec50spfinal, wsjPCFG.ser.gz, english.tar.gz* respectively. Additionally we make use of Italian and Japanese from the CoNLL datasets as well for our ensemble experiments. They were chosen due to their high baseline and different language families.

2.2.2 Parsing Metrics

There are two standard metrics for comparing dependency parsing systems. *L*abeled *a*ttachment *s*core (LAS) and *u*nlabeled *a*ttachment *s*core (UAS). We mainly use UAS to study the structure of a dependency tree and assess whether the output has the correct head and dependency arcs (Buchholz and Marsi 2006).

2.3 Deep Transfer Syntax-Based MT

Deep transfer machine translation is similar to the notion of translating to an interlingua language. The idea being if you can translate to an intermediate language that has very detailed information, you can then translate that language into your target language. This idea developed into using tectogrammatics as an abstraction of a language peculiarities as it generalizes certain aspects of a language while keep very detailed information about dependencies as well. For our study we use the TectoMT (Popel et al. 2010) system as it directly uses tectogrammatics as well as an analytical layer in which we can directly manipulate the dependency trees.

TectoMT is a machine translation framework based on Praguian tectogrammatics (Sgall 1967) which represents four main layers: word layer, morphological layer, analytical layer, and tectogrammatical layer (Popel et al. 2010). This framework is primarily focused on the translation from English into Czech.

2.3.1   MT Data Sets

For our experiments we will be using data released for the Workshop in Machine Translation (WMT). In particular we used the WMT shared task data for English to Czech for the years 2010, 2011, and 2012.

2.3.2   MT Metrics

The BLEU (*BiLingual Evaluation Understudy*) (Papineni et al. 2002) and NIST, from the *National Institute of Standards and Technology*, to determine the strength of our machine translation and compare the result with our parsing UAS.

3   Hybrid Dependency Parsers

Ensemble methods are often used when we want models trained on different data. We will look at ways to combine models trained on the same or similar data. When looking at similar or identical data, we hope that the different models give complimentary views of the same data. Ideally you do not want the models to be "good" at the same things. To get started with ensemble parsing, we have created an ensemble class in Treex that collects all analytical trees present and combines their structure into an edge matrix. An edge matrix is a simple structure to store a directed graph. Each edge is assigned some "weight". In the end, we have to generate a parse tree out of this matrix.

To generate a single ensemble parse tree, our system takes N parse trees as input. The inputs are from a variety of parsers as described in Sect. 2.1. We will call these parsers our **Base Parsers**. All edges in these parse trees are combined into a graph structure. This graph structure accepts weighted edges via **Graph Edge Weighting Algorithms**. So if more than one parse tree contains the same tree edge, the graph will be weighted appropriately according to a chosen weighting algorithm. One could imagine many ways of combining edges through additive and multiplicative methods but our specific weighting algorithms used in our experiments are described in Sect. 3.1.

Fig. 1 General flow to create
an Ensemble parse tree

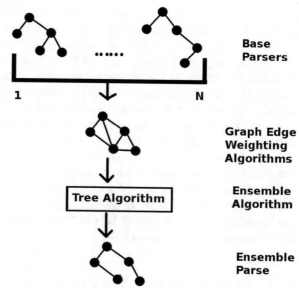

Once the system has a weighted graph, the system then uses an algorithm to find a corresponding tree structure by a selected **Tree Algorithm** so there are no cycles. In our set of experiments, we constructed a tree by finding the minimum spanning tree using ChuLiu/Edmonds' optimization algorithm, which is a standard choice for MST tasks. The result should be our final **Ensemble Parse**. Figure 1 graphically shows the decisions one needs to make in this framework to create an ensemble parse.

3.1 Minimum Spanning Tree Combination

To start with, we will apply a minimum spanning tree algorithm, ChuLiu/Edmonds' algorithm. For a combination of two supervised parses, this may return an "average" parse. This does not suit our concept of hybrid systems well. Since these algorithms work best with many inputs we can use many "baseline" parsers as well as the same parsers retrained with different data sets. The theory being, the more parsers and the more different types of parsers used, the better chance we have to get an accurate ensemble parse.

3.1.1 Parsers

For English, we use 5 of the most commonly used parsers which enables us to have a wide scope for ensemble learning. They range from graph-based approaches to transition-based approaches to constituent parsers. Constituency output is converted to dependency structures using PennConverter (Johansson and Nugues 2007). All parsers are integrated in the Treex framework (Žabokrtský et al. 2008; Popel et al. 2011) using the publicly released parsers from the respective authors but with Perl wrappers to allow them to work on a common tree structure. For testing we use section 23 of the WSJ for comparability reasons with other papers. This test data contains 56,684 tokens. For tuning we use section 22.

In addition to the UAS score of the enumerated parsers, we also report the accuracy of an Oracle Parser. This parser is simply the best possible parse composed only of edges offered by the individual dependency parsers. If the reference, gold standard, tree has an edge that any of the parsers contain, we include that edge in the Oracle parse. Initially all nodes of the tree are connected to an artificial root. Since only edges that exist in a reference tree are added, the Oracle Parser maintains the acyclic constraint. For English we ran 2^5 model combinations but only report on combinations of three or more models.

3.1.2   Weighting Schemes for Parsing Combination

For this experiment we are applying four weighting algorithms to the graph structure. All three of these are simple weighting techniques but even in their simplicity we can see the benefit of this type of combination.

- **Uniform Weights**: an edge in the graph gets incremented +1 weight for each matching edge in each parser. If an edge occurs in four parsers, the weight is 4.
- **UAS Weighted**: Each edge in the graph gets incremented by the value of its parsers individual accuracy. So based on the UAS baseline parsing results from Table 2, an edge in Charniak's tree gets 0.92 added while MST gets 0.86 added to every edge they share with the resulting graph. This weighting should allow us to add poor parsers with very little harm to the overall score.
- **Plural Voting Weights**: In Plural Voting, the parsers are rated and each gets a "vote" based on their quality. With N parsers the best parser gets N votes while the last place parser gets one vote. In this experiment, Charniak received five votes, Stanford received four votes, MSTParser received three votes, MaltParser received two votes, and Zpar received one vote. Votes in this case are added to each edge as a weight.
- **UAS^{10}**: For this weighting scheme we took each UAS value to the 10th power. This gave us the desired effect of making the differences in accuracy more apparent and giving more distance from the best to worst parser. This exponent was empirically found and the results are shown in Table 3.

Table 1 Our baseline parsers
and corresponding UAS used
in our ensemble experiments

Parser	UAS
Charniak	92.08
Stanford	87.88
MST	86.49
Malt	84.51
Zpar	76.06

3.1.3 Results

Table 2 contains the results of different parser combinations of the five parsers in Table 1. The results seem to indicate that using two parsers will give you an "average" score. Ensemble learning seems to start to have a benefit around three parsers with a few combinations having a better UAS score than any of the baseline parsers, these cases are in bold throughout the table. When we add a 4th parser to the mix almost all configurations lead to an improved score when the edges are not weighted uniformly. The only case in which this does not occur is when Stanford's Parser is not used. When all five parsers are used together with Plural Voting, the ensemble parser improves over the highest individual parser's UAS score. For UAS^{10} voting, the five parser combination gives the second highest accuracy score. The top overall score is when we use UAS^{10} weighting with the four top individual parsers. For parser combinations that do not feature Charniak's parser, we also find an increase in overall accuracy score compared to each individual parser, although never beating Charniak's individual score.

To see the maximum accuracy an ensemble system can achieve, we include an Oracle Ensemble Parser in Table 2. As we can see in Table 2, the ceiling of ensemble learning is 97.41 % accuracy. Because of this high value, ensemble learning should be a very prosperous area for dependency parsing research.

To discover the best exponential value in UAS^X we looked at our combining all parsers at different exponential values. We empirically test different values on our tuning data. UAS^{10} is the top scoring weight for English. The results are in Table 3. We only discover this weight using the "all" parser setting and only on English. If this setup was used in production it would be wise to relearn this exponential value through new tuning data for the model combination choice and particular language each time.

3.1.4 Dependency Errors Per POS Tag

We looked at the error distribution for all five parsers along with our best ensemble parser configuration. Much like the previous work we expect different types of errors, given that our parsers are from three different parsing techniques. To examine if the ensemble parser is substantially changing the parse tree or is just taking the best parse tree and substituting a few edges, we examine the part-of-speech errors in Table 4.

Table 2 Initial Results of the minimum spanning tree algorithm on a combined edge graph

System	Uniform weighting	UAS weighted	Plural voting	UAS^{10} weighted	Oracle UAS
Charniak-Stanford	89.84	92.08	92.08	92.08	94.85
Charniak-Mst	89.14	92.08	92.08	92.08	95.33
Charniak-Malt	88.15	92.08	92.08	92.08	95.4
Charniak-Zpar	84.10	92.08	92.08	92.08	94.49
Stanford-Mst	86.92	86.49	87.88	86.49	94.29
Stanford-Malt	86.05	87.88	87.88	87.88	94.09
Stanford-Zpar	81.86	87.88	87.88	87.88	93.02
Mst-Malt	85.54	86.49	86.49	86.49	90.38
Mst-Zpar	81.19	86.49	86.49	86.49	92.03
Malt-Zpar	80.07	84.51	84.51	84.51	91.46
Charniak-Stanford-Mst	91.86	**92.27**	**92.28**	**92.25**	96.48
Charniak-Stanford-Malt	91.77	**92.28**	**92.3**	92.08	96.49
Charniak-Stanford-Zpar	91.22	91.99	92.02	92.08	95.94
Charniak-Mst-Malt	88.80	89.55	90.77	92.08	96.3
Charniak-Mst-Zpar	90.44	91.59	92.08	92.08	96.16
Charniak-Malt-Zpar	88.61	91.3	92.08	92.08	96.21
Stanford-Mst-Malt	87.84	**88.28**	**88.26**	**88.28**	95.62
Stanford-Mst-Zpar	**89.12**	**89.88**	88.84	**89.91**	95.57
Stanford-Malt-Zpar	**88.61**	**89.57**	87.88	87.88	95.47
Mst-Malt-Zpar	**86.99**	**87.34**	86.82	86.49	93.79
Charniak-Stanford-Mst-Malt	90.45	**92.09**	**92.34**	**92.56**	97.09
Charniak-Stanford-Mst-Zpar	91.57	**92.24**	**92.27**	**92.26**	96.97
Charniak-Stanford-Malt-Zpar	91.31	**92.14**	**92.4**	**92.42**	97.03
Charniak-Mst-Malt-Zpar	89.60	89.48	91.71	92.08	96.79
Stanford-Mst-Malt-Zpar	**88.76**	**88.45**	**88.95**	**88.44**	96.36
All	91.43	91.77	**92.44**	**92.58**	97.41

Scores are in **bold** when the ensemble system increased the UAS score over all individual systems

As we can see the range of POS errors varies dramatically depending on which parser we examine. For instance for *CC*, Charniak has 83 % while MST is only 71 % accurate. There are also POS errors that are almost always universally bad such as the left parenthesis (. Given the large difference in POS errors, weighting an ensemble system by POS is a logical choice, which we will address further in Sect. 3.2. The varying POS accuracies indicate that the parsing techniques we have incorporated into our ensemble parser, are significantly different. In almost every case in Table 4, our ensemble parser achieves the best dependency accuracy for each POS, while reducing the average relative error rate by 8.64 %.

Table 3 UAS scores of our ensemble parser with all parsers included at different exponential values (UAS^x)

X	UAS^X
0.5	91.77
2	91.84
4	91.98
6	92.44
8	92.47
9	92.52
10	**92.58**
11	92.57
12	92.57
16	92.43

The bold value indicates the highest empirically found result

Table 4 Dependency errors per POS tag for each of our systems that are used in the ensemble system

POS	Charniak	Stanford	MST	Malt	Zpar	Best ensemble	Relative error reduction
PDT	88.890	77.78	83.33	88.89	77.78	88.89	0.00
CC	83.540	74.73	71.16	65.84	20.39	**84.63**	6.64
NNP	94.590	92.16	88.04	87.17	73.67	**95.02**	7.81
,	84.450	78.02	63.13	60.12	65.64	**85.08**	3.99
WP$	90.480	71.43	85.71	90.48	0.00	90.48	0.00
VBN	91.720	89.81	90.35	89.17	88.26	**93.81**	25.27
WP	83.780	80.18	80.18	82.88	2.70	81.08	−16.67
RBR	77.680	62.50	75.00	76.79	68.75	**78.57**	4.00
CD	94.910	92.67	85.19	84.46	82.64	**94.96**	1.02
RP	96.150	95.05	97.25	95.60	94.51	**97.80**	42.86
JJ	95.410	92.99	94.47	93.90	89.45	95.85	0.00
PRP	97.820	96.21	96.68	95.64	95.45	**98.39**	26.09
TO	94.520	89.44	91.29	90.73	88.63	94.35	−2.94
EX	96.490	98.25	100.00	100.00	96.49	**98.25**	50.00
WRB	63.910	60.90	68.42	73.68	4.51	63.91	0.00
RB	86.260	79.88	81.49	81.44	80.61	**87.19**	6.74
FW	55.000	45.00	60.00	25.00	35.00	55.00	0.00
WDT	97.140	95.36	96.43	95.00	9.29	**97.50**	12.50
VBP	91.400	83.29	80.92	75.81	50.87	91.27	−1.45
JJR	88.380	80.81	74.75	70.20	68.18	87.37	−8.70
VBZ	91.970	87.35	83.86	80.78	57.91	**92.46**	6.06
NNPS	97.620	95.24	100.00	95.24	69.05	100.00	100.00
(	73.610	75.00	54.17	58.33	15.28	73.61	0.00

(continued)

Table 4 (continued)

POS	Charniak	Stanford	MST	Malt	Zpar	Best ensemble	Relative error reduction
UH	87.500	62.50	75.00	37.50	37.50	87.50	0.00
POS	98.180	96.54	98.54	98.72	0.18	**98.36**	10.00
$	82.930	80.00	67.47	66.40	52.27	**84.27**	7.81
``	83.990	79.66	76.08	58.95	74.01	**84.37**	2.35
:	77.160	72.53	45.99	44.44	53.70	**79.63**	10.81
JJS	96.060	90.55	88.19	86.61	82.68	93.70	−60.00
LS	75.000	50.00	100.00	75.00	75.00	75.00	0.00
.	96.060	93.48	91.07	84.89	87.56	**97.08**	25.81
VB	93.040	88.48	91.33	90.95	84.37	**94.24**	17.27
MD	89.550	82.02	83.05	78.77	51.54	**89.90**	3.28
NNS	93.100	89.51	90.68	88.65	78.93	**93.67**	8.26
NN	93.620	90.29	88.45	86.98	83.84	**94.00**	6.00
VBD	93.250	87.20	86.27	82.73	64.32	**93.52**	4.03
DT	97.610	96.47	97.30	97.01	92.19	**97.97**	14.78
#	100.000	80.00	0.00	0.00	0.00	100.00	0.00
,	88.280	83.79	81.84	69.92	79.88	**90.04**	15.00
RBS	90.000	76.67	93.33	93.33	86.67	90.00	0.00
IN	87.800	78.66	83.45	80.78	73.08	87.48	−2.66
SYM	100.000	100.00	100.00	0.00	0.00	100.00	0.00
PRP$	97.640	96.07	47.22	96.86	93.12	97.45	−8.33
)	70.830	77.78	96.46	55.56	12.50	**72.22**	4.76
VBG	85.190	82.13	82.74	82.25	81.27	**89.35**	28.10
Average							**7.79**

We also our best ensemble system which is the combination of all parsers using UAS^{10}. All POS errors are calculated using the testing data provided by section 23 of the WST. The ensemble system that generated these errors was parametrized on tuning data, section 22 of the WSJ. Scores are in bold when the ensemble system increased the UAS score over all individual systems for that given POS

The current weighting systems don't simply default to the best parser or to an average of all errors. In the majority of cases our ensemble parser obtains the top accuracy. The ability of the ensemble system to use maximum spanning tree on an edge graph allows the ensemble parser to connect previously unconnected nodes for an overall gain, which is preferable to techniques which only select the best model for a particular tree. In all cases, our ensemble parser is never the worst parser. In cases where the POS is less frequent, our ensemble parser seems to average out the error distribution.

We demonstrated that using parsers of different techniques, especially including transformed constituent parsers, can lead to the best accuracy within this ensemble framework. The improvements in accuracy are not simply due to a few edge changes but can be seen to improve the accuracy of the majority of POS tags over all individual systems. We also show a theoretical maximum oracle parser which indicates that much more work in this field can take place to improve dependency parsing accuracy toward the oracle score of 97.41 %.

To amplify the effect of POS error reduction further, we will look to learn the ensemble weights though our POS error distribution. To do this we will cluster the POS accuracies of our parsers and combine in a similar fashion. These experiments are detailed in Sect. 3.2.

3.2 Fuzzy Clustering

Each technique above achieves this success via different error distribution. To minimize these errors and to increase state-of-the-art parsing accuracy, we now examine ensemble techniques that weight graph edges based on part-of-speech errors. To do this, we cluster all dependency parsing models on part-of-speech error counts. This leads us to have a different weighting scheme between dependency parsers for each individual part-of-speech.

3.2.1 Weighting Schemes for Clustering

We apply three weighting algorithms to the graph structure. First we give each parser uniform weight. Second we weight each particular edge by a combination of models weights determined by the part-of-speech error distribution. Finally we apply exponential scaling to the POS weights (POS^{10}) to amplify the differences between models.

- **Uniform**: This is the same as our previous fixed weight experiments with each edge in the graph getting incremented +1 weight for each matching edge in each parser.
- **POS**: Each edge of the graph is weighted by a combination of weighting schemes determined by the particular part-of-speech. This is described in more detail in Sect. 3.2.2.
- **POS^{10}**: For this weighting scheme, we took each POS model score from the previous weighting scheme and raised it to the 10th power at run time which was empirically chosen. This was once again an opportunity to exaggerate the differences in each parser when it came to each part-of-speech.

3.2.2 Determining Part-of-Speech Clustering Weights

To automatically learn the weights of our models, we turn to part-of-speech error analysis. We obtain a dependency error distribution by POS from our tuning data. Using fuzzy clustering with the cosine distance metric over 20 iterations we find

$$Weight_{edge} = \sum_{i=1}^{N} c_i \sum_{j=1}^{M} w_j$$

Fig. 2 Equation for calculating the weight of one edge across N POS clusters each with their own weight c and M models each with their own weight w, where each M predicts the edge

Table 5 Cluster weights for each model when averaged based across centroids for our English models

Models	Cluster 1 (%)	Cluster 2 (%)	Cluster 3 (%)
Charniak	21.48	26.46	31.68
Stanford	20.47	24.91	27.62
Mst	20.29	24.25	21.57
Malt	19.38	20.47	10.43
Zpar	18.38	3.91	8.70

three clusters. For a particular part-of-speech we get a weight corresponding to each cluster that sum to 1. In N clusters, we have M weights corresponding to each M models. So for a particular edge, we get its weight by summing each cluster multiplied by all model weights as seen in Fig. 2. If a part-of-speech did not occur in the tuning data, the weights are equally split across all clusters.

Our clustering algorithm is based on Fuzzy-Cmeans algorithm. This algorithm allows for a "data point" to exist partially in many clusters. The cluster centroid is iteratively calculated. For our data points we will use a count of correctly predicted dependencies based on POS's tags for each parser so for one entry we would have NOUN⇒Parser1⇒10, Parser2⇒20 Parser3⇒5, Parser4⇒6. The clusters will then specify the centroids of different clusters of these data points. We use three clusters which gives use three combinations of model weights.

- Determine clusters for a POS
- Multiply each corresponding cluster weight against each model that predicts the edge
- Sum the result
- Repeat for each cluster
- Sum results from all cluster

For instance for Tables 5 and 6 we will look at a node which has the POS VBZ. Let us assume that the edge we are looking at is only predicted by ZPar and Charniak. Step one we see that Cluster 1 has a weight of 0.971. We would then sum the weights of the models with the predicted edge $(21.48*0.971)+(18.38*0.971) = 38.7$. We then repeat this for Cluster 2 $((26.46 * 0.025) + (3.91 * 0.025) = 0.75)$ and Cluster 3 $((31.68 * 0.0036) + (8.70 * 0.0036) = 0.14)$. For the final weight we combine these weights $38.7 + 0.75 + 0.14 = 39.59$. As you can see Cluster 2 and Cluster 3 provide little weight to the final result. This is because Zpar did relatively well on this POS compared to its poor results on others. Cluster 1 gives a higher score to ZPar in this situation.

Table 6 The weights of each cluster for selected POS tags

POS	Cluster 1	Cluster 2	Cluster 3
(	0.007	0.9928	0.0007
)	0.043	0.9508	0.0067
CC	0.008	0.9904	0.0019
JJ	1.000	0.0001	0
MD	0.804	0.182	0.0136
NN	1.000	0	0
NNP	1.000	0.0001	0
NNPS	0.007	0.9917	0.0013
PDT	0.210	0.7277	0.0618
PRP	1.000	0.0001	0.0001
VB	1.000	0	0
VBD	0.981	0.0153	0.0036
VBZ	0.971	0.025	0.0041
WDT	0.003	0.9963	0.0005

3.2.3 Fuzzy Clustering Results

This weighting system models the POS tag in a fashion similar to the dependency error per POS distribution. For instance the POS tag "CC" has high weights for Cluster 1. Cluster 1 gives very little weight to Zpar. If we examine the POS errors in Table 4, Zpar did very poorly on these tags. Overall, it does appear that the clusters tend towards a more balanced weighting scheme while only pointing out true outliers.

Table 7 shows the results of the run on our testing data in which the fuzzy clusters were determined on our tuning data. The accuracies are higher but comparable to what is seen with a basic uniform weighting scheme. The weights were a combination of the fuzzy clustering weights based on POS errors shown in Table 6. This score, **92.54 %**, which occurred when all parsers were used, is the best accuracy of all our ensemble techniques and model combinations with English.

3.2.4 POS Error Reduction

Next in Table 8 we look at the relative POS error reduction rate and its average across all parts-of-speech. The table indicates that while the POS clustering ensemble system did reduce error on an edge by edge level in terms of POS error. This indicates that locally the system makes better decisions but the overall structure of the parse tree may be incorrect. To correct this we must look at combining POS clustering with an ensemble method that will favor an overall structure. To see if can get a better overall structure, we now look at a more describe ensemble system in which only one parser determines the edge.

Table 7 UAS scores of our ensemble parser using POS fuzzy clustering weights for English

Parser	Uniform	POS	POS[10]	Oracle
Charniak-Stanford-Mst	91.86	**92.27**	92.08	96.48
Charniak-Stanford-Malt	91.77	**92.28**	92.08	96.49
Charniak-Stanford-Zpar	91.22	92.00	92.08	95.94
Charniak-Mst-Malt	88.80	89.55	92.08	96.3
Charniak-Mst-Zpar	90.44	91.59	92.08	96.16
Charnial-Malt-Zpar	88.61	91.30	92.08	96.21
Stanford-Mst-Malt	87.84	**87.94**	87.88	95.62
Stanford-Mst-Zpar	**89.12**	**89.89**	87.88	95.57
Stanford-Malt-Zpar	**88.61**	**89.60**	**89.58**	95.47
Mst-Malt-Zpar	**86.99**	**87.34**	86.49	93.79
Charniak-Stanford-Mst-Malt	90.45	**92.09**	**92.45**	97.09
Charniak-Stanford-Mst-Zpar	91.57	**92.24**	**92.49**	96.97
Charniak-Stanford-Malt-Zpar	91.31	**92.15**	92.08	97.03
Charniak-Mst-Malt-Zpar	89.60	89.53	92.08	96.79
Stanford-Mst-Malt-Zpar	**88.76**	**88.40**	87.88	96.36
All	91.43	91.84	**92.54**	97.41

Values are bolded wherever the result is greater than any individual model within the ensemble system

3.3 Model Classification

Here we will use a meta-classifier to select which model will choose each node's parent. A dependency tree in this situation may be made up of many different parsers but each node will only be determined by one parser each. This is contrary to the previous section where each node took input and weights from each individual parser.

Morphologically rich languages are often short on training data or require much higher amounts of training data due to the increased size of their lexicon. This section examines a new approach for addressing morphologically rich languages with little training data to start.

Using Tamil and Indonesian as our test languages, we create nine dependency parse models with a limited amount of training data. Using these models we train an SVM classifier using only the model agreements as features. We use this SVM classifier on an edge by edge decision to form an ensemble parse tree. Using only model agreements as features allows this method to remain language independent and applicable to a wide range of morphologically rich languages.

Table 8 POS errors for each of our systems that are used in the ensemble system for English

POS	Charniak	Stanford	MST	Malt	Zpar	Best ensemble	Relative error reduction
PDT	88.890	77.78	83.33	88.89	77.78	88.89	0.00
CC	83.540	74.73	71.16	65.84	20.39	**84.63**	6.64
NNP	94.590	92.16	88.04	87.17	73.67	**95.02**	7.81
VBN	91.720	89.81	90.35	89.17	88.26	**93.81**	25.27
JJ	95.410	92.99	94.47	93.90	89.45	95.85	0.00
PRP	97.820	96.21	96.68	95.64	95.45	**98.39**	26.09
TO	94.520	89.44	91.29	90.73	88.63	94.35	−2.94
RB	86.260	79.88	81.49	81.44	80.61	**87.19**	6.74
FW	55.000	45.00	60.00	25.00	35.00	55.00	0.00
WDT	97.140	95.36	96.43	95.00	9.29	**97.50**	12.50
VB	93.040	88.48	91.33	90.95	84.37	**94.24**	17.27
MD	89.550	82.02	83.05	78.77	51.54	**89.90**	3.28
NNS	93.100	89.51	90.68	88.65	78.93	**93.67**	8.26
NN	93.620	90.29	88.45	86.98	83.84	**94.00**	6.00
DT	97.610	96.47	97.30	97.01	92.19	**97.97**	14.78
Average							**7.79**

We also include the POS error distribution for our best ensemble system. All POS errors are calculated using the testing data, section 23 of the WST. The ensemble system that generated these errors was parametrized on tuning data, section 22 of the WSJ. We only display a reduced set of POS tags for space but the Average is over all POS tags including those not shown. Scores are in bold when the best ensemble system increased the UAS score over all individual systems for that given POS

3.3.1 Process Flow

When dealing with small data sizes, it is often not enough to show a simple accuracy increase. This increase can be very reliant on the training/tuning/testing data splits as well as the sampling of those sets. For this reason our experiments are conducted over eight training/tuning/testing data split configurations. For each configuration we randomly sample without replacement the training/tuning/testing data and rerun the experiment 100 times. These 800 runs, each on different samples, allow us to better show the overall effect on the accuracy metric as well as the statistically significant changes as described in Sect. 3.3.4. Figure 3 shows this process flow for one run of these experiments.

3.3.2 Parsers

For this section, we generate two models using MSTParser (McDonald et al. 2005a), one projective and one non-projective to use in our ensemble system. Additionally we generate many transition-based parsers. We make use of MaltParser (Nivre et al.

Fig. 3 Process Flow for one
run of our SVM ensemble
system. This Process in its
entirety was run 100 times for
each of the eight data set
splits

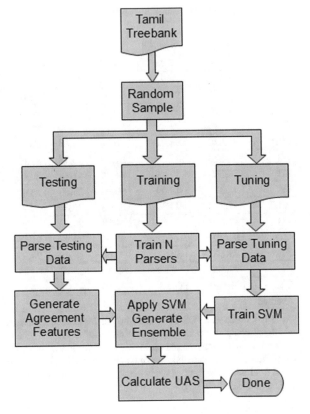

2007), which in the CoNLL shared tasks was often tied with the best performing
systems. For this parser, we generate seven different models using different training
parameters and use them as input into our ensemble system along with the two
graph-based models described above.

3.3.3 Ensemble SVM System

We train our SVM classifier using only model agreement features. Using our tuning
set, for each predicted dependency edge, we create $\binom{N}{2}$ features where N is the
number of parsing models. We do this for each model which predicted the correct
edge in the tuning data. So for $N = 3$ the first feature would be a 1 if model 1 and
model 2 agreed, feature 2 would be a 1 if model 1 and model 3 agreed, and so on.
This feature set is novel and widely applicable to many languages since it does not
use any additional linguistic tools.

Table 9 Node predictions for SVM based meta-classifier

Model	Head prediction
1	Node 3
2	Node 4
3	Node 2
4	Node 3
5	Node 2

Table 10 SVM agreement matrix

	Model 1	Model 2	Model 3	Model 4	Model 5
Model 1	1	0	0	1	0
Model 2	0	1	0	0	0
Model 3	0	0	1	0	1
Model 4	1	0	0	1	0
Model 5	0	0	1	0	1

In Table 9, we can see an example of five models/parsers and their prediction for a head of a node. Let us say in this example that Model 2 is correct and the correct head is Node 4. We would create a feature sets based on Table 10 in which our features would describe a few scenarios. First (10010) would say that when Model 1 and Model 4 agree, Model 2 is correct. Second (01000) when Model 2 disagrees with everyone, Model 2 is correct. Third (00101) when Model 3 and Model 5 agree, Model 2 is correct. These are all feature sets that are used in our SVM. For each edge in the ensemble graph, we use our classifier to predict which model should be correct, by first creating the model agreement feature set for the current edge of the unknown test data. The SVM predicts which model should be correct and this model then decides to which head the current node is attached. At the end of all the tokens in a sentence, the graph may not be connected and will likely have cycles. Using a Perl implementation of minimum spanning tree in which each edge has a uniform weight, we obtain a minimum spanning forest, where each subgraph is then connected and cycles are eliminated in order to achieve a well formed dependency structure. Figure 4 gives a graphical representation of how the SVM decision and maximum spanning tree algorithm create a final ensemble parse tree which is similar to the construction used in Hall et al. (2007) and Green and Žabokrtský (2012a).

3.3.4 Evaluation

To test statistical significant, we use Wilcoxon paired signed-rank test. For each data split we have 100 iterations each with different sampling. Each model is compared against the same samples so a paired test is appropriate in this case. We report statistical significance values for $p < 0.01$ and $p < 0.05$.

Fig. 4 General flow to create
an Ensemble parse tree for a
discrete SVM selection

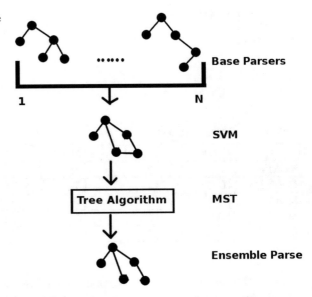

Base Parsers

SVM

MST

Ensemble Parse

Table 11 Average increases
and decreases in UAS score
for different
Training-Tuning-Test samples

Data split	Average SVM UAS (%)	% Increase over avg (%)	% Increase over best (%)
70-20-10	76.50	5.13	0.52
60-20-20	76.36	5.68	0.72
60-30-10	75.42	5.44	0.52
60-10-30	75.66	4.83	0.10
85-5-10	75.33	3.10	−1.21
90-5-5	75.42	3.19	−1.10
80-10-10	76.44	4.84	0.48

The average was calculated over all nine models while the best
was selected for each data split

3.3.5 Results and Discussion

For each of the data splits, Table 11 shows the percent increase in our SVM
system over both the average of the nine individual models and over the best
individual model. As Table 11 shows, our approach seems to decrease in value
along with the decrease in tuning data. In both cases when we only used 5 %
tuning data we did not get any improvement in our average UAS scores. Examining
Table 12, shows that the decrease in the 90-5-5 split is not statistically significant
however the decrease in 85-5-10 is a statistically significant drop. However, the
increases in all data splits are statistically significant except for the 60-20-20 data
split.

It appears that the size of the tuning and training data matter more than the size
of the test data. Given that the TamilTB is relatively small when compared to other
CoNLL treebanks, we expect that this ratio may shift more when additional data is

Table 12 Statistical significance table for different training-tuning-test samples in Tamil

Model	70-20-10	60-20-20	60-30-10	60-10-30	85-5-10	90-5-5	80-10-10
2planar	*	*	*	*	*	*	**
mstnonproj	*	*	*	*	*	*	**
mstproj	*	*	*	*	*	*	**
nivreeager	*	*	*	*	**	x	*
nivrestandard	*	*	**	x	*	*	*
planar	*	*	*	*	*	*	**
stackeager	*	*	*	x	*	**	*
stacklazy	*	*	*	x	*	**	*
stackproj	**	*	*	x	**	**	**

Each experiment was sampled 100 times and Wilcoxon Statistical Significance was calculated for our SVM model's increase/decrease over each individual model.
$* p < 0.01$, $** p = < 0.05$, $x = p \geq 0.05$

supplied since the amount of out of vocabulary, OOV, words will decrease as well. As OOV words decrease, we expect the use of additional test data to have less of an effect.

The traditional approach of using as much data as possible for the training does not seem to be as effective as partitioning more data for tuning an SVM. For instance, the high test training percentage we use is 90% applied to training with 5% for tuning and testing each. In this case the best individual model had a UAS score 76.25% and the SVM had a UAS of 75.42%. One might think using 90% of the data would achieve a higher overall UAS score than using less training data. On the contrary, we achieve a better UAS score on average using only 60%, 70%, 80%, and 85% of the data towards training. This additional data spent for tuning appears to be worth the cost.

To further examine the tuning/training data trade off, we turn to a new language to see if the results are replicated. For this we will look at Indonesian.

For each of the data splits, Table 13 shows the percent increase in our SVM system over both the average of the seven individual models and over the best individual model. As Table 13 shows, we obtain above average UAS scores in every data split. The increase is statistical significant in all data splits except one, the 90-5-5 split. This seems to be logical since this data split has the least difference in training data between systems, with only 5% tuning data. Our highest average UAS score was with the 70-20-10 split with a UAS of 62.48%. The use of 20% tuning data is of interest since it was significantly better than models with 10–25% more training data as seen in Fig. 5. This additional data spent for tuning appears to be worth the cost.

The selection of the test data seems to have caused a difference in our results. While all our ensemble SVM parsing systems have better UAS scores, it is a lower increase when we only use 5% for testing. Which in our treebank means we are only using five sentences randomly selected per experiment. This does not seem to be enough to judge the improvement.

Table 13 Average increases and decreases in Indonesian UAS score for different Training-Tuning-Test samples

Data split	Average SVM UAS (%)	% Increase over average (%)	% Increase over best (%)	Statistical significant
50-40-10	60.01	10.65	4.34	Y
60-30-10	60.28	10.35	4.41	Y
70-20-10	62.25	10.10	3.70	Y
80-10-10	60.88	8.42	1.94	Y
50-30-20	61.37	9.73	4.58	Y
60-20-20	62.39	9.62	3.55	Y
70-10-20	62.48	7.50	1.90	Y
50-20-30	61.71	9.48	4.22	Y
60-10-30	62.57	7.89	2.47	Y
90-5-5	60.85	0.56	0.56	N
85-10-5	61.15	0.56	0.56	Y
80-15-5	59.23	0.54	0.54	Y
75-20-5	60.32	0.54	0.54	Y
70-25-5	59.54	0.54	0.54	Y
65-30-5	59.76	0.54	0.54	Y
60-35-5	59.31	0.53	0.53	Y
55-40-5	57.27	0.50	0.50	Y
50-45-5	57.72	0.51	0.51	Y

The average was calculated over all seven models while the best was selected for each data split. Each experiment was sampled 100 times and Wilcoxon Statistical Significance was calculated for our SVM model's increase/decrease over each individual model. $Y = p < 0.01$ and $N = p \geq 0.01$ for all models in the data split

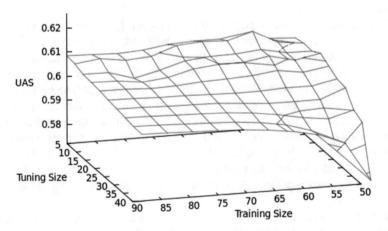

Fig. 5 Surface plot of the Indonesian UAS score for the tuning and training data split

We have shown a new SVM based ensemble parser that uses only dependency model agreement features. The ability to use only model agreements allows us to keep this approach language independent and applicable to a wide range of morphologically rich languages. We show a statistically significant 5.44 % improvement over the average dependency model and a statistically significant 0.52 % improvement over the best individual system for Tamil. We reproduced the results on a smaller Indonesian corpus with an improvement on individual accuracy of 4.92 % on average.

4 MT with a Hybrid Parsing Approach

Evaluating ensemble parsing systems on UAS alone is not enough. We further studied their effect in machine translation using the Treex system. We evaluated our three approaches in ensemble parsing against each baser parser. All tests are done in English and Czech. We evaluated 3 years of data WMT 2010–2012. Doing so, we find a strong correlation between our parsing scores and our machine translation scores. We now want to look at two things. One, how our ensemble structures effect machine translation and two, how a gold standard parse will effect the translation result.

To find the maximum effect that dependency parsing can have on the NLP pipeline, we annotated English dependency trees to form a gold standard. Annotation was done with two annotators using a tree editor, TrEd (Pajas and Fabian 2011), on data that was preprocessed using MSTParser. For the annotation of our gold data, we used the standard annotation standards described in the Prague Dependency Treebank (PDT) (Hajič 1998). PDT is annotated on three levels, morphological, analytical, and tectogrammatical. For our gold data, we do not touch the morphological layer, we only correct the analytical layer (i.e. labeled dependency trees). For machine translation experiments later in the chapter, we allow the system to automatically generate a new tectogrammatical layer based on our new analytical layer annotation. Because the Treex machine translation system uses a tectogrammatical layer, when in doubt, ambiguity was left to the tectogrammatical layer to handle.

4.1 Data Sets

4.1.1 Evaluation Set

For the annotation experiments, we use text provided by the 2012 Workshop for Machine Translation (WMT2012). The data consists of 3003 sentences. We automatically tokenized, tagged, and parsed these sentences. This data set was also chosen since it is disjoint from the usual dependency training data, allowing researchers to use it as a out-of-domain testing set. The parser used is an implementation of MSTParser. We then hand corrected the analytical trees to have a "Gold" standard dependency structure. Analytical trees were annotated on the PDT standard. Most manual corrections involved coordination construction along with prepositional phrase attachment.

Having only two annotators has limited us to evaluating our annotation only through spot checking and through comparison with other baselines. Annotation happened sequentially one after another. Possible errors were additionally detected through a set of automatic tests. As a comparison we will evaluate our gold data set versus other parsers in respect to their performance on previous data sets, namely the Wall Street Journal (WSJ) section 23.

4.1.2 Training Set

All the parsers were trained on sections 02–21 of the WSJ converted to dependencies using the PennConverter, except the Stanford parser which also uses section 01. We retrained MST and Malt parsers and used pre-trained models for the other parsers. Machine translation data was used from WMT 2010, 2011, and 2012. Using our gold standard we are able to evaluate the effectiveness of different parser types from graph-base, transition-based, constituent conversion to ensemble approaches on the 2012 data while finding data trends using previous years data.

4.2 Translation Components

Our dependency models are evaluated using the TectoMT translation system (Popel et al. 2010). This system, as opposed to other popular machine translation systems, makes direct use of the dependency structure during the conversion from source to target languages via a tectogrammatical tree translation approach.

We use the different parsers in separate translation runs each time in the same Treex parsing block. So each translation scenario only differs in the parser used and nothing else. The parsers used are as follows:

- **MST**: Implementation of Ryan McDonald's Minimum spanning tree parser (McDonald et al. 2005b)
- **MST with chunking**: Same implementation as above but we parse the sentences based on chunks and not full sentences. For instance this could mean separating parentheticals or separating appositions (Popel et al. 2011)
- **Malt**: Implementation of Nivre's MaltParser trained on the Penn Treebank (Nivre 2003)
- **Malt with chunking**: Same implementation as above but with chunked parsing
- **ZPar**: Yue Zhang's statistical parser. We used the pretrained English model (english.tar.gz) available on the ZPar website for all tests (Zhang and Clark 2011)

- **Charniak**: A constituent based parser (ec50spfinal model) in which we transform the results using the PennConverter (Johansson and Nugues 2007)
- **Stanford**: Another constituent based parser (Klein and Manning 2003) whose output is converted using PennConverter as well (wsjPCFG.ser.gz model)
- **Fixed Weight Ensemble**: Our stacked ensemble system combining five of the parsers above (MST, Malt, ZPar, Charniak, Stanford). The weights for each tree are assigned based on UAS score (Green and Žabokrtský 2012a)
- **Fuzzy Cluster**: Our stacked ensemble system as well but weights are determined by a cluster analysis of POS errors (Green and Žabokrtský 2012b)
- **SVM**: Our hybrid system in which each individual edge is picked by a meta classifier from the same five parsers as the other ensemble systems (Green et al. 2012a,b).

4.3 Evaluation

For machine translation, we report two automatic evaluation scores, BLEU and NIST. We examine parser accuracy using UAS. We compare a machine translation system, integrating 10 different parsing systems, against each other using these metrics. We report UAS scores for each parser on section 23 of the WST and BLEU and NIST scores for the WMT test set in Table 14.

Table 14 Scores for each machine translation run for each dataset (WMT 2010, 2011 and 2012 results are given in both columns)

Parser	UAS	NIST(10/11/12)	BLEU(10/11/12)
MST	86.49	5.4038/5.5898/5.1956	12.99/13.58/11.54
MST w chunking	86.57	5.4364/5.6346/5.2364	13.43/14.00/11.96
Malt	84.51	5.3747/5.5702/5.1484	12.90/13.48/11.27
Malt w chunking	87.01	5.4110/5.6025/5.1904	13.39/13.80/11.73
ZPar	76.06	5.2676/5.4635/5.0846	11.91/12.48/10.53
Charniak	92.08	5.4750/5.6561/5.2816	13.49/13.95/**12.26**
Stanford	87.88	5.4000/5.5970/5.1892	13.23/13.63/11.74
Fixed weight	92.58	**5.4911**/5.6831/**5.2902**	**13.53**/14.04/12.23
Fuzzy cluster	92.54	5.4730/5.6820/5.2672	13.47/14.06/12.06
SVM	92.60	5.4846/**5.6837**/5.2891	13.45/**14.11**/12.22

Scores in bold indicate the best result for each given dataset

4.4 Results and Discussion

4.4.1 Type of Changes in WMT Annotation

Since our gold annotated data was preprocessed with MSTParser, our baseline system at the time, we started with a decent baseline and only had to change 9 % of the dependency arcs in the data. These 9 % of changes roughly increases the BLEU score by 7 %.

4.4.2 Parsers vs Our Gold Standard

On average, our gold data differed in head agreement from our base parser 14.77 % of the time. When our base parsers were tested on the WSJ section 23 data they had an average error rate of 12.17 % which is roughly comparable to the difference with our gold data set which indicates overall our annotations are close to the accepted standard from the community. The slight difference in percentage fits into what is expect in annotator error and in the errors in the conversion process of the WSJ by PennConverter.

4.5 MT Results in WMT Using Hybrid Parsing Approaches

- **WMT 2010**: As seen in Table 14, the highest resulting BLEU score for the 2010 data set is from the fixed weight ensemble system. The other two ensemble systems are beaten by one component system, Charniak. However, this changes when comparing NIST scores. Two of the ensemble method have higher NIST scores than Charniak, similar to their UAS scores.
- **WMT 2011**: The 2011 data corresponded the best with UAS scores. While the BLEU score increases for all the ensemble systems, the order of systems by UAS scores corresponds exactly to the systems ordered by NIST score and correlates strongly (Table 15). Unlike the 2010 data, the MSTParser was the highest base parser.
- **WMT 2012**: The ensemble increases are statistically significant for both the SVM and the Fixed Weight system over the MSTParser with 99 % confidence, our previous baseline and best scoring base system from 2011. We examine our data versus MST instead of Charniak since we have preprocessed our gold data set with MST, allowing us a direct comparison in improvements. The fuzzy cluster system achieves a higher BLEU evaluation score than MST, but is not significant. In pairwise tests, it wins approximately 78 % of the time. This is the first dataset we have looked at where the BLEU score is higher for a component parser and not an ensemble system, although the NIST score is still higher for the ensemble systems.

Table 15 Pearson
correlation coefficients for
each year and each metric
when measured against UAS

	NIST	BLEU
2010	0.98	0.93
2011	0.98	0.94
2012	0.95	0.97

Overall NIST has a stronger correlation to UAS scores, however both show a strong relationship

Table 16 Pairwise
agreement between
annotators for our SVM and
baseline systems

	+	=	−
+	12	12	0
=		3	7
−			7

(−,−) all annotators agreed the baseline was better, (+,+) SVM was better, (+,−) annotators disagreed

4.5.1 Human Manual Evaluation: SVM vs the Baseline System

We selected 200 sentences at random from our annotations and they were given to seven native Czech speakers. Seventy seven times the reviewers preferred the SVM system, 48 times they preferred the MST system, and 57 times they said there was no difference between the quality of the sentences. On average each reviewer looked at 26 sentences with a median of 30 sentences. Reviewers were allowed three options: sentence 1 is better, sentence 2 is better, both sentences are of equal quality.

Table 16 indicates that the SVM system was widely preferred. When removing annotations marked as equal, we see that the SVM system was preferred 24 times to the Baseline's 14.

Although a small sample, this shows that using the ensemble parser will at worse give you equal results and at best a much improved result.

4.5.2 MT Results with Gold Data

In the perfect situation of having gold standard dependency trees, we obtained a NIST of 5.3003 and a BLEU of 12.39. For our gold standard system run, the parsing component was removed and replaced with our hand annotated data. These are the highest NIST and BLEU scores we have obtained including using all base parsers or any combinations of parsers.

5   Conclusion

In this chapter we have taken the idea of hybrid approaches to machine translation and examined three unique hybrid dependency techniques as a form of source side analysis. We have shown that ensemble parsing techniques have an influence on syntax-based machine translation both in manual and automatic evaluation. Furthermore we have shown a stronger correlation between parser accuracy and NIST rather than the more commonly used BLEU metric. We have also introduce a gold set of English dependency trees based on the WMT 2012 machine translation task data, which shows a larger increase in both BLEU and NIST. While on some datasets it is inconclusive whether using an ensemble parser with better accuracy has a large enough effect, we do show that practically you will not do worse using one and in many cases do much better. In an NLP world with increasing amounts of tools and techniques, hybridity plays an important part in combining efforts and developing a more sophisticated analysis of text. We have shown just one example here with dependency parsing but other source side procedures might additionally benefit from a similar analysis.

References

Bick, E. 2007. Hybrid ways to improve domain independence in an ML dependency parser. In *Proceedings of the CoNLL Shared Task Session of EMNLP-CoNLL 2007*, 1119–1123. http://www.aclweb.org/anthology/D/D07/D07-1120.

Buchholz, S., and E. Marsi. 2006. CoNLL-X shared task on multilingual dependency parsing. In *Proceedings of the Tenth Conference on Computational Natural Language Learning, CoNLL-X '06*, 149–164. Stroudsburg, PA: Association for Computational Linguistics. http://portal.acm.org/citation.cfm?id=1596276.1596305.

Charniak, E., and M. Johnson. 2005. Coarse-to-fine n-best parsing and maxent discriminative reranking. In *Proceedings of the 43rd Annual Meeting on Association for Computational Linguistics, ACL '05*, 173–180. Stroudsburg, PA: Association for Computational Linguistics. http://dx.doi.org/10.3115/1219840.1219862.

Dietterich, T.G. 2000. Ensemble methods in machine learning. In *Proceedings of the First International Workshop on Multiple Classifier Systems, MCS '00*, 1–15. London: Springer. http://dl.acm.org/citation.cfm?id=648054.743935.

Eisner, J. 1996. Three new probabilistic models for dependency parsing: an exploration. In *Proceedings of the 16th International Conference on Computational Linguistics (COLING-96)*, 340–345. Copenhagen: Association for Computational Linguistics. http://www.aclweb.org/anthology/N10-1004.

Green, N., and Z. Žabokrtský. 2012a. Hybrid combination of constituency and dependency trees into an ensemble dependency parser. In *Proceedings of the EACL 2012 Workshop on Innovative Hybrid Approaches to the Processing of Textual Data*, Avignon.

Green, N., and Z. Žabokrtský. 2012b. Ensemble Parsing and its Effect on Machine Translation. Technical Report 48.

Green, N., S.D. Larasati, and Z. Žabokrtský. 2012a. Indonesian dependency treebank: Annotation and parsing. In *Proceedings of the 26th Pacific Asia Conference on Language, Information, and Computation*, 137–145. Bali: Faculty of Computer Science, Universitas Indonesia. http://www.aclweb.org/anthology/Y12-1014.

Green, N., L. Ramasamy, and Z. Žabokrtský. 2012b. Using an SVM ensemble system for improved tamil dependency parsing. In *Proceedings of the ACL 2012 Joint Workshop on Statistical Parsing and Semantic Processing of Morphologically Rich Languages*, 72–77. Jeju, Republic of Korea: Association for Computational Linguistics. http://www.aclweb.org/anthology/W12-3410.

Gusmita, R.H., and R. Manurung. 2008. Some initial experiments with Indonesian probabilistic parsing. In *Proceedings of the 2nd International MALINDO Workshop*.

Haffari, G., M. Razavi, and A. Sarkar. 2011. An ensemble model that combines syntactic and semantic clustering for discriminative dependency parsing. In *Proceedings of the 49th Annual Meeting of the Association for Computational Linguistics: Human Language Technologies*, 710–714. Portland, OR: Association for Computational Linguistics. http://www.aclweb.org/anthology/P11-2125.

Hajič, J. 1998. Building a syntactically annotated corpus: The Prague dependency treebank. In *Issues of valency and meaning. Studies in honor of Jarmila Panevová*, ed. E. Hajičová, 12–19. Prague Karolinum: Charles University Press.

Hall, J., J. Nilsson, J. Nivre, G. Eryigit, B. Megyesi, M. Nilsson, and M. Saers. 2007. Single malt or blended? A study in multilingual parser optimization. In *Proceedings of the CoNLL Shared Task Session of EMNLP-CoNLL 2007*, 933–939. http://www.aclweb.org/anthology/D/D07/D07-1097.

Johansson, R., and P. Nugues. 2007. Extended constituent-to-dependency conversion for English. In *Proceedings of NODALIDA 2007*, Tartu, 105–112.

Joice, J. 2002. Pengembangan lanjut pengurai struktur kalimat bahasa indonesia yang menggunakan constraint-based formalism. Undergraduate thesis. Master's thesis, Faculty of Computer Science, University of Indonesia.

Klein, D., and C.D. Manning. 2003. Accurate unlexicalized parsing. In *Proceedings of the 41st Annual Meeting on Association for Computational Linguistics - Volume 1, ACL '03*, 423–430. Stroudsburg, PA: Association for Computational Linguistics.

Kübler, S., R. McDonald, and J. Nivre. 2009. *Dependency parsing*. Synthesis lectures on human language technologies. San Rafael, CA: Morgan & Claypool. http://books.google.com/books?id=k3iiup7HB9UC.

Marcus, M.P., M.A. Marcinkiewicz, and B. Santorini. 1993. Building a large annotated corpus of English: The Penn Treebank. *Computational Linguistics* 19:313–330. http://portal.acm.org/citation.cfm?id=972470.972475.

McDonald, R., and J. Nivre. 2007. Characterizing the errors of data-driven dependency parsing models. In *Proceedings of the 2007 Joint Conference on Empirical Methods in Natural Language Processing and Computational Natural Language Learning (EMNLP-CoNLL)*, 122–131. http://www.aclweb.org/anthology/D/D07/D07-1013.

McDonald, R., F. Pereira, K. Ribarov, and J. Hajic. 2005a. Non-projective dependency parsing using spanning tree algorithms. In *Proceedings of Human Language Technology Conference and Conference on Empirical Methods in Natural Language Processing*, 523–530. Vancouver, BC: Association for Computational Linguistics. http://www.aclweb.org/anthology/H/H05/H05-1066.

McDonald, R., F. Pereira, K., Ribarov, and J. Hajič. 2005b. Non-projective dependency parsing using spanning tree algorithms. In *Proceedings of the Conference on Human Language Technology and Empirical Methods in Natural Language Processing, HLT '05*, 523–530. Morristown, NJ: Association for Computational Linguistics. http://dx.doi.org/10.3115/1220575.1220641.

Nivre, J. 2003. An efficient algorithm for projective dependency parsing. In *Proceedings of the 8th International Workshop on Parsing Technologies (IWPT)*, 149–160.

Nivre, J., and R. McDonald. 2008. Integrating graph-based and transition-based dependency parsers. In *Proceedings of ACL-08: HLT*, 950–958. Columbus, OH: Association for Computational Linguistics. http://www.aclweb.org/anthology/P/P08/P08-1108.

Nivre, J., J. Hall, J. Nilsson, A. Chanev, G. Eryigit, S. Kübler, S. Marinov, and E. Marsi. 2007. MaltParser: A language-independent system for data-driven dependency parsing. *Natural Language Engineering* 13(2):95–135.

Pajas, P., and P. Fabian. 2011. TrEd 2.0 - Newly refactored tree editor. http://ufal.mff.cuni.cz/tred/. Institute of Formal and Applied Linguistics, MFF.

Papineni, K., S. Roukos, T. Ward, and W.J. Zhu. 2002. Bleu: A method for automatic evaluation of machine translation. In *Proceedings of the 40th Annual Meeting on Association for Computational Linguistics, ACL '02*, 311–318. Morristown, NJ: Association for Computational Linguistics. http://dx.doi.org/10.3115/1073083.1073135.

Popel, M., Z. Žabokrtský, and J. Ptáček. 2010. Tectomt: Modular nlp framework. In *IceTAL*, 293–304.

Popel, M., D. Mareček, N. Green, and Z. Žabokrtský. 2011. Influence of parser choice on dependency-based mt. In *Proceedings of the Sixth Workshop on Statistical Machine Translation*, 433–439. Edinburgh: Association for Computational Linguistics. http://www.aclweb.org/anthology/W11-2153.

Ramasamy, L., and Z. Žabokrtský. 2011. Tamil dependency parsing: Results using rule based and corpus based approaches. In *Proceedings of the 12th International Conference on Computational Linguistics and Intelligent Text Processing - Volume Part I, CICLing'11*, 82–95. Berlin, Heidelberg: Springer.

Sagae, K., and A. Lavie. 2006. Parser combination by reparsing. In *Proceedings of the Human Language Technology Conference of the NAACL, Companion Volume: Short Papers*, 129–132. New York City, NY: Association for Computational Linguistics. http://www.aclweb.org/anthology/N/N06/N06-2033.

Sagae, K., and J. Tsujii. 2007. Dependency parsing and domain adaptation with LR models and parser ensembles. In *Proceedings of the CoNLL Shared Task Session of EMNLP-CoNLL 2007*, 1044–1050. Prague: Association for Computational Linguistics. http://www.aclweb.org/anthology/D/D07/D07-1111.

Sgall, P. 1967. *Generativní popis jazyka a česká deklinace*. Prague: Academia.

Surdeanu, M., and C.D. Manning. 2010. Ensemble models for dependency parsing: Cheap and good? In *Human Language Technologies: The 2010 Annual Conference of the North American Chapter of the Association for Computational Linguistics, HLT '10*, 649–652. Stroudsburg, PA: Association for Computational Linguistics. http://dl.acm.org/citation.cfm?id=1857999.1858090.

Žabokrtský, Z., J. Ptáček, P. Pajas. 2008. TectoMT: Highly modular MT system with tectogrammatics used as transfer layer. In *Proceedings of the 3rd Workshop on Statistical Machine Translation, ACL*, 167–170.

Zeman, D., and Z. Žabokrtský. 2005. Improving parsing accuracy by combining diverse dependency parsers. In *Proceedings of the 9th International Workshop on Parsing Technologies*.

Zhang, Y., and S. Clark. 2011. Syntactic processing using the generalized perceptron and beam search. *Computational Linguistics* 37(1):105–151

Using WordNet-Based Word Sense Disambiguation to Improve MT Performance

Špela Vintar and Darja Fišer

Abstract We report on a series of experiments aimed at improving the machine translation of ambiguous lexical items by using WordNet-based unsupervised Word Sense Disambiguation (WSD) and comparing its results to three MT systems. Our experiments are performed for the English-Slovene language pair using UKB, a freely available graph-based word sense disambiguation system. Since the fine granularity of WordNet is often reported as problematic, we compare the performance of UKB using all WordNet senses with using sense clusters. Results are evaluated in three ways: a manual evaluation of WSD performance from MT perspective, an analysis of agreement between the WSD-proposed equivalent and those suggested by the three systems, and finally by computing BLEU, NIST and METEOR scores for all translation versions. Our results show that WSD performs with a MT-relevant precision of 71 % and that 21 % of sense-related MT errors could be prevented by using unsupervised WSD. We also show that sense clusters improve MT-relevant precision.

1 Introduction

Ambiguity continues to be a tough nut to crack in Machine Translation. In most known languages certain lexical items can refer to more than a single concept, meaning that MT systems need to choose between several translation equivalents representing different senses of the source word. Wrong choices often result in grave translation errors, as words often refer to several completely unrelated concepts. The adjective *striking* can mean *beautiful, surprising*; *delivering a hard blow* or *indicating a certain time*, and the noun *course* can be *something we give, take, teach* or *eat*.

In traditional statistical machine translation (SMT) systems lexical choice is governed largely by the target language model, giving preference to phrases with a higher probability in the target language. Several problems arise from the so-called

Š. Vintar (✉) • D. Fišer
University of Ljubljana, Ljubljana, Slovenia
e-mail: spela.vintar@ff.uni-lj.si; darja.fiser@ff.uni-lj.si

© Springer International Publishing Switzerland 2016
M.R. Costa-jussà et al. (eds.), *Hybrid Approaches to Machine Translation*,
Theory and Applications of Natural Language Processing,
DOI 10.1007/978-3-319-21311-8_8

191

static phrase model; firstly, distant dependencies are not taken into account, secondly, the context used to choose the translation equivalent is limited to a few words only, and thirdly, the source context which is most relevant for disambiguation is not taken into account in current SMT systems (Haque et al. 2011). Approaches to integrate WSD into traditional SMT initially yielded limited success, but since 2007 several authors have reported significant improvements using context-dependent or dynamic lexicons (Chan et al. 2007; Gimenez and Marquez 2007; Carpuat and Wu 2007).

In rule-based systems lexical selection is performed in a number of ways, but most RBMT systems rely either on hand-crafted rules, semantic lexica or probabilistic models acquired from corpora, and some systems employ no explicit WSD at all. Because ambiguous words may have a number of equivalents with unrelated meanings but similar syntactic behavior, some sentences are extremely difficult to disambiguate without looking at a broader context; e.g. *Let us wait for the next course* might refer to taking classes or eating a meal.

The experiments we describe below were performed for the English-Slovene language pair, whereby Slovene can be considered a less-resourced language at least concerning MT and semantically annotated corpora. Our aim was to assess the performance of three MT systems and to see whether WordNet-based Word Sense Disambiguation (WSD) could improve performance and assist in avoiding grave sense-related translation errors. We test one statistical system (Google[1]), one "linguistically informed" hybrid system (Bing,[2] although the amount and nature of language resources employed for Slovene remain questionable) and one rule-based system (Presis[3]), whereby we envisage the implementation of our method as a post-processing step rather than its integration into the translation engine.

For WSD we use UKB (Agirre and Soroa 2009), a graph-based algorithm that uses WordNet (Fellbaum 1998) and computes the probability of each sense of a polysemous word by taking into account the senses of context words. In our experiment we use Orwell's notorious novel *1984* as the source and its translation into Slovene as the reference translation. We then disambiguate the English source with UKB, assign each disambiguated English word a Slovene equivalent from sloWNet (Fišer 2009) and compare these with the equivalents proposed by Google, Bing and Presis.

Because many authors report that the WordNet sense inventory is too fine-grained for many NLP tasks (Mihalcea and Moldovan 2001), we performed the experiment with two settings, using the full sense inventory and using automatically induced coarser-grained sense clusters that were based on the mapping to a manually crafted dictionary encoding sense hierarchies, namely the Oxford Dictionary of English (Navigli 2006).

---

[1] http://translate.google.com

[2] http://www.bing.com/translator

[3] http://presis.amebis.si/prevajanje/?jezik=en

Evaluation is performed in three ways. First, WSD performance is evaluated manually from MT perspective and both settings are compared. Then we analyse the agreement between each of the MT systems and the UKB/WordNet-derived translation, whereby we also give an estimate of the cases where MT performance could effectively be improved by our method. Finally we generate our own raw translation using the equivalents proposed by WSD and compare BLEU, NIST and METEOR scores achieved with each translation version.

Our results show that the ad hoc WSD strategies used by the evaluated MT systems can definitely be improved by a proper WSD algorithm, and that WordNet-based WSD could be useful as a post-processing step. Evaluation with metrics however does not show any significant improvement.

The remainder of this paper is structured as follows: in Sect. 2 we give an overview of approaches to WSD in the context of MT, focusing in particular on unsupervised and knowledge-based methods. Section 3 describes the experimental setup and presents all the resources and tools we use. Section 4 lists the results of all experiments and of all evaluation procedures, and we conclude with a thorough discussion in Sect. 5.

2   Word Sense Disambiguation and Machine Translation

WSD for Machine Translation purposes slightly differs from traditional WSD, because distinct source language senses which share the same translation equivalent need not be differentiated in MT (Vickrey et al. 2005). This phenomenon is known as parallel ambiguities and is particularly common among related languages (Resnik and Yarowsky 2000). Still, lack of explicit WSD in MT can lead to grave translation errors such as the one made by Google in our experiment when translating the first sentence of Orwell's 1984 from English into Slovene (*It was a bright cold day in April, and the clocks were striking thirteen. Bilo je svetlo mrzel dan v aprilu, in ure so bile trinajst presenetljiv.*), where *striking* was translated as *surprising*.

Reviewing approaches to WSD in traditional Machine Translation, we find that a distinction is usually made between interlingual systems and transfer systems (Resnik 2007, p. 313). Interlingual systems require explicit WSD in order to identify the correct meaning representation for a concept expressed in the source language. This monolingual analysis task produces an interlingual representation which in turn maps to a surface realization in the target language. Transfer-based systems similarly face the need to determine which sense of the source word to use for mapping to the target language, however they have an opportunity to avoid explicit WSD and map directly from words to words, in effect treating the set of target-language translations of a word as if it is the word's sense inventory (Resnik 2007, p. 314).

In statistical MT, the issue of selecting the right sense of a word is usually subsumed under lexical choice governed by the translation model and the target language model employed by the SMT engine. The move from words in the early

SMT models to phrases (Koehn et al. 2003) was motivated in part by the observation that local context in the source language provides strong cues for lexical selection, and as a consequence phrase-to-phrase mappings produce less sense-related errors. Nevertheless, many researchers continued to explore the potential of integrating "true" WSD into SMT. Early experiments by Carpuat and Wu (2005) failed to provide convincing proof; their attempt to integrate WSD using an external sense inventory into an IBM-style SMT system resulted in worse BLEU scores. However, in later experiments Carpuat and Wu (2007) train their WSD system on the same corpora as the SMT system and incorporate WSD into the lexical choice task faced by the multi-word phrasal translation engine, and in this setting performance was consistently improved according to all common evaluation metrics. Similar results were reported independently by Cabezas and Resnik (2005) and Chan et al. (2007), and in the following years different authors have proposed alternative methods of integrating WSD into statistical or hybrid MT (Gimenez and Marquez 2007; Ali et al. 2009; Meyer and Popescu-Belis 2012).

WordNet-based approaches to improving MT have been employed by numerous authors, on the one hand using WordNet as a semantic resource to help resolve ambiguity, and on the other hand as a rich source of domain-specific translation equivalents. As early as 1993 (Knight 1993), WordNet was used as the lower ontology within the PANGLOSS MT system. Yuseop et al. (2002) have employed LSA and the semantic similarity of WordNet literals to translate collocations, while Salam et al. (2009) used WordNet for disambiguation and the choice of the correct translation equivalent in an English to Bengali SMT system.

Still, using WordNet as the source of sense inventories has been criticized not just in the context of MT (Apidianaki 2009) where unsupervised approaches seem to yield better results (Soltani and Faili 2012), but also within other language processing tasks. The most notorious arguments against WordNet are its high granularity and—as a consequence—high similarity between some senses, but its global availability and universality seem to be advantages that prevail in many cases (Edmonds and Kilgarriff 2002).

Our experiments lie somewhat in between; on the one hand we demonstrate the potential of WSD in MT, especially for cases where different MT systems disagree, and on the other hand we attribute most WSD errors to the inadequacy of the sense splitting in WordNet (see Sect. 5).

3 Experimental Setup

3.1 Corpus and MT Systems

Our corpus consists of George Orwell's novel *1984*, first published in English in 1949, and its translation into Slovene by Alenka Puhar, first published in 1967. While it may seem unusual to be using a work of fiction for the assessment of MT systems, literary language is usually richer in ambiguity and thus provides a more complex semantic space than non-fiction.

We translated the entire novel into Slovene with Google Translate, Bing and Presis, the first two belonging to the family of statistical systems and the latter being a rule-based MT system developed by the Slovenian company Amebis.

For Google and Bing lexical choice is governed by a combination of the target language model containing the probabilities of phrases and the translation model proposing various equivalents (Cabezas and Resnik 2005). In Presis, on the other hand, the choice of words in a given context is ruled by verb templates encoding all possible combinations of verbs and their objects together with their semantic properties (animate/inanimate). The semantic lexicon additionally contains common Adjective + Noun patterns, prepositional phrases, and in cases of coordination resolves ambiguity by looking for a common hypernym (e.g. *ošpice in koze [measles and smallpox]—> disease* vs. *ovce in koze [sheep and goats]—> domestic animals).*

For the purposes of further analysis and comparison with our disambiguated corpus all texts—original and translations—have been PoS-tagged and lemmatized using the JOS web service (Erjavec et al. 2010) for Slovene and ToTaLe (Erjavec et al. 2005) for English. Because we can only disambiguate content words, we retained only nouns, verbs, adjectives and adverbs and discarded the rest. After all these preprocessing steps our texts end up looking as follows (Fig. 1).

English:
It was a bright cold day in April and the clocks were striking thirteen.
English-preprocessed:
be bright cold day April clock be strike
Slovene-reference:
Bil je jasen, mrzel aprilski dan in ure so bile trinajst.
Slovene-reference-preprocessed:
biti biti jasen mrzel aprilski dan ura biti biti
Slovene-Google:
Bilo je svetlo mrzel dan v aprilu, in ure so bile trinajst presenetljiv.
Slovene-Google-preprocessed:
biti biti svetlo mrzel dan april ura biti biti presenetljiv
Slovene-Bing:
Je bil svetlo hladne dan aprila in v ure so bili presenetljivo trinajst.
Slovene-Bing-preprocessed:
biti biti svetlo hladen dan april ura biti biti presenetljivo
Slovene-Presis:
Svetal hladen dan v aprilu je bilin so ure udarjale trinajst.
Slovene-Presis-preprocessed:
svetel hladen dan april biti bilin biti ura udarjati

Fig. 1 Corpus preprocessing

Table 1 Corpus size and
number of ambiguous words

Corpus size in tokens	103,769
Corpus size in types	10,982
Ambiguous tokens	48,632
Ambiguous types	7627
Synsets with no equivalent in sloWNet	3192
Contexts with no equivalent in sloWNet	8073
Contexts with no cluster assignment	25,810

As can be seen in Table 1, almost half of all the tokens in the corpus are considered to be ambiguous according to the English WordNet. Since the Slovene WordNet is considerably smaller than the English one, almost half of the different ambiguous words occurring in our corpus have no equivalent in sloWNet. This could affect the results of our experiment, because we cannot evaluate the potential benefit of WSD if we cannot compare the translation equivalent from sloWNet with the solutions proposed by different MT systems. We therefore restricted the research to the words and sentences for which an equivalent exists in sloWNet.

3.2 Disambiguation with UKB and WordNet

The aim of semantic annotation and disambiguation is to identify polysemous lexical items in the English text and assign them the correct sense based on their context. Once the sense of the word has been determined, we can exploit the cross-lingual links between WordNets of different languages and propose a Slovene translation equivalent from the Slovene WordNet.

We disambiguated the English corpus with UKB, which utilizes the relations between synsets and constructs semantic graphs for each candidate sense of the word. The algorithm then computes the probability of each graph based on the number and weight of edges between the nodes representing semantic concepts. Disambiguation is performed in a monolingual context for single- and multiword nouns, verbs, adjectives and adverbs, provided they are included in the English WordNet.

Figure 2 shows the result of the disambiguation algorithm for the word *face,* which has as many as 13 possible senses in WordNet. We are given the probability of each sense in the given context (e.g. *0.173463*) and the ID of the synset (e.g. *eng-30-05600637-n*), and for the purposes of clarity we also added the literals (words) associated with this particular synset ID in the English (*face, human face*) and Slovene (*fris, obraz, faca*) WordNet respectively.

WSD: ctx_Oen.1.1.2 24   !! face

- W: 0.173463   ID: eng-30-05600637-n   ENGWN: face, human face, (the front of the human head from the forehead to the chin and ear to ear)   SLOWN: fris, obraz, faca, človeški obraz
- W: 0.116604   ID: eng-30-08510666-n   ENGWN: side, face, (a surface forming part of the outside of an object)   SLOWN: stranica, ploskev
- W: 0.0956895   ID: eng-30-03313602-n   ENGWN: face, (the side upon which the use of a thing depends (usually the most prominent surface of an object))   SLOWN: sprednja stran, prava stran, zgornja stran, lice
- W: 0.0761554   ID: eng-30-04679738-n   ENGWN: expression, look, aspect, facial expression, face, (the feelings expressed on a person's face)   SLOWN: izraz, pogled, obraz, izraz na obrazu
- W: 0.0709513   ID: eng-30-03313456-n   ENGWN: face, (a vertical surface of a building or cliff)   SLOWN: stena, fasada
- W: 0.0653514   ID: eng-30-06825399-n   ENGWN: font, fount, typeface, face, case, (a specific size and style of type within a type family)   SLOWN: font, pisava, črkovna družina, vrsta črk, črkovna podoba, črkovni slog
- W: 0.0629878   ID: eng-30-04838210-n   ENGWN: boldness, nerve, brass, face, cheek, (impudent aggressiveness) SLOWN: predrznost, nesramnost
- W: 0.0610286   ID: eng-30-06877578-n   ENGWN: grimace, face, (a contorted facial expression) SLOWN: spaka, grimasa
- W: 0.0605221   ID: eng-30-03313873-n   ENGWN: face, (the striking or working surface of an implement) SLOWN: čelo, podplat, udarna površina
- W: 0.0579952   ID: eng-30-05601198-n   ENGWN: face, (the part of an animal corresponding to the human face)   SLOWN: obraz
- W: 0.0535548   ID: eng-30-05168795-n   ENGWN: face, (status in the eyes of others) SLOWN: ugled, dobro ime
- W: 0.05303   ID: eng-30-09618957-n   ENGWN: face, (a part of a person that is used to refer to a person)   SLOWN: obraz
- W: 0.0526668   ID: eng-30-04679419-n   ENGWN: face, (the general outward appearance of something)   SLOWN: podoba

Fig. 2 Disambiguation result for the word face with probabilities for each of the 13 senses

3.3   Disambiguation with Sense Clusters

As can be seen from this example, WordNet is—in most cases—a very fine-grained sense inventory, and looking at the Slovene equivalents clearly shows that many of these senses may partly or entirely overlap, at least in the context of translation. For this reason we performed a second round of disambiguation using sense clusters (Agirre and Lacalle 2003). In this setting, each of the possible senses of an ambiguous lexical item is assigned a cluster, with the aim of grouping similar meanings into the same cluster. We can now join the translation equivalents belonging to the same cluster and re-evaluate WSD performance in a translation-relevant context. Sense clustering can only be applied to about one half of all ambiguous tokens (see Table 1).

If we look at the sentence below containing the ambiguous word *place*:

People were leaping up and down in their places and shouting at the tops of their voices in
an effort to drown the maddening bleating voice that came from the screen.

Out of 16 possible senses of *place* in WordNet, UKB will select the sense
labeled eng-30-08664443-n with the definition *a point located with respect to*
surface features of some region and listing the literals *topographic point, place,*
spot. Because this sense is assigned the cluster labeled *life10*, we add to the original
4 Slovene equivalents *kraj, mesto, prostor, točka* additional 10 equivalents belonging
to the same cluster: *dom, bivališče, posest, stanovanje, domovanje, sedež, trg,*
posestvo, položaj, sedišče.

4 Evaluation

The aim of our experiments was to see whether explicit WSD could improve
Machine Translation, whereby we wished to compare the three English-Slovene MT
systems and to evaluate the role of sense clusters in unsupervised WordNet-based
WSD. The task in itself is not trivial because the number of meanings a word can
have, the degree of translation equivalence or the quality of the target text are all
extremely disputable and vague notions. For this reason we wished to evaluate our
results from as many angles as possible, both manually and automatically.

4.1 Manual Evaluation of WSD Precision in the Context of MT

Firstly, we were interested in the performance of the UKB disambiguation tool in
the context of MT. Since UKB uses WordNet as a sense inventory, the algorithm
assigns a probability to each sense of a lexical item according to its context in
an unsupervised way. The precision of UKB for unsupervised WSD is reported at
around 58 % for all words and around 72 % for nouns, but of course these figures
measure the number of cases where the algorithm selected the correct WordNet
synset from a relatively fine-grained network of possible senses (Agirre and Soroa
2009).

In manual evaluation we use the notion of translation-based Mirrors method
(Dyvik 2005; Lyse 2011), which means that we are concerned only with sense
distinctions of the source word that call for a different translation in the target
language. For example, the English word *breast* has four senses in WordNet: (1) the
upper frontal part of a human chest, (2) one of the two soft milk-secreting glands of
a woman, (3) meat carved from the breast of a fowl and (4) the upper front part of an
animal corresponding to the human chest. For the English sentence *Winston nuzzled*
his chin into his "breast" … UKB suggested the second sense, which is clearly

Table 2 Manual evaluation of WSD performance for MT with and without sense clusters

	Correct (%)	Incorrect (%)	Borderline (%)
No sense clusters	345 (69)	126 (25)	29 (6)
With sense clusters	420 (82)	55 (11)	35 (7)

wrong, but since the ambiguity is preserved in Slovene and the word *prsi* can be used for all of the four meanings, we consider this a case of successful disambiguation for the purposes of MT.

Manual evaluation was performed with a single evaluator (a translator) who was presented with 500 randomly selected examples of disambiguated words and their context. The evaluator examined the source word in context and then evaluated the Slovene equivalents offered for the sense that had been chosen by UKB without sense clusters. The results of this manual evaluation show the precision of WSD to be 69 %, with 6 % borderline cases (see Table 2). The latter include cases where the equivalent is semantically correct but had been assigned the wrong part of speech by the POS-tagger (eg. **glass** *door* -> **steklo* instead of **steklen**).

In a similar manner we manually evaluated 500 randomly selected words and their contexts using sense clusters. In this second setting we expected a higher number of correct cases because, on average, clusters considerably broaden the range of possible equivalents, but on the other hand they are only available for about one half of all the ambiguous contexts. The random selection of examples therefore included only those for which a sense cluster had been assigned. The improvement is nevertheless significant because we now achieve 82 % WSD precision, meaning that in 82 % of the cases at least one of the Slovene equivalents suggested by the WordNet-based WSD and sense clustering was correct for the given context.

It must be noted here that evaluation examples included a number of potentially highly ambiguous words in English which in fact need no disambiguation in their current syntactic role. We refer mostly to auxiliary verbs and copula (be, can, have, do) where the sense inventory for them used as lexical verbs may be very broad, but to disambiguate them when occurring in a purely functional role makes no sense at all. We therefore disregarded such cases in our manual evaluation.

4.2 Agreement Between Each of the MT Systems and the Disambiguated Equivalent

It is interesting to compare the equivalents we propose through our WordNet-based WSD procedure with those suggested by the three MT systems: Presis, Google and Bing. For this comparison we considered it a positive case if any of the Slovene words proposed by our WSD procedure matched the word used by the MT system and by the reference translation respectively.

Table 3 Comparison of WSD/WordNet-based equivalent and the translations proposed by Presis, Google, Bing and the reference translation, not using and using sense clusters

	No sense clusters	Using sense clusters
Total no. of disambiguated tokens	40,560	42,157
Synsets with no sloWNet equivalent	8073	6476
WSD = reference	18,544	20,277
WSD = Presis	19,858	21,866
WSD = Google	20,522	22,471
WSD = Bing	20,112	21,963
WSD = ref = Presis = Google = Bing	12,815	14,126
WSD = ref $\neq$ Presis $\neq$ Google $\neq$ Bing	1041	1061

Of the over 48k ambiguous tokens we obviously considered only those which had an equivalent in sloWNet, otherwise comparison with the MT systems would have been impossible. If we use clusters, around 1500 additional contexts can be considered because the previously empty Slovene synset now receives Slovene equivalents from similar synsets belonging to the same cluster (Table 3). The WSD/WordNet-based equivalents most often agree with the Google translation, and in just under one third of the cases all systems agree with each other and with the reference translation.

If we also look at the number of cases where our WSD-WordNet-based equivalent is the only one to agree with the reference translation, it is safe to assume that these are the cases where WSD could clearly improve MT. There are over one thousand such cases in our corpus, and slightly more if we use sense clusters (1041 and 1061).

4.3 Evaluation with Metrics

One method of evaluating the performance of WSD in the context of Machine Translation is through metrics for automatic evaluation (BLEU, NIST, METEOR etc.). We thus generated our own translation version similar to the one in Fig. 1 consisting only of content words in their lemmatized form. We translated the disambiguated words with WordNet, exploiting the cross-language universality of the synset ID. If the Slovene synset contained several possible translations we selected the first one. However, since we can only propose translation equivalents for the words which are included in WordNet, we had to come up with a translation solution for those which were not. Such words include proper names (*Winston, Smith, London, Oceania*), hyphenated compounds (*pig-iron, lift-shaft, gorilla-faced*) and Orwellian neologisms (*Minipax, Newspeak, thoughtcrime*). We translated these words with three alternative methods:

- Using a general bilingual dictionary,

- Using the English-Slovene Wikipedia and Wiktionary,
- Using the automatically constructed bilingual lexicon from the English-Slovene parallel Orwell corpus.

The fourth option was to leave them untranslated and simply add them to the generated Slovene version.

Finally, we wanted to see how the WSD/WordNet-based translation compares with the three MT systems using the BLEU, NIST and METEOR scores. For the purposes of this comparison we pre-processed all five versions of our corpus—original, reference translation, Presis, Google and Bing translation—by lemmatization, removal of all function words, removal of sentences where the alignment was not 1:1, and finally by removal of the sentences which contained lexical items for which there was no equivalent in sloWNet.

We then generated the so-called WSD version by translating all ambiguous words with sloWNet (see Sect. 3), and for the words not included in the English WordNet we used four alternative translation strategies; a general bilingual dictionary (dict), wiktionary (wikt), a word-alignment lexicon (align) and amending untranslated words to the target language version (amend).

Table 4 shows the results of automatic evaluation; the corpus consisted of 2428 segments. We can see that our generated version using disambiguated equivalents does not outperform any of the MT systems on any metric, except when the WSD-align version outperforms Presis on the NIST score and comes fairly close to the Bing score.

It is possible that the improvement we are trying to achieve is difficult to measure with these metrics because our method operates on the level of single words, while the metrics typically evaluate entire sentences and corpora. We are using a stripped version of the corpus, i.e. only content words which can potentially be ambiguous, whereas the metrics are normally used to calculate the similarity between two versions of running text. Whenever the Slovene WordNet proposed several equivalents for the selected sense we had chosen the first for our generated translation. This means—and indeed we had seen such examples in our data—that the WSD equivalent might have been synonymous to the reference translation but would not be recognized by the metrics. Finally, the corpus we are using for automatic evaluation is very small.

Table 4 Evaluation with metrics

	BLEU (n = 1)	NIST	METEOR
Bing	0.506	3.594	0.455
Google	0.579	4.230	0.481
Presis	0.485	3.333	0.453
WSD	0.440	3.258	0.429
WSD-amend	0.410	3.308	0.430
WSD-dict	0.405	3.250	0.427
WSD-align	0.448	**3.588**	0.434
WSD-wikt	0.442	3.326	0.429

Because this evaluation method yielded no obvious improvement, we did not proceed to test it with sense clusters because it seems that metrics are not an ideal way of measuring what we are trying to measure.

5 Discussion

Although employing unsupervised WSD and comparing WordNet-based translation equivalents to those proposed by the MT systems scored no significant improvement with standard MT evaluation metrics, we remain convinced that the other two evaluation methods show the potential of using WSD, particularly with homonyms and coarse-grained sense distinctions rather than those where sense distinctions are slight or vague. A manual inspection of the examples where MT systems disagreed and our WSD-based equivalent was the only one to agree with the reference translation shows that these are indeed examples of grave MT errors. For example, the word *hand* in the sentence *The clock's "hands" said six meaning eighteen* can only be translated correctly with a proper WSD strategy and was indeed mistranslated as *roka* (body part) by all three systems. If a relatively simplistic and unsupervised technique such as the one we propose can prevent as many as 20 % of these mistakes, it is certainly worth employing at least as a post-processing step.

The fact that we explore the impact of WSD on a work of fiction rather than domain-specific texts may also play a role in the results we obtained, although it is not entirely clear in what way. We believe that in general there is more ambiguity in literary texts meaning that a single word will appear in a wider range of senses in a work of fiction than it would in a domain-specific corpus. This might mean that WSD for literary texts is more difficult, however our own experiments so far show no significant difference in WSD performance.

A look at the cases where WSD goes wrong shows that these are typically words with a high number of senses which are difficult to differentiate even for a human. To return to the example from Sect. 2, the first sentence of Orwell's novel (*It was a bright cold day in April and the clocks were striking thirteen.*) caused a grave translation blunder in both Google and Bing, since *striking* was interpreted in its more expressive sense and translated into Slovene as *presenetljiv [surprising]*. However, UKB also got it wrong and chose the sense defined as *deliver a sharp blow, as with the hand, fist, or weapon* instead of *indicate a certain time by striking*. While these meanings may seem quite easy to tell apart, especially if the preceding word in a sentence is *clock*, *strike* as a verb has as many as 20 senses in Princeton WordNet, and many of these seem very similar. In this case, the Slovene translation our method proposed is "less wrong" than the *surprising* solution offered by Google or Bing, because *udarjati* may actually be used in the *clock* sense as well.

Using sense clusters does bring some relief from the notorious high granularity of WordNet, and our evaluation results show a moderate improvement in performance using clusters. A manual inspection of some clustering results however shows that the effect of joining related senses may also be exaggerated, which is to be expected from automatic clustering; thus the sense cluster labeled *lecture3* for the word *speech* resulted in Slovene equivalents as distinct as *jezik [language], ustna komunikacija [oral communication]* and *pridiga [sermon]*. This brings us to the important issue of lexical selection which our experiment does not address; if the number of proposed equivalents is high and their meanings are fairly distinct it is not trivial to choose between them.

We might also assume that statistical MT systems will perform worse on fiction; results in Table 4 show that both statistical systems outperform the rule-based Presis. Then again, Orwell's 1984 has been freely available as a parallel corpus for a very long time and it is therefore possible that both Google and Bing have used it as training data for their SMT model.

6 Conclusion

We described an experiment in which we explore the potential of WSD to improve the machine translation of ambiguous words for the English-Slovene language pair. We utilized the output of UKB, a graph-based WSD tool using WordNet, to select the appropriate equivalent from sloWNet. Manual evaluation showed that the correct equivalent was proposed in 69 % of the cases, and using sense clusters we managed to achieve 82 % precision. We then compared these equivalents with the output of three MT systems. While the benefit of WSD could not be proven with the standard MT evaluation metrics, the correspondence of the WSD/WordNet-based equivalent with the reference translation was high. Furthermore it appears that in cases where MT systems disagree WSD can help choose the correct equivalent.

As future work we plan to redesign the experiment so as to directly use WSD as a post-processing step to machine translation instead of generating our own translation version. This would provide better comparison grounds. In order to improve WSD precision we intend to combine two different algorithms and use it only in cases where both agree. Also, we intend to experiment with different text types and context lengths to be able to evaluate WSD performance in the context of MT on a larger scale.

References

Agirre, Eneko, and Aitor Soroa. 2009. Personalizing PageRank for word sense disambiguation. In *Proceedings of the 12th Conference of the European Chapter of the Association for Computational Linguistics*, 33–41. Association for Computational Linguistics.

Agirre, Eneko, and Oier Lopez De Lacalle. 2003. Clustering WordNet word senses. *RANLP* 260: 121–130.

Ali, Ola Mohammad, Mahmoud Gad Alla, and Mohammad Said Abdelwahab. 2009. Improving machine translation using hybrid dictionary-graph based word sense disambiguation with semantic and statistical methods. *International Journal of Computer and Electrical Engineering* 1(5): 618–623.

Apidianaki, Marianna. 2009. Data-driven semantic analysis for multilingual WSD and lexical selection in translation. In *Proceedings of the 12th Conference of the European Chapter of the ACL*, 77–85. Association for Computational Linguistics.

Cabezas, Clara, and Philip Resnik. 2005. Using WSD techniques for lexical selection in statistical machine translation. Technical report CS-TR-4736/LAMP-TR-124/UMIACS-TR-2005-42. http://lampsrv01.umiacs.umd.edu/pubs/TechReports/LAMP_124/LAMP_124.pdf.

Carpuat, Marine, and Dekai Wu. 2005. Word sense disambiguation vs. statistical machine translation. In *Proceedings of the 43rd Annual Meeting on Association for Computational Linguistics*, 387–394. Association for Computational Linguistics.

Carpuat, Marine, and Dekai Wu. 2007. Improving statistical machine translation using word sense disambiguation. In *Proceedings of the 2007 Joint Conference on Empirical Methods in Natural Language Processing and Computational Natural Language Learning (EMNLP-CoNLL)*, 61–72. Association for Computational Linguistics.

Chan, Yee Seng, Hwee Tou Ng, and David Chiang. 2007. Word sense disambiguation improves statistical machine translation. In *Proceedings of the 45th Annual Meeting of the Association of Computational Linguistics*, 33–40.

Dyvik, Helge. 2005. Translations as a semantic knowledge source. In *Proceedings of the Second Baltic Conference on Human Language Technologies*, 27–38. Tallinn University of Technology.

Edmonds, Philip, and Adam Kilgarriff. 2002. Introduction to the special issue on evaluating word sense disambiguation systems. *Natural Language Engineering* 8(4): 279–291.

Erjavec, Tomaž, Camelia Ignat, Bruno Pouliquen, and Ralf Steinberger. 2005. Massive multilingual corpus compilation: Acquis Communautaire and totale. *Archives of Control Science* 15(4): 529.

Erjavec, Tomaž, Darja Fišer, Simon Krek, and Nina Ledinek. 2010. The JOS linguistically tagged corpus of Slovene. In *Proceedings of the 7th International Conference on Language Resources and Evaluation (LREC'10)*. Malta.

Fellbaum, Christiane. 1998. *WordNet: An electronic lexical database*. Cambridge, MA: MIT.

Fišer, Darja. 2009. Leveraging parallel corpora and existing Wordnets for automatic construction of the slovene Wordnet. *Human language technology: challenges of the information society, (LNCS 5603)*, 359–368. Berlin, Heidelberg: Springer.

Giménez, Jesús, and Lluís Màrquez. 2007. Context-aware discriminative phrase selection for statistical machine translation. In *Proceedings of the Second Workshop on Statistical Machine Translation*, 159–166. Association for Computational Linguistics.

Haque, Rejwanul, Sudip Kumar Naskar, Antal van den Bosch, and Andy Way. 1993. Integrating source-language context into phrase-based statistical machine translation. *Machine Translation* 3(25): 239–285.

Knight, Kevin. 1993. Building a large ontology for machine translation. In *Proceedings of the ARPA Human Language Technology Workshop*. Plainsboro, NJ.

Koehn, Philipp, Franz Josef Och, and Daniel Marcu. 2003. Statistical phrase-based translation. In *Proceedings of the Human Language Technology Conference (HLT-NAACL)*, 48–54. Edmonton.

Lyse, Gunn Inger. 2011. *Translation-based Word Sense Disambiguation*. Doctoral dissertation. University of Bergen. https://bora.uib.no/handle/1956/5731?show=full

Meyer, Thomas, and Andrei Popescu-Belis. 2012. Using sense-labeled discourse connectives for statistical machine translation. In *Proceedings of the Joint Workshop on Exploiting Synergies between Information Retrieval and Machine Translation (ESIRMT) and Hybrid Approaches to Machine Translation (HyTra)*. Association for Computational Linguistics.

Mihalcea, Rada, and Dan I. Moldovan. 2001. EZ. WordNet: Principles for automatic generation of a coarse grained WordNet. In *FLAIRS Conference*, 454–458.

Navigli, Roberto. 2006. Meaningful clustering of senses helps boost word sense disambiguation performance. In *Proceedings of the 21st International Conference on Computational*

Linguistics and the 44th annual meeting of the Association for Computational Linguistics. Association for Computational Linguistics.

Resnik, Philip. 2007. WSD in NLP applications. In *Word sense disambiguation: algorithms and applications*, eds. Eneko Agirre and Philip Edmonds, vol. 33, 299–337. Berlin: Springer.

Resnik, Philip, and David Yarowsky. 2000. Distinguishing systems and distinguishing senses: New evaluation methods for word sense disambiguation. *Natural Language Engineering* 5(2): 113–133.

Salam, Khan Md. Anwarus, Mumit Khan, and Tetsuro Nishino. 2009. Example based English-Bengali machine translation using WordNet. In *Proceedings of the TriSA'09*. Japan.

Soltani, Mahmood, and Heshaam Faili. 2012. Target word selection in English to Persian translation using unsupervised approach. *International Journal of Artificial Intelligence and Soft Computing* 3(2): 125–142.

Vickrey, David, Luke Biewald, Marc Teyssier, and Daphne Koller. 2005. Word-sense disambiguation for machine translation. In *Proceedings of the Human Language Technology Conference/Conference on Empirical Methods in Natural Language Processing (HLT/EMNLP-2005)*. Vancouver.

Yuseop, Kim, Jeong-Ho Chang, and Byoung-Tak Zhang. 2002. Target word selection using WordNet and data-driven models in machine translation. In *Proceedings of the Conference PRICAI'02: Trends in Artificial Intelligence.*